Coleridge, Language and the Sublime

Coleridge, Language and the Sublime

From Transcendence to Finitude

Christopher Stokes

palgrave
macmillan

First published 2011 by
PALGRAVE MACMILLAN

Palgrave Macmillan in the UK is an imprint of Macmillan Publishers Limited, registered in England, company number 785998, of Houndmills, Basingstoke, Hampshire RG21 6XS.

Palgrave Macmillan in the US is a division of St Martin's Press LLC, 175 Fifth Avenue, New York, NY 10010.

Palgrave Macmillan is the global academic imprint of the above companies and has companies and representatives throughout the world.

Palgrave® and Macmillan® are registered trademarks in the United States, the United Kingdom, Europe and other countries.

ISBN: 978–0–230–27811–0 hardback

This book is printed on paper suitable for recycling and made from fully managed and sustained forest sources. Logging, pulping and manufacturing processes are expected to conform to the environmental regulations of the country of origin.

A catalogue record for this book is available from the British Library.

Library of Congress Cataloging-in-Publication Data

Stokes, Christopher, 1981–
Coleridge, language and the sublime: from transcendence to finitude/ by Christopher Stokes.
p. cm.
Includes bibliographical references and index.
ISBN 978–0–230–27811–0 (alk. paper)
1. Coleridge, Samuel Taylor, 1772–1834—Criticism and interpretation. 2. Sublime, The, in literature. I. Title.
PR4487.S92S76 2011
821'.7—dc22

2010034431

10 9 8 7 6 5 4 3 2 1
20 19 18 17 16 15 14 13 12 11

Printed and bound in Great Britain by
CPI Antony Rowe, Chippenham and Eastbourne

Contents

Acknowledgements

This research began as a DPhil thesis at the University of Sussex in 2004, in relation to which I must thank the AHRC (who provided a full scholarship), my two original examiners, Andrew Bennett and Sophie Thomas, and above all Nicholas Royle, who helped lay so much of the groundwork for this book with his unfailingly helpful and incisive supervisions. I would also like to thank my fellow DPhils at Sussex, who helped constitute a great community of scholarship and friendship: in particular, Miles Mitchard, Karen Schaller, Heba Youssef, Tatiana Kontou, Josh Vazquez, Jennifer Cooke and Peter Blake.

In bringing this study to completion, I owe a series of further debts. The staff at the British Library and the library of the Cornwall campus provided the spaces where this manuscript was hewn into shape, whilst my current colleagues at the University of Exeter have always been on hand, aiding this monograph both directly and indirectly. In particular, I'd like to thank Adeline Johns-Putra, Jason Hall, Alex Murray and Nick Groom, as well as the contingent of postgraduates on the University of Exeter's Cornwall campus. I should also acknowledge my fantastic undergraduate students, who have helped keep me sane (and intellectually sharp) throughout.

Finally, I would like to offer my gratitude to Palgrave Macmillan, notably Paula Kennedy, Benjamin Doyle and my thorough, but generous, anonymous reader.

Abbreviations and Textual Note

The following abbreviations are used throughout this book:

CP Samuel Taylor Coleridge, *The Complete Poems*, ed. William Keach (Harmondsworth: Penguin, 1997). Citations are given by line number, although the complete page range of the poem is indicated in the first citation.

CL Samuel Taylor Coleridge, *Collected Letters of Samuel Taylor Coleridge*, ed. E. L. Griggs, 6 vols (Oxford: Clarendon Press, 1956–71).

N Samuel Taylor Coleridge, *The Notebooks of Samuel Taylor Coleridge*, ed. Kathleen Coburn, 5 vols (London: Routledge, 1957–2002). Citations are given by note number (e.g. *N*1234). Numbering of notes is consecutive between volumes.

The following journal titles are also abbreviated:

ELH *English Literary History*

JAAC *Journal of Aesthetics and Art Criticism*

NLH *New Literary History*

MLN *Modern Language Notes*

The reader should also note that:

- Citations from multi-volume works include the volume number even if pagination is consecutive.
- With the exception of the medial ſ, all quotations from original editions are presented with non-modified spelling and punctuation.
- All biblical citations refer to the *Authorized King James Version* (1611).

Introduction

There is currently no full-length study of Coleridge and the sublime. This fact is rather surprising. The topic is central to histories and theories of Romanticism, and monographs entitled 'Poet X and the Sublime' are predictably common.[1] If we look at the recent Coleridge's Writings series, the sublime was chosen as a theme equal in importance to those of politics, humanity, language and religion.[2] And given Coleridge's immersion in German thought, as well as his authorship of what Paul Magnuson calls the nightmare poems, one would assume a dialogue is waiting to happen with a tradition whose major eighteenth-century proponents are Edmund Burke and Immanuel Kant.[3] However, one of the reasons that the sublime has not received systematic attention is precisely because it is not a systematic category as such in Coleridge's work. Unlike tropes such as the imagination or the symbol, it does not provide a centre around which he articulates a poetics, aesthetics or metaphysics. There is no grand statement to match the deduction of the imagination in the *Biographia Literaria*, or the definition of the symbol in *The Statesman's Manual*.

The closest he gets to an explicit theory of the sublime occurs in two 1814 fragments, which are involved in my analysis in Chapter 6. They are disappointingly brief. However, the fact that the sublime is not a systematic term in his writings is, for me, that which makes it most interesting and most valuable to study. Rather than being a centre in Coleridge's work, it is a fault-line, subject to a persistent ambiguity. The sublime is a category that has always involved a certain double-edgedness: its etymological and philosophical history alike attest to an experience of the limit, and we should remember every limit has both an inside and an outside edge. Characteristically, the sublime involves the opposites of pain and pleasure, the visionary and the invisible: it intimates the whole and yet is often fragmented or non-realised. As Longinus establishes, it expresses a taste for the infinite, yet it also evokes the finitude of human categories and perceptions. What the double-edgedness of the sublime does, I argue, is to expose the double-edgedness of Coleridge himself.

The main thrust of this study is to show that whilst Coleridge was always driven by the transcendence hoped for by the so-called Romantic ideology, he also had a sense of finitude every bit as profound as more openly sceptical Romantics like Byron or Keats. Moreover, he brought an intellectual range and strength unmatched by other English poets in coming to face that sense of finitude – to write and think *through* it. In many ways, in fact, he was as much a post-Romantic as he was a Romantic, someone who experienced a seemingly endless series of crises – the end of his Unitarian faith, the trauma of the French Revolution, the sense of his own poetic death, his struggles with metaphysical monism, his religious guilt, his existential isolation – each of which affected and undermined Romantic idealism. As I show in the readings that follow, the sublime is the discourse where much of this internal struggle is played out. The sublime implicates his grandest ambitions and desires (be they poetical, ethical, political or metaphysical) and yet also comes to inscribe the failure of those ambitions and desires, and the more finite positions articulated in the wake of these failures. There are transcendent, confident forms of the sublime, borne aloft by the grandeur of the Romantic ideology, but there are also weaker, more fragile and finite forms.

By attesting to both, this monograph aims to follow the lesson of Seamus Perry's *Coleridge and the Uses of Division*: there are always two sides to Coleridge, and the 'counter-current opposing Coleridge's idealist progress ... [is] too often overlooked'.[4] Certainly, this is true of nearly all existing work that analyses the sublime in Coleridge's poetry and thought. David Vallins, writing his introduction to the volume on the sublime from the *Coleridge's Writings* series, stakes out the following claim as cardinal:

> Coleridge ... is the foremost advocate of the aesthetic of transcendence ... No other British Romantic focuses so consistently as Coleridge on the importance of transcending the material, the everyday, or the mundanely comprehensible in favour of a confrontation with ... infinite forces.[5]

This monograph, in essence, argues that this is (less than) half the story. Defining the sublime exclusively as a category of transcendence not only forecloses what can be read in the texts and traditions of the sublime, but occludes a vital part of Coleridge.

Nevertheless, Vallins is merely summing up a broad critical consensus. The sublime is nearly always taken only in its positive aspect by Coleridgeans. For instance, Raimonda Modiano's discussion in *Coleridge and the Concept of Nature* begins with the proposition that 'at the centre of the Romantic sublime is the belief that man can transcend the boundaries of the phenomenal world'.[6] Her central thesis is based around a trope of reconciliation: the idea that Coleridge minimised the sense of rupture and crisis so prominent in the Kantian sublime in favour of a more composed, harmonious sublime. With serene infinitude, the mind is expanded without any violence or discontinuity, and the supersensible is evoked as informing a transfigured nature in a fashion which parts Coleridge fundamentally from Kant. As Modiano puts it, he 'wants to take nature along in the experience'.[7] The sublime, as a boundless force of reconciliation, is ultimately assigned to familiar centres of Coleridgean thought: the symbol and Christian doctrine. It is hard to detect any negativity or finitude in Modiano's conclusion: 'the essential and unique character of Coleridge's conception of the sublime rests on the integration of nature in an experience of transcendence tending towards a Christian "I AM"'.[8]

Of course, Modiano's analysis identifies many things about the Coleridgean sublime correctly, but it is one-sided. Those ideological centres – imagination, symbol, faith – are in an almost perpetual state of crisis and reconstruction from the very earliest stages of Coleridge's career and this is where I feel different forms of sublimity emerge. Yet, time and again, the sublime is posited only in its positivity. Steven Knapp, in his book *Personification and the Sublime*, sees the sublime primarily as a mediating and reconciliatory category, parallel to the symbol. Thus, just as the symbol balances the dangers of allegory (which loses touch with life) and literalism (which is too empirical), the sublime balances the supersensible locus of selfhood (which, again, may lose touch with life) and the threatened, physical self (which, again, is too empirical).[9] Once more the sublime is assimilated to another, more central, category, and it exists to successfully connect the finite to a transcendent ground beyond it.

Even where critics are ready to see the double-edgedness of the sublime, Coleridge receives much the same treatment. Thus, Thomas Weiskel's classic *The Romantic Sublime* is famously organised around a positive and a negative sublime. Yet the limited discussion of Coleridge largely positions him as proposing a positive theology of the self, and reads his theory of the imagination as a narcissistic mechanism.[10] Even Seamus Perry, who I have already cited as being alert to Coleridge's differences with himself, does not really advance over Modiano's conclusions made nearly twenty years earlier. He too places the Coleridgean sublime in the same positive frame, as a trope of reconciliation, success and transcendence:

> Coleridge's devotion to a totalising sublime is *more than satisfied* by the notion of a ubiquitous, divine creativity, subsuming the plurality of the world into unity, while at the same time his tenacious sensibility is gratified by the centrality reserved for nature in the new theology.[11]

Ironically it is perhaps David Vallins, writing in his own study *Coleridge and the Psychology of Romanticism*, who comes closest to the kind of reading that I wish to broach. Having emphasised a scission between thought and expression, he identifies a recurrent concern with obscurity as sublimity in Coleridge's writings. However, his conclusion turns from potentially transcendent ideas to the facticity of writing itself: 'the effect of his writing is primarily to draw attention to itself, and to the effort involved in producing it, rather than to the sublime ideas which it explicitly invokes'.[12] It is this kind of shift towards the finite that comes much closer to my own argument.

Too often, any thought of finitude in Coleridge's poetry has been analysed merely as a kind of de-sublimation. Thus, for example, Thomas Weiskel identifies certain lyrics ('Dejection: An Ode' and 'The Nightingale') as de-idealising the lyric ego and undercutting the sublime.[13] A similar point is made by Jerome McGann in identifying a disillusioned, revisionary phase in Coleridge's writing: in a poem like 'Constancy to an Ideal Object', there is no 'avenue for making or even anticipating new ideological affirmations'.[14] He praises the poem for exposing Romantic idealism as 'the ignorant pursuit of an illusion'.[15] When Coleridge is not being the Romantic ideologist *par excellence*, the advocate of transcendence, it seems he must instead be disenchanted. Finitude seems to mean nothing more than a *lack* of transcendence. A false dichotomy emerges between a sublime that is reduced to its transcendent moment and a sense of the finite that is seen purely as the end of an illusion.

What the false dichotomy overlooks is precisely the possibility for a more fragile sublimity, a sublimity that arises in the space where desire for transcendence is revised or relinquished. One can, after all, inscribe a limit without necessarily crossing *over* that limit. I want to make a threefold affirmation about this more restricted sublimity. Firstly, it has been far too often overlooked in Coleridge studies, in favour of the simplistic dichotomy between transcendence and disenchantment mentioned above, a dichotomy that drastically oversimplifies the aesthetics of the sublime. Secondly, new and interesting things happen within it: Coleridge articulates new poetics, new ethics and even new metaphysics based on a renewed experience of the limit. Thirdly, it remains something best analysed through the category of the sublime. A new formation of the sublime occurs, rather than a de-sublimation or a crossing into a different aesthetic category. In asserting these positions, I have drawn on contemporary analyses of the sublime rendered by recent literary theory: not least because they articulate a reading of the sublime not dominated by the assumption of transcendence. However, in the context of a dominant historicist approach in Romantic studies today, this methodological decision deserves further, more elaborate comment.

A conversation about finitude: Romanticism, theory, sublimity

Literary theory, in its most fundamental sense, is nothing more than a philosophical approach to literature: a conceptual rather than historical interrogation of its types, effects and consequences that is as old as Plato and Aristotle. It is, moreover, something that the Romantics, including Coleridge, pursued more extensively than virtually any other generation of writers. Shelley on poetry and legislation, Wordsworth on language and society, Keats on literature and negativity: these are all explicit examples of literary theorising. The *Biographia Literaria*, no less, is one of the most fascinating works of literary theory we possess. Consequently, it is a shame that this wider sense of theory has been lost because of the overexposure of a certain, very narrow, type of theoretical enquiry. In this study, I draw to a greater or lesser extent throughout on a body of ideas associated with continental philosophy and aesthetics, with phenomenology and with deconstruction. However, I aim to do so with a light touch, without too much jargon and with a due attention to history and the findings of historicist criticism.[16] I also want to keep the primary texts always in the foreground: someone like Paul de Man is, for me, most valuable as a way of continuing the tradition of close reading. Above all, I have attempted to be guided by two methodological principles. Firstly, to go beyond the narrow, textualist conclusions which dominated and doomed the period of high theory, and, secondly, to always treat theory as a reading of traditions and texts, rather than as a master-discourse.

Let me address the first principle first, for I believe it is precisely in a turn towards the aesthetics of the sublime – as in parallel turns towards ethics and theology – that we see a fuller sense of theory's scope inscribed.[17] Jean-Luc Nancy remarked in 1988 that 'one may be tempted to imagine that our epoch is rediscovering the *sublime*'.[18] As shown by a glance through the contributors to the collection that Nancy's observation prefaces, translated into English as *Of the Sublime: Presence in Question*, this rediscovery implicated a considerable swathe of theorists: Jean-François Lyotard would be the obvious and pre-eminent example, but the sublime was addressed directly by many others.[19] One interesting thing about this chronology is that the juncture when the aesthetics of the sublime became a dominant concern for French theorists was also roughly the high-water mark for theory in literary studies, at least in Anglo-American departments.

Indeed, what we might term the first wave of theory was rather hostile to the sublime. The major deconstructive readings of Coleridge from the period of high theory – texts like Tilottama Rajan's *Dark Interpreter* (1980) and *The Supplement of Reading* (1990), Jerome Christensen's *Coleridge's Blessed Machine of Language* (1981) and Susan Eilenberg's *Strange Power of Speech* (1992) – are largely indebted to the type of deconstruction practised by Paul de Man. They share with de Man a consuming interest in the operation of figures and tropes, and the notion that language is ultimately rhetorical rather than referential. The endpoint of any de Manian analysis tends to be an avowal of textual irony. Thus, two of Rajan's major conclusions are that 'Romanticism accepts the arbitrariness of its own signs, yet constantly seeks ways to deny the traumatic implications' and that Coleridge was 'perhaps too committed to the legacy of a transcendental poetics'.[20] Eilenberg's analysis of the relationship between Coleridge and Wordsworth argues that 'each body of writing ... aggressively allegorizes the other ... Wordsworth demystifies the Coleridgean uncanny; Coleridge deconstructs the Wordsworthian matter-of-fact'.[21] And Christensen's analysis of the *Biographia Literaria* and other texts is rooted in identifying an endless linguistic deferral operating mechanistically against Coleridge's stated intentions.[22]

As Derrida accurately observed in a eulogy, 'Paul [de Man] was irony itself'.[23] Given this preference for irony – irony being, perhaps, one of sublimity's obvious opposites – it is perhaps unsurprising that de Man himself found the sublime a discourse that was too idealist.[24] We see this in an essay like 'Phenomenality and Materiality in Kant'.[25] De Man argues that the crucial thing about the Kantian analysis lies in a narrative of sacrifice imposed to permit the relationship between imagination and reason to become meaningful. His objection is that this is not 'an argument, [but] ... a story, a dramatized scene of the mind'.[26] The shift between the terms of the mathematical sublime (number, extension and quantity) to those of the dynamical (power, morality and mortality) allows the different faculties of the human mind to be cast as personifications in a tragic scene: 'the story of an exchange, of a negotiation, in which powers are lost and gained in an economy of sacrifice and recuperation'.[27] When the imagination plays the role of Antigone or Iphigenia, then its failure to comprehend the sublime object can be invested with meaning as a sacrifice. Yet what does it mean for a part of the mind to *sacrifice* itself? How can a psychological faculty be said to take up a part in this way? De Man's point – and the nub of his deconstruction – is that the Kantian sublime is essentially a figural construction. The sublime is revealed as an effect of allegory: in essence, Kant is ironised.

However, if irony seems the natural outcome of a de Manian deconstruction, I would like to draw attention to what Derrida calls 'a certain beyond-of-irony'.[28] Although Derrida identifies this beyond-of-irony as a subtle side of de Man's own work, the phrase perhaps better represents the drift of his own practice of deconstruction, as one can see from the following interview with Richard Kearney:[29]

> It is totally false to suggest that deconstruction is a suspension of reference. Deconstruction is deeply concerned with the 'other' of language. I never cease to be surprised by critics who see my work as a declaration that there is nothing beyond language, that we are imprisoned in language; it is, in fact, saying the exact opposite.[30]

Recent French theory, in its various 'turns' as well as through thinkers who are more phenomenological and Heideggerian than Derrida, could be described as increasingly pursuing a 'beyond-of-irony' and the '"other" of language'. Rather than halting at the exposure of a vertiginous textual irony, it has pursued instead a certain *sublime* logic: theorising experiences at the limits of signification and phenomenality. It is no surprise that theory turned to the sublime as a topic as its own logic became increasingly sublime itself. It is perhaps unfortunate that literary studies turned away from theory – on the understandable grounds that avowals of textual irony were becoming clichéd and tired – at more or less this point. Yet even when important works of theoretically informed Romantic criticism have appeared since the heyday of theory, they still tend to privilege the tropes of text, reference, figure, reading, writing and voice. Angela Esterhammer's *The Romantic Performative*, for instance, is innovative because it looks at the performative, but still, of course, remains primarily locked within an analysis of language.

In this book I attempt to exploit the recent theoretical turns made by theorists and continental thinkers in order to reconnect analyses of language with other kinds of narrative intertwined with the sublime. My initial chapters, on language, are perhaps predictably the most de Manian of my readings: yet I have also tried to use Rei Terada's interpretation of emotion to bring questions of passion, affect and feeling back into the picture. Theory need not imply pure scepticism – that emotions do not exist – as David Vallins suggests when avowing his own emotional essentialism.[31] In my chapters on terror, particularly in my reading of 'The Rime of the Ancient Mariner', I am heavily influenced by the recent engagement of theory with questions of freedom, evil and guilt: again, themes that might seem unusually traditional given the textualist theory familiar to Romantic studies. And in my fifth and sixth chapters, where the invocation of recent theorists such as Jean-Luc Nancy and Jean-Luc Marion is at its most explicit, I am indebted to the so-called theological turn in phenomenology. This reconnects theory to that most vexed topic of all: God.

More generally, my methodology has a phenomenological drift. I do not treat the subject merely as a rhetorical or textual category (as it threatens to be, incidentally, in Knapp's analysis of sublime personification). In many ways, a subjectivity that is estranged from itself is the most recurrent motif of this study, and I am keen not to posit it merely as a signifier 'I' adrift in language. In this, I am influenced by the more Heideggerian and Husserlian side of recent French theory, as well as a renewed interest in the question as to who or what succeeds the so-called death of the subject.[32] A more phenomenological engagement with subjectivity – particularly evident at the end of my second and fourth chapters – offers an alternative to more essentialist notions of the subject, as well as to the misconception that theory implies that the subject simply doesn't exist, or is just a grammatical fiction.

Yet, all this is more or less ungrounded or anachronistic if we do not remember the second methodological principle – that theory is not a master-discourse, but readings of – and *inside* – a tradition. In general, I have only invoked theorists when their readings are rooted in texts from Coleridge's influences or contemporaries. For instance, it is via

Terada's references to John Keats that I put her concept of *pathos* into play with Coleridge, and it is Immanuel Kant who triangulates my readings of Coleridge, Jean-Luc Nancy and Jean-Luc Marion in Chapter 6. At times, we must also accept that certain texts remain ahead, as it were, of their readers. I exploit this kind of dynamic in my fifth chapter, for instance, when I argue that deconstructive scepticism directed against the Romantic nature sublime has already been anticipated by Immanuel Kant's strictures against visionary rapture, and Kant's text not only manages this, but offers a further set of resources (neglected by de Man and others) to understand the relationship between aesthetics and theology.

Positioning theorists in this way, as readers of and participants in tradition, is to acknowledge two crucial things about a justifiable use of theory. Firstly, we see that theory need not be merely the intellectual wing of some postmodern *zeitgeist*, committed only to issues of the text – as the reproduction of French thought through the Yale School and in turn the imitators of the Yale School might suggest. Rather, serious theory is part of a lineage of continental philosophy: engaged with the major figures of the European tradition (Descartes, Kant, Hegel, Heidegger) and with the perennial issues of philosophy, such as emotion, evil and theism/atheism. Secondly, it is to recognise that theory itself is shaped by philosophical history, not least the philosophical history of the Romantic period.[33] The grand axis from Kant to Hegel, the very axis in which Coleridge himself was so deeply immersed, is the legacy that modern literary theory of whatever stripe continues to work through. One of the most valuable assumptions of theory is that we have not finished reading Kant or the German Romantics, or exhausting the continued power and relevance of those texts – and I would affirm exactly the same of Coleridge.

To return specifically to the sublime, we must recall that it is readings of the *Critique of Judgment* – and to a lesser but still important extent, Burke and Longinus – that continue to be the site for contemporary meditations on the sublime. As Nancy remarks 'the sublime properly constitutes our tradition ... not *an* aesthetics ... [but] the aesthetic as question'.[34] This is not a question that is going to go away, at least not whilst we are held by a broadly Romantic or post-Romantic intellectual legacy. What I have found particularly useful and provocative about the various theoretical returns to the sublime is that they identify the sublime as a privileged moment in the philosophical and aesthetic thinking of the limit – of what it means to confront a boundary of what is cognisable or representable – and identify a need to continue a dialogue with that thinking. In this sense, we may describe the sublime as a conversation about finitude. Longinus, Burke and Kant take part in this conversation, as do Derrida, Nancy and Lyotard: and as do the English Romantics, including Coleridge.

Coleridge, in short, belongs to an ongoing tradition. In the same way that Paul Hamilton has recently identified a philosophically vibrant Coleridge who contributed to a Hegelian moment that is, in some important ways, still *our* moment, I see Coleridge's thought as representing a fascinating conjunction between transcendence and finitude which implicates our own condition as a post-Romantic age.[35] He has a pivotal role as one of the great Romantic architects of transcendence, and throughout this book my readings tend to set off from one or another desire for transcendence. Yet, we must remember the double-edgedness of Coleridge and the sublime alike: this desire for transcendence was often a torn one. Moreover, in the wake of failures and crises, Coleridge does not merely revert to disillusion but tends to emerge with a renewed sense of the finite. The following quotation from his late work *Aids to Reflection* could act as a motif for this study: 'the Life, we seek after, is a mystery; but so both in itself and in its origin is the Life we have'.[36] The strange presence of mystery in 'the Life we have', of an immanence divided against itself, is crucial to this other side of Coleridge, so occluded by existing criticism. Jean-François Lyotard claims that the sublime 'does not reside in an over there, in another world, or another time, but in this: in that (something) happens', and there is something of this always accompanying the more conventional, transcendentalising Coleridge.[37] Finitude is always inherent in the motif of transcendence. It is this doubleness which makes Coleridge's voice far more subtle, interesting and intellectually challenging than has previously been acknowledged.

The tradition of the sublime: Longinus, Burke, Kant

Foregrounding the notion of a tradition of the sublime demands that we understand the constitution of whatever tradition is in question. It was noted earlier that the sublime was not a systematic category: perhaps that has something to do with its excessive and ambivalent nature as a concept – the aforementioned double-edgedness – but it also has to do with what Peter de Bolla describes as a discursive tendency to overrun those discourses adjoining it.[38] The sublime, by the Romantic period, was everywhere, which is why a study like this could cover a potentially limitless set of concerns and texts. Nevertheless, we can identify three figures as by far the most influential pivots around which the tradition of the sublime is articulated. These are the anonymous third-century rhetorician known as Longinus, the British philosopher Edmund Burke, and Immanuel Kant. It is in acknowledgement of this that this study is structured around these figures and the three broad areas they helped define in sublime terms: language by Longinus, terror by Burke, and representation by Kant.

My opening section takes its bearings from Longinus's treatise *Peri Hypsous*, arguing that in defining the sublime as the highest intensity of linguistic expression, he gave to the eighteenth century a troubling double legacy. Firstly, he set up a model of a discourse that could not be governed by normal, formal rules, but was instead referred to an exceptional subjectivity: the impassioned transport of the great poet or orator. However, he also theorised the technical manipulation of figures which threatened to falsify that very aesthetic of sincerity. I trace the presence of both legacies in some of Coleridge's earliest poetry, and his first poetic persona, via the so-called effusions found in 1796's *Poems on Various Subjects*. These effusions suggested an outburst of genuine feeling and yet also increasingly engaged with a certain theatricality or fabulosity of the passions. Given that Longinus's texts obviously involve a more complex reception history than Burke or Kant, I also look at two mid-century writers who help, albeit partially and incompletely, to bridge the gap between the remote classical context and the 1790s.

The problem of passion continues in a political register, as I explore in my second chapter's reading of the 1798 *Fears in Solitude* quarto. The value of passion *per se*, and its relation to wider discourses on justification, principle and conviction, is raised in 'France: An Ode', and in 'Fears in Solitude' itself. By the quarto's final poem, 'Frost at Midnight', Coleridge has radically refigured his speaking position into a more private space. Making a fresh case for the lyric element of this poem (whilst acknowledging more recent historicist and political readings), I use Rei Terada's notion of pathos as a second-order emotion to explore the way that Coleridge confronts the experience of affect as destabilising, rather than being possessed by, an 'I'. This re-engages Coleridge with another side of the Longinian tradition: the negativity of the Sapphic lyric, founded on dispossession, fragmentation and the non-coincidence of feeling with itself.

My third chapter begins by noting the central importance of terror in the wake of Burke's *A Philosophical Enquiry into the Origin of Our Ideas of the Sublime and Beautiful*. However, by comparing the empiricist philosophies of Burke and associationist thinker David Hartley, we can understand why Coleridge never adopts a Burkean sublime. He uses Hartleian thinking in the context of Unitarian radicalism to develop a sublime that is not a passion of self-preservation (as Burke theorises), but a social, political passion rooted in an experience of sympathy, and the binding of individuals into a wider ethical community. The unfinished poem 'The Destiny of Nations' exemplifies this ethical terror-sublime. However, its unfinishedness marks a certain problem: the intractability of evil and suffering proves difficult to assimilate into a Unitarian framework, motivating a turn to archaic images of divine vengeance and violence at odds with political and ethical optimism. In fact, such images of God as raw power revert back to a Burkean conception of terror as pure physical force.

The problem of evil continues to menace Coleridge, as I explore in my fourth chapter and a reading of his most famous creation, 'The Rime of the Ancient Mariner'. In an interpretation which overturns the usual characterisation of the Christian content of the poem, I argue that the oft-noted strangeness and obscurity is best attributed to the irrationality of the doctrines of original sin and originary guilt. I also argue that contemporary reactions to the excessive and disturbing nature of the ballad can be attributed to a fundamental difference in kind between Coleridge's terror-sublime in the 'Rime', and the standard eighteenth-century taste for terror. Whereas the Burkean model places the terrors firmly outside a perceiving subject (hence the recurrent motif of a necessary distance), the 'Rime' places the terrors *inside* a subject. The subject, confronting an irreducible yet inexplicable sense of guilt at its very root, terrifies itself. This, I believe, is why the poem still continues to speak so powerfully to the contemporary world: Coleridge's reconceptualisation of original sin, abandoning a legalistic model in favour of a kind of haunting responsibility for evil, is strikingly contemporary.

My third section, following Kant, explores the relationship between presentation and sublimity. Chapter 5 offers an interpretation of Coleridge's perhaps most archetypally sublime text, 'Hymn Before Sun-Rise'. I show initially how Coleridge's sublime differs from that theorised in *The Critique of Judgment,* chiefly in its desire for a positive representation of the supersensible and concomitant religious transcendence (as noted by Modiano, although not in a reading of this text). I then pursue a de Manian reading that deconstructs the way that Coleridge figures the landscape for his own ends, but note that Kant himself has anticipated many of deconstruction's own anti-visionary and anti-transcendent gestures. With this in mind, I return to the Kantian text, and examine the motif of the divine name. A reconsideration of the divine name in the 'Hymn' shows that its referential function is increasingly displaced by an experience of the appellative or prayer, attesting to God's alterity to nature. I conclude the chapter by looking at two further poems that privilege an experience of prayer (and divine withdrawal) over a more conventional natural sublimity (and divine presence).

Chapter 6 also looks at the relationship between presentation and a possible beyond-of-presentation. It begins by analysing Coleridge's 1814 definitions of the sublime as the suspension of the comparative power, and links them to a long-running valorisation of wholeness and totality in Coleridge's work. All-ness is the key trope here. However, examining various texts, one finds that the thought of a presentation of all-ness can quickly become nihilistic. Being may revert to nothingness, as all-ness threatens to absorb everything into a single, undifferentiated, stagnant perception. After linking this to Coleridge's travails with monism, I identify a rather different kind of the sublime in *The Friend*, which moves forcefully beyond the paradigm of presentation. What provokes wonder is not a given form, even one that stretches perception to its limits, but that forms – being, existence – are at all. Coleridge anticipates the Heideggerian question *par excellence* – why is there something, rather than nothing? Defining this as a sublime of givenness, I conclude the chapter by comparing Coleridge's work with two contemporary readings of Kant's sublime that focus on givenness, and assess the relationship between givenness, theology and philosophy.

My final chapter acts as a conclusion in so far as the texts considered neatly encapsulate the movement from transcendence to finitude, and the emergence of a more fragile sublime in the spaces where the Romantic ideology has been challenged, fractured or abandoned. It poses the *Biographia Literaria* against the Limbo poems. The *Biographia* can be read, I argue, as trying to merge the beautiful with the sublime into one absolute aesthetic category. It represents the grandest ambitions of Romanticism. Yet, at the same time, Coleridge was writing in his notebooks a poetry of almost pure finitude, characterised by a strange fragmentary form, lack of unity and recurrent gestures of *apophasis*. Coleridge describes the Limbo fragments as a sublimity dashed to pieces. Yet, this motif could stand for the entire thrust of this study: fragment, divide, limit and render finite the sublime and what you are left with is still sublime, since fragmentation, division, liminality and finitude are merely the alternative moments of an always double-edged discourse.

Again and again, we find Coleridge's texts articulating a similar set of issues, as a path is traced from Romantic idealism towards a more complex sense of the finite. He begins by articulating a desire for transcendence, and in many senses that desire accompanies him throughout his career. It is an irreducible component of Romanticism. However, it is also true that every articulation of transcendence, whether poetic, ethical, theological or in any other discourse, tends to be in a constant state of disarticulation: whether due to internal contradiction or outside trauma, under the pressure of Coleridge's keen awareness of weakness and lack, or the critical gaze of his mobile intelligence. In turn, we see newly finite considerations of existence and a reiteration of the strangeness of the life we have. That may make itself felt in the shape of the lyric restlessness of 'Frost at Midnight', the abyssal guilty subject of the 'Rime', or in some of most sophisticated Romantic theology that the era produced. We should not overlook the finite thinking and finite poetics that this side of Coleridge poses against his better-known reputation as a transcendent thinker. If we possess, as I think we do, the task of becoming a truly post-Romantic age, working through both the lure and the impossibility of its aesthetic and intellectual programme, then there are few figures more provocative and invaluable. The double-edgedness of our legacy is mirrored by a profoundly double-edged Coleridge. Rather than being held up by the confident self-representations of concepts such as the symbol or the imagination, it is time to map the fault-line of the sublime.

Part I
Language, Longinus, Emotion

1
'Violently Agitated by a Real Passion': Longinus and Coleridge's Effusions

The sublime was originally a rhetorical category: the highest and most powerful language. The classical treatise *On Sublimity*, attributed to Longinus, considers it very simply as 'a kind of eminence or excellence of discourse'.[1] Although the Longinian sublime has now receded somewhat from view, it was formerly central, as one can see from Theodore Wood's classic survey of usage or a representative anthology like that edited by Andrew Ashfield and Peter de Bolla.[2] It was Nicolas Boileau's translation of Longinus from 1674 that arguably reinserted sublimity into the heart of the European critical vocabulary. John Milton's *Paradise Lost* won its reputation as archetypally sublime not just because it represented the unrepresentable divine, but also because of genre, linguistic effect and daring use of figure and personification. Powerful language on the most powerful themes, rhetoric magnified to its greatest pitch, poetry that seized its readers' imaginations with no uncertain violence: this was just as much the core of the sublime for an early eighteenth-century reader as any thought of mountains or storms. It is thus important, I think, to be faithful to this history, and to give the matter of language and a Longinian tradition their due place in any study of the sublime.[3]

Whilst the work of Edmund Burke and others had already set the sublime on a perceptual footing by the late eighteenth century, the linguistic aspect of sublimity would have been familiar to Coleridge from his university studies in rhetoric. This is true even if he had never studied Longinus directly, for Longinian ideas were common rhetorical currency.[4] Indeed, if we look at Coleridge's use of the word 'sublime' in his first published collection – *Poems on Various Subjects* – only once does it appear unambiguously in reference to an object of perception.[5] More commonly, it describes grandeur of thought, emotion or expression, often with a political edge, as in the following sonnet to jurist Thomas Erskine:

> When British Freedom for an happier land
> Spread her broad wings, that flutter'd with affright,
> ERSKINE! thy voice she heard, and paus'd her flight
> Sublime of hope![6]

Therefore, it appears that Coleridge was just as likely to consider sublimity as intensity of discourse (or indeed voice), as he was to define it as intensity of perception.

I am going to argue in this chapter that the notion of a sublime speaking position, derived ultimately from Longinus, was a major preoccupation for Coleridge in the 1790s. Such a speaking position is based on the production of an irregular, seemingly spontaneous discourse. Normal rules of judgement are suspended and transcended as the audience or reader is seized by the power of the speaker: the very excess over rules becomes the defining feature. However, a conflict between the veracity of the language (said to stem from its intimate relation to the speaker's own emotional state) and the technical manipulation of figures runs throughout the Longinian tradition, and can be seen to problematise Coleridge's early poetics of the *effusion*. Thus, whilst the young Coleridge is very keen to appropriate a speaking position where the outpouring of emotion is paramount, and truth to the speaker's inner state is the foremost measure of worth, the extensive use of figures in the poems suggests a language not of truth, but of dissimulation. Moreover, by turning to recent theories of emotion developed from a de Manian position on figures, we can see that Coleridge's effusive lyric subject has its all important truth value threatened not only because it stages its emotions to auditors or readers, but also because it stages its emotions to itself.

Force and origin: genius in Longinus's *On Sublimity*

What seems characteristically sublime about the discourse analysed in Longinus's *Peri Hypsous* is *intensity*, that is, a performative moment of concentrated power rather than the structural extension of a discourse arranged into parts. Thus, the Longinian sublime appears as a kind of anti-composition, based on ravishment in an instant rather than cumulative persuasion:

> Experience in invention and ability to order and arrange material cannot be detected in single passages; we begin to appreciate them

> only when we see the whole context. Sublimity, on the other hand, produced at the right moment, tears everything up like a whirlwind, and exhibits the orator's whole power at a single blow. (pp. 143–4)

It is a point of force, legible because of the way it tears into the fabric or syntax (from the Greek, *syn-taxis*, to arrange together) of language itself. The tropes of sublimity analysed by Longinus are those that disrupt syntax: asyndeton, polyptoton and hyperbaton. An irregularity in arrangement characterises the highest poetry or oratory, with 'oversights let fall at random ... with the negligence of genius' (p. 176). As such, the sublime in language threatens to be illegal: its intension becomes a withdrawal from an order that could be entirely formalisable and rule-bound. Longinus recognises this with some alarm: 'grandeur is particularly dangerous when left on its own ... abandoned to mere impulse and ignorant temerity. It often needs the curb as well as the spur' (p. 144).

Sublime language is de-structured, and hence the rules of rhetorical composition are not necessarily effective in either describing or prescribing the nature of sublime utterance. Fundamentally, this is because linguistic sublimity is not amenable to laws of spatiality, being itself defined by *temporality*. As Jacques Derrida points out in his essay 'Force and Signification', 'the notion of structure refers only to space, geometric or morphological space, the order of forms and sites'.[7] By contrast, sublime speech is temporal: it is a force, it strikes in a single moment and as Longinus notes 'makes a strong and ineffaceable impression on the *memory*' (p. 148, my emphasis). Sublime rhetoric is not meant to be an elegant spatial arrangement; rather it is a series of all-consuming temporal apexes bursting *through* normal structures. As such, rhetorical principles governing the structure or syntax of a discourse – its spatiality – have only limited relevance to sublime oratory and the temporality of its force. Indeed, as Longinus's section on sublimity versus mediocrity argues, genius tends towards 'that bursting forth of the divine spirit which is so hard to bring under the rule of law' (p. 176). Although he has not entwined the two to the same extent, say, as Immanuel Kant, genius maintains a systematic relation with the exceeding of rules. There arises, therefore, a problem in how sublime force might be regulated, given that Longinus has already admitted that linguistic sublimity is potentially dangerous.

The answer is to turn away from trying to legislate sublime discourse through its spatial form, through rules or conventions, but rather to address its temporality: Longinus assigns sublime force an *origin*. The necessary regulation for sublime utterance is provided by a constant recourse to the notion of *genius*, which – as its etymology suggests – is a genealogical concept: 'sublimity is the echo of a noble mind' (p. 150). Supposedly only the greatest of human beings have the capacity to reflect on, and thus to express, the greatest of thoughts:

> those whose thoughts and habits are trivial and servile all their lives cannot possibly produce anything admirable or worthy of eternity. (p. 150)

Force, therefore, expresses its origin.[8] Regardless of how much rhetorical grandeur is applied to language, if one does not have a soul naturally inclined to reflection and greatness – what Longinus later describes as 'an irresistible desire for anything which is great, and in relation to ourselves, supernatural' (p. 178) – then any force rendered into language will be illicit: 'a show of grandeur which, for all its accidental trappings, will, when dissected, prove vain and hollow' (p. 148). Hence, the genealogy of force allows one to certify that a sublime discourse is ultimately in the service of the noble and good, and thus not dangerous. Genius acts as a safeguard at the origin of rhetorical force.

The genealogy of genius to which Longinus appeals goes as far back as possible, to the very root of the orator's selfhood. Genius is not a culturally acquired identity or role that, once gained, allows one to produce sublime discourse: it is rather an innate, natural inheritance and a given at birth. One cannot become or learn to be a genius. Indeed perhaps this is logically impossible, in that the acquirable implies transmission and thus formalisation, and the sublime is on the very edge of what is formalisable. This natural element to genius can be seen in the metaphors used when Longinus justifies the transgression of artistic decorum characteristic of sublime genius: Pindar and Sophocles are compared to fire, Demosthenes to a thunderbolt. It is notable that Longinus's most prominent reference to the *natural sublime* – the sublimity of oceans, stars and volcanoes that become archetypal *topoi* for Burke and Kant – occurs at the conclusion of this discussion. Although Longinus is careful not to slight cultural rules – choice of figures, noble diction and elevated word-arrangement are three of his five sources for sublimity – these rest on a natural foundation prior to rhetorical education: 'the power to conceive great thoughts' and 'strong and inspired emotion' (p. 149). This naturalness is of course highly reassuring, since if nobility cannot be learned or acquired, then it leads one to hope that it cannot be faked. As such, the resistance of sublime discourse to codification under cultural structures (i.e. the rules of rhetorical composition) is transcended by appealing to an origin in nature.

One modern commentator on Longinus who has paid special attention to the relation between origins and sublimity is French critic Michel Deguy. He describes the Longinian sublime as 'the simulation of a primordial, exalted state of language'.[9] The sublime, he argues, is tinged with nostalgia for a sacred source: 'the "phenomenological" return to the things themselves', to the things which had 'meaning for one's ancestors'.[10] Thus, Longinus reads Homer because Homer is the zero degree, the origin, of Western poetry. Homer is exalted because he is writing an epic poem before, as it were, the art of poetry existed. Our discussion of genius is analogous because sublime language has a genealogy rendering it prior to the arts of rhetoric. What is at stake in Homer and the great orators alike is rooting sublime language, which seems to exist outside of cultural propriety, in a pre-cultural origin. Deguy, however, goes on to deconstruct this appeal to a natural origin. The sacred source, Deguy claims, is a simulation; it is *not real*. The sublime is a moment where all the arts that go towards framing a linguistic statement (words, figures, rhythms and so forth) consume themselves to leave the *impression* of an exalted state of language – for in fact the elements of language have done nothing more than conceal their artificiality. Sublime language would no longer be grounded in the natural, but is rather a disguised form of art. Yet this is not merely a hermeneutic of suspicion on Deguy's part: it is Longinus's own definition. Deguy specifies exactly the point in Longinus's treatise that serves to undermine his appeal to a natural origin: the concealed figure. For *Peri Hypsous* is also a rhetorical manual and chapters in this vein give it a rather self-divided structure: an opening and, to a lesser extent, a conclusion which highlight the innate or natural nobility of genius; and a middle section which teaches the art of rhetoric and how an orator may wield the many figures of the sublime.

It is the moment when Longinus instructs the orator on how to conceal figures that threatens to open a radical breach between nature and artifice, between a language of expression or exhibition and of concealment:

> A figure is therefore generally thought to be best when the fact that it is a figure is concealed ... sublimity and emotion are a defence and a marvellous aid against the suspicion which the use of figures engenders. The artifice of the trick is lost to sight in the surrounding brilliance ... and it escapes all suspicion. (p. 164)

Ironically, given that emotion is the second of Longinus's pre-cultural or natural sources of sublimity, his treatment of figures (the third source) defines them largely as the studied *simulacra* of emotions.

Thus, Longinus states that 'the figure of question and answer arrests the hearer and cheats him into believing that all the points made were raised and are being put into words on the spur of the moment' (p. 165). Asyndeton (the omission of conjunctions) and hyperbaton (inversion) are both marshalled as good ways to give the impression of agitation and unpremeditated emotion; they are commended for being, ironically, 'a very real mark of urgent emotion' (p. 166). Sublimity thus becomes characterised by dissimulation; its naturalness a studied effect of rhetorical art. The origin in the high emotion of a noble soul is ultimately fictive. As Deguy emphasises, the apparent destruction of all that is rhetorical and artificial in a given discourse is itself rhetorical and artificial. What we actually have is figures disguising themselves as natural: 'the denegated figure, the figure of the denegation of figure'.[11]

In fact, Longinus's tactic here may be said to mirror a certain sublime logic of the concealed figure. Securing sublime discourse is a matter of giving force – which outstrips the spatial regulation of rhetorical convention – a temporal regulation in an origin. To do this, a transparently expressive relation is said to hold between a discourse that can be barely held in limits and a mind that is similarly expansive. With scale as his primary term (elevation, enlargement, expansion), he assumes that the greatest of ideas and the greatest of emotional effects can only be produced by a great soul, one with ethical and noble qualities. Of course, it does not logically follow that a noble discourse should be the exclusive property of the noble. Rather, it follows *figurally*. As such, there is a transfer of qualities circulating in a chiasmic fashion between the text and the genius that supposedly lies behind it. As already mentioned, Longinus relies on an expressive relation maintaining that 'sublimity is the echo of a noble mind' (p. 150). However, the discursive excesses of sublime texts are cited for 'the greatness of spirit they reveal' (p. 176). This creates a chiasmus in that the sublimity of the text is determined through the existence of genius, and the existence of genius is inferred from the sublimity of the text. Although genius is invoked to offer a genealogy, an origin and ultimately a validation to sublime discourse, it turns out to be purely specular. It is a mirror image of the rule-breaking in the text – 'the universe ... is not wide enough for the range of human speculation and intellect' (p. 178) – for which it supposedly provides legitimacy. Just as individual emotional origins can be dissimulated by concealed figures, here the origin of sublimity *per se* is dissimulated by the subtle force of the chiasmus just discussed.[12]

If the soul of the genius is inferred from the very textual effects it supposedly guarantees, this leads Longinus's sublime towards a more general crisis in the validity of subjective interiority similar to that identified by Paul de Man in *Allegories of Reading*. In de Man's analysis of Rainer Maria Rilke, he shows that the qualities of inwardness which we feel belong to the poetic subject in fact reside metaphorically in objects of perception: 'the figure of chiasmus ... crosses the attributes of inside and outside'.[13] Indeed, the notion of interiority being surreptitiously and chiastically constructed out of its own objects is a recurrent one in *Allegories of Reading*: Marcel Proust's inner space of contemplation recuperating the warmth of a sensate outside, for instance, or the self in Jean-Jacques Rousseau being figured by a fashioned object or a beloved other.[14] The consequences for a privileged subjectivity are radical, in so far as exposing interiority as just a figure intimates 'the loss, the disappearance of the subject as subject'.[15] As such, when Longinian style of passionate interiority became the foundation for a poetic 'I' in Romanticism (as I shall argue below), the problem of figures and figurality raises high stakes around the emotional authenticity of the speaking subject.

This is where the recent work of Rei Terada is especially useful.[16] De Manian deconstruction still holds as perhaps the most sophisticated analysis of figurality we have, but Terada's invocation of deconstruction as a powerful theory of emotion pushes our readings beyond the merely textual and linguistic in a way that has not been fully appreciated or utilised in literary criticism. Essentially, Terada challenges the so-called *expressive hypothesis*, which analyses emotions as intentional properties of unified subjects. The privileged and occult interiority, so important as an originary and creative point in Longinus, is displaced by a subject who feels (itself) through tropes, theatricality and performativity. I intend to keep Terada's re-reading of de Man in mind in what follows, both because it pushes my deconstructive methodology into more interesting territories, but also because it keeps our own analysis close to the terms important to Longinus: emotion, subjectivity and interiority. (A third reason will become apparent in the next chapter, when I take Terada's reading of pathos as a second-order emotion and apply it to the lyric subjectivity of 'Frost at Midnight'.) However, before going on to Coleridge, I want to turn first to two representative eighteenth-century thinkers: James Burgh and John Lawson. Such a discussion not only helps elaborate how Coleridge may have inherited a certain Longinian tradition through cultural movements earlier in the century, but also identifies a subtle change of emphasis (from rhetoric to poetics, from manipulation of figures to a more diffuse notion of the imaginative and fabular) which will prove important to the effusive 'I' that Coleridge eventually fashions as his first mature literary identity.

Longinian genius in eighteenth-century Britain

The cultural currency of Longinus was arguably at its height in the first half of the eighteenth century, when discussions of sublime discourse often used the Longinian treatise as a reference point. Thus, although as already noted Coleridge may not have studied Longinus directly, his influence would have been impossible to avoid through a corpus of British texts, a few of which are worth surveying to provide a bridge between Longinus and Coleridge's contemporary context. A particularly clear example, from Ashfield and De Bolla's useful collection of sources, is Sir Richard Blackmore, who paraphrases Longinus slavishly:

> It is impossible for a man inured only to base and vulgar thoughts, to reach that elevation of mind which is necessary for an orator of the first rank ... [Longinus] advises men to nourish in their minds a generous temper, that will always incline them to form high and noble ideas ... he should not grovel in the dust, nor breathe in thick impure air, but keep above, and inure himself to lofty contemplation, till by a constant correspondence and intercourse with superior objects, he gets a habit of thinking in the great and elevated manner.[17]

Yet although eighteenth-century writings recapitulate the Longinian position, they also recapitulate its paradoxes. Genius supposedly offers a genealogy for force, seeing it as the natural product of a great soul, and thus ensuring its sincerity. However, as we have seen, the close relation between sublimity and figurality associates it with performativity and staging.

One good example of these issues is the mid-century essay 'The Art of Speaking' by educationalist James Burgh, which prefaces a set of exercises designed to instil, unsurprisingly enough, the arts of rhetoric in the young. He expresses clearly, in Longinian terms, the force of sublime language:

> True eloquence does not wait for cool *approbation*. Like irresistible *beauty*, it *transports*, it *ravishes*, it *commands* the *admiration* of all, who are within its reach. If it allows us *time* to *criticise*, it is not genuine.[18]

Indeed, Burgh claims that the combination of image and sound makes sublime language the most powerful force that can be applied to the human mind. He goes even further than Longinus in depicting a situation of absolute dominance: the orator is said to actually take possession of the passions of the audience, and work them as he pleases. Every thought is driven out of the minds of the hearers but that which the orator wishes to impress: an oratorical point is described as something to be carried, as if it was a military assault.

No doubt Burgh intended such force to be used only in ethical ways: his closing concerns in the essay are with preaching and the church, and he considers it shameful that an age enlightened by modern science and Christian revelation cannot produce a Plato or a Cicero.[19] It is all part of the thesis of the 'Art of Speaking' that oratory will improve general intercourse, the professions and particularly the pulpit. Yet how is such rhetorical power to be policed? Burgh repeats, as might be expected, the Longinian position that sublime expression is limited to the ethically elevated: 'the consummate *speaker*' displays 'all that is noble in human nature'.[20] Yet equally, Burgh carries over from Longinus the problem of the concealed figure: it appears that although the consummate speaker is noble and ethical, he must be prepared to manipulate, and manipulate well, for *'art, seen through*, is *execrable'*.[21] Indeed, Burgh comments in vivid terms that it would be preferable for a speaker to be as lifeless and dull as an Egyptian mummy, than for him to *appear* affected. Since manipulation and dissimulation appear such key moments of the sublime oration, it appears impossible to fully accept the transparent sincerity of expression that the appeal to natural genius involves.

The issue of manipulation is also raised by John Lawson in his *Lectures Concerning Oratory* (1758), where the propriety of the appeal to the passions is a running concern. Lawson admits that:

> As the End of Eloquence is Persuasion, and strictly speaking, all Persuasion ought to be founded in Conviction alone, it must be acknowledged, that all Address to the Passions is grounded in the Imperfection of Mankind.[22]

Yet Lawson too has little more to offer against this admission than, once more, the Longinian genealogy whereby exalted discourse expresses an exalted genius: 'Stile is truly a Part of Genius ... determined by Thought, and this Power of Thinking arising from the Frame of the Soul' (p. 327). He does appeal to Plato's argument in *Phaedrus* that 'if the Appearance of Truth perswades, must not Truth itself more effectually perswade?' (p. 333). Yet, this is another appeal which finds itself foundering on the Longinian position that orators must dissimulate figures: 'figures are strong Instruments of Persuasion, because strong Proofs of Sincerity'

(p. 257). This is exactly what the modern critic Suzanne Guerlac terms a *sincerity effect* – artful rhetoric looking as if it is artless and natural.[23] It is this effect which fools the audience into thinking that they are watching a natural outpouring of emotion, and thus confuses the distinction between what is properly one's own, and what is performed. The *Phaedrus* argument depends on judgement, and it is the effect of the sublime to ravish judgement.

The *Lectures* are also interesting in raising further issues of truth and falsity when discourse ventures into the poetic, or, as Lawson terms it, 'this your unbounded region of Fable' (p. 280). He introduces a dialogue considering how limits can be set to the imagination which 'is never so well pleased as when fully indulged, and left free to rove in all the Luxuriancy of wild uncontrolled Irregularity' (p. 285). The discussion focuses largely on the matter of rhetorical technique, but in questioning whether the poetic (figures, appeals to the passions, vehemence, fictions – all the things associated with the Longinian sublime) should be introduced into oratory, it raises more general issues about sincerity and dissimulation. Philemon represents the sceptical voice. Although he accepts his interlocutor Eubulus's contention that poetic elements are necessary to make a discourse attractive, especially to the common man, he questions whether the power thus released can be adequately legislated: 'who can stop precisely within these Limits?' (p. 284).

Eubulus's answer is slightly disingenuous, since he appears to reduce Philemon's objection to the issue of style. Eubulus simply refers to the Longinian commonplace of sublimity possessing an irregular form; Philemon's question arguably raises wider issues which are not answered in Eubulus's answer on transgression of literary form. The limits in question do not merely concern figures as devices of style, but as threats to truth. Eubulus then uses some lengthy citations from great poets, but this precisely ignores Philemon's point. Philemon *accepts* that poetic tropes can be used effectively by noble souls, but he is querying the possibility that the sublime mode may exceed appropriate limits in other hands: 'you take no Notice of the mighty Dangers which attend these Advantages' (p. 300). When considering, specifically, the appropriation of the poetic by oratory, Philemon claims that 'the Skilful only can extract Medicines from Poisons' (p. 276). This is an objection left unresolved by Eubulus's answers.

The discussion ends in a rather unsatisfactory way: Eubulus refers to Quintilian, in a citation appealing to the figure of the teacher, who is to instruct and tame the ardour of the young orator. As such, the mighty dangers which attend the sublime are simply policed by invoking authority: Quintilian, a great teacher of oratory, discoursing about the teaching of oratory. This movement is further continued when Philemon himself defers to Eubulus: 'what may be wanting in your Arguments to convince me ... [is] abundantly made up in your Authority' (p. 312). Although Lawson's dialogue primarily concerns rhetorical technique (and thus Eubulus's answer on transgression of form is certainly not out of place), there is a genuine, underlying fear of dissimulation, Philemon objecting to the fictions of poetry as 'Enemies to Reason and common Sense' (p. 275).

The dialogue between Philemon and Eubulus does not only remind us that Longinus was as much a theorist of literature as he was of oratory, it brings the troublesome fictionality of the poetic to the fore in a specifically eighteenth-century way. There is perhaps a shift in the way that the expressive relation between great genius and a great discourse is menaced in Longinus and in Lawson. In Longinus's text, the problem of figures is more or less worked out within the technical bounds of rhetorical tropes. Conversely, the 'region of Fable' in Lawson arguably suggests a broader anxiety about the intrinsic falseness of poetic and figural materials, described by Philemon as a potential 'Infection' (p. 280) and 'Ornaments ... poetick Dress' (p. 281). This broader problem is something that can also be carried forward to Coleridge's work of the 1790s. Although he is obviously positioning himself as a lyric poet, which is a minor part of Longinus's discussion of the sublime, a number of key qualities sought by Coleridge's early lyric voice can be broadly interpreted as inheritances of the Longinian tradition. However, the invocation of such a speaking position also courts the dangers of 'Fable'. Given Terada's analysis of a self who must imagine their way into themselves, it may be that the very experience of emotion so fundamental to such a lyric subject may also be fundamentally fabular.

Coleridge, the sonnet and the effusion

The kinship between Coleridge's early speaking position and the Longinian tradition can be seen by looking at his two most comprehensive, early statements of poetic theory: the prefaces to *Poems on Various Subjects* and *A Sheet of Sonnets* (both 1796). The *Sheet of Sonnets*' status as an authorial patchwork – including poems from Coleridge, his friends, and his most important contemporary influences – creates something that is both text and context in relation to the voice and speaking position sought by the young Coleridge.[24] Initially, the argument of the *Sheet*'s preface would hardly seem to suggest that this context involved the Longinian tradition. 'The Sonnet ... is a small poem', Coleridge informs us, 'in which some lonely feeling is developed'.[25] Given the tendency of the Longinian tradition to privilege the epic and large-scale, the privacy and intimacy of the sonnet seems to count against its sublimity.

Yet this is misleading. Firstly, although the 'lonely feeling' of the sonnet seems to lack the conspicuous audience of the oratorical scene, this also holds true of, say, Sappho's lyrics analysed in *On Sublimity*. Moreover, the effect *on* the reader is consonant with sublimity. Sonnets are the expressions of peaks of feeling, and Coleridge's gesture to the reader lies with the hope that the sonnet will evoke a common experience of such intense feeling. Whilst the sonnet is small, it is a precise instrument with which to score a permanent mark on the heart and memory: it is telling that Coleridge considers the sonnet to be a slightly longer form of epigram (from the Greek *epi-graphein*, to inscribe upon). Longinus holds that 'real sublimity contains much food for reflection ... and makes a strong and ineffaceable impression on the memory' (p. 148), and Coleridge repeats the notion:

> Easily remembered from their briefness, and interesting alike to the eye and the affections, these are the poems which we can 'lay up in our heart, and our soul,' and repeat them 'when we walk by the way, and when we lie down, and when we rise up'. (II.1139)

Equally, just as Longinus notes that 'we come to believe we have created what we have only heard' (p. 148), Coleridge believes the sonnet 'domesticate[s] with the heart, and *becomes[s], as it were, a part of our identity*' (II.1139, my emphasis).

The Longinian tendency of Coleridge's poetic ideal, however, really becomes apparent in the depiction of the author and manner of utterance. The sonnet

> will ever be cultivated by those who write on tender, pathetic subjects. It is peculiarly adapted to the state of a man violently agitated by a real passion, and wanting composure and vigor [sic] of mind to methodize his thought. It is fitted to express a momentary burst of passion. (II.1140)

Violent agitation barely fused into a whole ('wanting' implying both desire and lack) recalls both the primacy of passion in genius's outpourings, and more specifically Longinus's discussion of Sappho's lyrics: 'she is cold and hot, mad and sane, frightened and near death, all by turns. The result is that we see in her not a single emotion, but a complex of emotions' (p. 154). However, it is the spontaneity (and by extension temporality) that is the fundamental Longinian *topos*: like the single blow of the orator's power, here is a 'momentary burst of passion', a concentration of 'real passion'.

Turning to Coleridge's *Poems on Various Subjects*, we find that the same Longinian qualities are valorised. Many of the poems in the edition are indeed sonnets and Coleridge's analysis of the form mirrors that given above: 'after the more violent emotions of Sorrow, the mind demands solace'.[26] As in all forms of the Longinian tradition, the temporality of the moment is foremost, and Coleridge laments that 'POEMS ON VARIOUS SUBJECTS written at different times and prompted by very different feelings; but which will be read at one time and under the influence of one set of feelings – this is an heavy disadvantage' (p. v). As with the sonnets, the sincere 'I' of the poet is strongly valorised. Other writers are attacked for the textual manipulations – indeed *figural* manipulations – involved in depersonalisation: 'now he transforms himself into a third person, – "the present writer" – now multiplies himself and swells into "we"' (p. ix). By contrast, the touchstone for the position Coleridge claims is the primacy of the 'I'. He values sincerity and naturalness of expression, even at the cost of solipsism: 'to censure [egotism] in a Monody or Sonnet is almost as absurd as to dislike a circle for being round' (pp. v–vi).

The poetic voice sought by Coleridge in the 1796 *Poems* is thus, like Longinian sublimity, genealogical rather than legal: it defines the poetry through its temporal origin, as opposed to a set of rules. Although in a lower key, a constellation emerges around the temporally momentary, affectively intense and expressively sincere: all inheritances of the Longinian tradition. Coleridge's chosen designation for his poems eschews established generic definitions in order to relocate the poems within this constellation of values: nearly all the poems in the collection are named *effusions*, Coleridge claiming that 'I could recollect no title more descriptive of the manner and matter of the Poems'. The effusion privileges the discharge of emotion, even at the cost of '*oneness* of thought' (p. x): the structural irregularity, although Coleridge apologises for it, is yet another familiar Longinian trope.

The essential concerns of the two prefaces can be rather neatly summed up in the following passage from the *Sheet of Sonnets*, on the Petrarchan sonnet. Coleridge typifies the latter as binding the poet with oppressive rules, and sets up a polemical dichotomy between the natural expression of the 'I' and artificial demands of artistic convention:

> If there be one species of composition more difficult and artificial than another, it is an English Sonnet on the Italian Model. Adapted

> to the agitations of a real passion! Express momentary bursts of feeling in it! I should sooner expect to write pathetic *Axes* or *pour forth Extempore Eggs* and *Altars*! But the best confutation of such idle rules is to be found in the Sonnets of those who have observed them, in their inverted sentences, their quaint phrases and incongruous mixture of obsolete and spenserian words: and when at last, the thing is toiled and hammered into fit shape, it is in general racked and tortured Prose rather than anything thing resembling Poetry. (II.1140)

The opposition between artifice and 'idle rules' on the one hand, and nature and passion on the other, underlies everything Coleridge does in fashioning his effusive speaking position. However, as we have seen in Longinus and neo-Longinian writers alike, the place of nature and passion is never straightforward, especially if that passion is expressed through figurality and fable. Although the effusive genre valorises sincerity and the 'real passion' of the poet above all, we shall see that the problem of artifice and dissimulation is always close to the surface. This can be seen with particular clarity in two of Coleridge's effusions in the 1796 collection: 'Effusion XXIV' and 'Effusion XXXVI'.

'The living image of my dream': 'Effusion XXIV' and Romance

The first of the two poems that I wish to examine, the lightly comic 'Effusion XXIV: In the Manner of Spenser', was written to excuse Coleridge from missing a romantic liaison. Whilst engrossed with 'thoughts of my dissevered Fair', the speaker invokes sleep, but 'rejected SLUMBER' turns out to inaugurate a Spenserian dream world.[27] By beckoning the 'softly-breathing God' (l.28), the poem and its narrator enter into a realm of magic and romance. Unfortunately, if the speaker can call forth morphic powers, he is far from the only Archimago in this realm of fancy. As for the knights of *The Faerie Queene*, enchantment lies around every corner. Another personification, Love, hatches a plot and, by firing a magic arrow, keeps the poet bound to the dream images of sleep:

> Was there some Magic in the Elfin's dart?
> Or did he strike my couch with wizard lance?
> For strait so fair a Form did upwards start
> (No fairer deck'd the Bowers of old Romance)

That Sleep enamour'd grew, nor mov'd from his sweet Trance!
(ll.32–6)

This parodic Spenserian style allows the speaker to excuse his actions through gentle humour: by portraying the dream as a bewitchment from 'old Romance', it becomes an elaborate and somewhat endearing justification for missing his rendezvous.

By figuring the world of fancy as one of seductive illusions contrived by the 'too successful wile' (l.20) of the trickster-god, Love, Coleridge identifies it firmly as a realm of falsehood. This is legible as a split within the speaker: 'Chill Fancy droop'd, wreathing herself with willow, / As tho' my breast entomb'd a pining ghost' (ll.12–13). A ghostly inner world of dream and fancy divides the poet in two, suggesting that he is not fully responsible for his enchantment by the false images and disassociating his sleeping self from his sincere, waking self. Sleep also erects an opposition between a true and false Sara, setting up the somewhat flattering conceit that the speaker could not awake to meet his *real* lover because he was besotted with the *dream* lover. Such is the force of the dissimulation, that it appears copy and original exchange priorities, the flesh-and-blood Sara appearing as an 'Image' of the dream: 'Such joys with Sleep did 'bide, / That I the living Image of my Dream / Fondly forgot' (ll.42–4).

A major aspect of Coleridge's depiction of the realm of fancy lies in the adoption of the Spenserian idiom itself, Coleridge using not only the famous nine line stanza, but archaic vocabulary like 'ypluck'd' (l.4) and 'Wight' (l.9). The hyperbolic fictionality of Spenserian Romance is appropriate to emphasise the falseness of the world of dreaming, and disassociate the speaker's real life, emotions and beloved from it. However, this raises an interesting problem, since the poem implicitly links the poetic with dreaming and thus falsehood, whereas the preface demands a poetics of sincerity. Tropes and figures, marshalled by fancy, may overcome the 'I' of the poet, displacing passions and relations based on real events and people in favour of a purely fictive world. In 'Effusion XXIV', Coleridge deliberately courts this possibility, and it is the central conceit of the poem. Yet, can Coleridge really maintain such a strict division between the false poetic materials represented by a parodic Spenserianism and the good poetic materials that are the expressions of the effusive 'I'?

For example, the opening stanza voices desire for a 'soothing song' (l.6) in reparation for the false speech of Coleridge's broken vow: 'I would, that from the pinions of thy Dove / One quill withouten pain ypluck'd might be!' (ll.3–4). The quill plucked from the dove might suggest a natural writing, and thus sincerity, given that birdsong is an established lyric ideal. Yet in fact it is here that Coleridge's parody of the Spenserian style is at its heaviest. The dove belongs to an overwrought figural complex: itself a symbol for peace, it belongs in the poem to a personified Peace reclining under an equally symbolic olive tree – symbolism laid on top of, of course, the birdsong-as-poetry metaphor. The quill might promise a naturalness of expression, but lies deep within a series of tropes. As such, the 'soothing song' to be inscribed by the quill could be viewed as sincere speech (as supported by the Old English root *soþ*/truth), or merely as persuasive and artistically elaborate flattery, conjured up by poetic dexterity. The poem seems to be ensnared in fictions even as it seeks to demarcate a self-evidently false realm of Spenserian fancy and dream from true feelings and intentions.

A similar thing occurs when the speaker attempts to regulate the space between dreaming and waking. Addressing Sleep, the speaker exclaims:

> leave me with the matin hour, at most!
> Like snowdrop opening to the solar ray,
> My sad heart will expand, when I the Maid survey. (ll.16–18)

The fictions of dream are to be dismissed with the coming of the light and the real presence of Sara. Yet this moment is itself depicted with a trope taken from the botanic luxuriance of the Spenserian bower (compare 'lilied bank' (l.1) and 'wreathing herself with willow' (l.12)). The moment when dream is supposedly banished seems like an episode *from* the Spenserian dream. At this moment where reality is supposed to intervene, all we have are images. The poem remains bound to the very fancifulness supposedly repudiated at this very point. So much for the real Sara: the very opposition between true and imaginary seems to falter as Coleridge cannot avoid drawing her into the embrace of Spenserian figures.

In summary, 'Effusion XXIV' begins by associating fancy and falsity, but this association can threaten Coleridge's supposedly authentic poetic speaking position. It becomes apparent that the emotion is bound to a certain fabular, literary or even dreamlike experience of oneself. Terada's recent work on emotion opens up this problem into a theorisation of emotion that works against the commonplace assumption that we interpret the emotions of others mediately by comparing them to our own immediate experience. By contrast, she argues we experience our own emotions in reference to a cultural model: 'we feel not to the extent that ... other people's experiences remind us of our own, but to the extent that our own seem like someone else's ... we have to imagine our way into ourselves'. The fact that the poem has trouble disentangling the enactment of genuine love from the recapitulation or performance of Spenserian tropes would seem to suggest her logic is correct. Terada's analysis also has more far-reaching consequences. The differentiality characteristic of self-conscious experience (myself feeling myself) is read, in terms of emotion, as a kind of mental theatricality, where one stages imaginary representations of oneself to oneself, with all the inevitable uncanniness and self-dispossession that this entails: 'the Cartesian theatre as a zone of auditory hallucination and oblique self-approach'.[28] Once again, I think the problematics of dream and wakefulness – especially the inner ghost envisaged in Coleridge's second stanza – precisely suggest this kind of experience of the subject. To what extent does a certain oneiric element haunt the waking 'I'?

The rhetorical or staged nature of the emotional self, both to its auditors *and to itself*, undermines the effusive aesthetic. If the linguistic sublime is about power, then one needs the validation of true and authentic emotion – a sincere interior space of feeling – to authenticate the staging and transfer of affect performed by the effusive 'I'. But what happens when we begin to detect a certain staging *within* – and thus dividing – that originary and supposedly unitary 'I'? Given the association in 'Effusion XXIV' between false fancy and a particular poetic tradition or genre, could not the voice of the poet be subtly possessed (and divided) by given poetic traditions or genres, before its very enunciation? Could these genres overturn the sincerity that supposedly comes from the real passions of the 'I' – and would anyone notice? After all, 'Effusion XXIV' is an imitation: how does the poetics of the effusion relate to the poetics of the imitation? One can certainly say that the imitative mode is courted here for comic effect. Yet looking at the title page of *Poems on Various Subjects*, we see there are further imitations: two of Ossian (Effusions XXIX and XXX), and 'Effusion XXXI: Imitated from the Welch'. If we follow Terada in assuming a certain internal literariness to emotional experience, this clash between effusion and imitation, original authenticity and rhetorical staging, is crucial to understanding and interrogating the effusion as a genre.

Imitation in 'Effusion XXIV' is used to buttress the theme of artificiality: the possession of Coleridge's own voice by the Spenserian mode suggests and mirrors the entrancement of the speaker by dream images. If this is so, however, does the same suggestion of possession – the lyric self imagining its way into itself – not apply to the other imitations? There is a particularly sharp contradiction, for instance, in 'Effusion XXXI: Imitated from the Welch' which audaciously includes the following stanza on sincerity of expression, despite being itself closely copied from a 1784 anthology of translated Welsh verse:

> If, while my passion I impart,
>   You deem my words untrue,
> O place your hand upon my heart –
> Feel how it throbs for you![29]

If, as Coleridge's preface proclaims, the poems are built on a foundation of subjective sincerity – a language springing from real passion, unmediated as far as possible by mere learnt conventions – then how can imitations possibly earn the title of effusion? Moreover, if the effusion is the language of the 'I' above all, then why does Coleridge need to identify some as imitations in the first place: surely they should immediately stand out as not representing the true voice of the poet?[30] We might ask ourselves, could we identify the imitations from the non-imitations if they were not so marked? Might there not be imitations – conscious or unconscious – that are indeed unmarked, and which we thus read naively in terms of Coleridge's effusive poetics of sincerity? These questions begin to undermine the entire position of the preface and suggest, as Terada does, that in feeling we are imitating others and presenting the imitation to ourselves as our own original.

'I'd float a Dream by Night': 'Effusion XXXVI' and the fictive image

'Effusion XXIV' revolves around the speaker choosing an image over a reality, and the difference between the real and imaginary presence of a beloved is also at stake in the second poem that I wish to examine, 'Effusion XXXVI: Written in Early Youth'.[31] As in the other poem, fancy is characterised through surrogates such as dream, sorcery and Spenserian romance: 'Aid, lovely Sorceress! aid thy Poet's dream! / With faery wand O bid the MAID arise'.[32] However, here the speaker willingly invites his own bewitchment as consolation for the absence of the beloved, beckoning forward 'dear Deceit!' (l.23). Such willing self-deception is in clear contrast to the memory of the beloved's presence, the latter described with a vocabulary of sincerity:

> When as she twin'd a laurel round my brow,
> And met my kiss, and half return'd *my vow*,
> O'er all my frame shot rapid my thrill'd heart,

> And every nerve *confess'd* the electric dart. (ll.19–22, my emphases)

The speaker desires, despite its evident falsity, a simulation or repetition of this original moment, a point underscored by word for word repetition of the line 'Chaste Joyance dancing in her bright-blue Eyes' (l.16, also l.24). The willing acceptance of this fantasy is in tension with the principles of the preface, which demand expression of the real passions of the moment, and surely not their evasion in fantasy and memory. In the terms of Lawson's Philemon, the speaker has thrown himself into 'this your unbounded region of Fable' not in spite of, but *because of*, its narcotic properties.

In the Longinian tradition, figures were potentially false and concealed; here, they are openly sought for their falseness and, ironically, it is truth that is to be concealed. Yet the fact that the poem has chosen to sport in a realm of fictions over real things is not a seamless repression. Coleridge's description of the imagined scene has a haunted feel, much of its imagery filled with traces, images and signs. It is little wonder that this poem was sometimes titled as an ode to absence, since the absence of the real beloved is continually exerting itself on the tone of the fantasy. 'I trace her footsteps' (l.27), the speaker avows, 'I mark her glancing mid the gleam of dawn' (l.28). The 'mark' implies that each glance has already slid away (Old French *glaichier*, to slip) before even received, leaving just an indent or memory. She is 'in moon-beams clad' (l.32), an evanescent glow, only barely present in a landscape of soft half-light. It is telling that the central charm in the workings of fancy is but a name: thus not a presence but yet another *mark* working in the absence of its referent:

> SPIRITS OF LOVE! ye heard her name! Obey
> The powerful spell, and to my haunt repair. (ll.37–8)

Even when their paths do meet, her voice seems simultaneously present and distant:

> With her I list the warblings of the grove;
> And seems in each low wind her voice to float,
> Lone-whispering Pity in each soothing note! (ll.34–6)

Once again 'soothing', despite its etymology, has a hint of dissimulation about it. It is, after all, only a fantasised imitation of her voice, as one can see later when the speaker commands fancy to 'still that voice, those notes prolong' (l.54). This desire for a reified simulacrum once again reverses the ethos of the preface: instead of poetry acting as the expression of an emotive moment, the speaker submits his emotions to the consoling stasis of poetry. The temporal aspect fits well with Paul de Man's argument that a typically Romantic desire is the denial of temporality, or 'eternity in motion ... escaping from "the unimaginable touch of time"'.[33] However, unlike in de Man's prototypical scenario – where the stability of natural objects is appropriated – Coleridge has already linked the absence of his beloved with a *mutable* nature by setting the poem at evening. Instead, therefore, a purely internal dream world is invoked as the guarantor of permanence, even if this means a certain deliberate self-mystification on the part of the subject.

We can see the extent of this self-mystification in the speaker's sigh: 'were mine the wizard's rod, / Or mine the power of Proteus, changeful God!' (ll.57–8). The irony is that the poet *is* a Proteus. His lament is that he cannot change himself:

> A flower-entangled ARBOUR I would seem
> To shield my Love from Noontide's sultry beam:
> Or bloom a MYRTLE, from whose od'rous boughs
> My Love might weave gay garlands for her brows. (ll.59–62)

Yet, of course he can shape and form new realities, and has been doing so throughout the poem. Whilst he may not be able to create a myrtle, he can evoke one and use it to transfer beauty metaphorically from divine to human: 'Love lights her smile – in Joy's red nectar dips / His myrtle flower, and plants it on her lips' (ll.51–2). 'On Seraph wing I'd float a DREAM, by night' (l.67), the speaker wishes, 'And gaze upon her with a thousand eyes!' (l.70). The speaker has yet to realise his desire is already fulfilled: he has already created a dream, and gazed upon her through the rich prism of poetic figures (or eyes).[34]

However, the poem ends with a realisation of the insufficiency of this purely escapist aesthetic. The movement of the 'eye reverted' (l.78) to a lost past becomes apparent, and the speaker realises the distance that stands between him and his memories. The fantastic screen of images is broken:

> Dear native brook! where first young POESY
> Star'd wildly-eager in her noontide dream,
> ...
> No more your sky-larks melting from the sight
> Shall thrill th' attuned heart-string with delight. (ll.83–4, 93–4)

It is interesting that the mourning of the lost beloved is also entwined with a mourning for a more general scene of youth, and particularly the poetic endowment of youth. Thus Coleridge himself appears to link this poem's sense of absence and lack to the falling away of a certain poetic voice, 'wildly-eager', which is surely nothing else but the very effusive voice theorised in the preface and on to which the poem itself tries and fails to hold.

This is an entirely appropriate coda for a poem which haunts the Longinian voice of the collection with the figural and fabular nature of its own enunciation, driving the very same problems found in the first poem to the point where emotion is shown to persist and continue to affect the self despite being purely fictive. Far from being an intentional state directed at an object, love is shown to be capable of creating or figuring its own object. The poem mirrors amatory tales such as Narcissus and Echo or Pygmalion, which can be read as exposing a rhetorical self-deception inherent in *all* love, a figural projection from and across the experience of the self which fixes the beloved as beloved: 'the target, the usually empirical thing that may quite contingently cause an emotion, needs to be connected to an idealization'.[35] As Coleridge's poem indicates, this work of idealization can occur with or without an intentional object (Terada herself notes that 'literature often portrays the love object as absent ... or illusory', or indeed unrequited), raising the possibility that in normal love we may be as much in love with our act of loving, as with the target.[36]

'Effusion XXXVI', by portraying the deliberate choice of deceit over reality, deepens the threat to the effusive lyric self found in 'Effusion XXIV'. The affinity of the 1796 *Poems* to a Longinian tradition rests on a conception of utterance which departs from formal propriety in favour of the aforementioned triptych of a language temporally momentary, affectively intense and expressively sincere. However, in lieu of literary decorum and rules, it is the veracity of the speaking subject which is used to authenticate and value this language. What the two effusions I have examined bring to light is a problem with this speaking subject. Whilst the paramount issue for Longinus was the deception of the audience by a manipulative orator (ultimately, the security of the *polis*), Coleridge reflects an eighteenth-century anxiety about the falseness of figural materials and flights of fancy in so far as audience *and speaker* alike may become deceived by the allure of the poetic. However, one can go further still: this is not just about some authentic emotional self becoming distorted as it enters into a language of figures and images. Coleridge's descriptions of his own feelings suggest that the emotional self itself is not the unitary intentional subject that the Longinian tradition demands as the originary point for true and authentic feeling. Rather, as a reading of figurality such as Terada's suggests, one need not confine the poetic to the page: both poems we have examined suggest a certain staging of the self to itself, a detour through a kind of fabular mental theatre, which is necessary for emotion to be felt at all. Indeed, Terada's point is *not* that emotion is fictional, for this would only make sense if there could be an authentic, non-fabular emotion: to feel is to feel oneself, and Terada argues that this demands fabularity and a certain self-staging of self.

Arguably, the notion that feeling might actually be constituted through performativity lies behind Coleridge's ultimate rejection of the effusive genre (the term was not used in subsequent collections). In 1797, as Daniel Robinson notes, he effectively abandons the effusive sonnet by penning comic imitations of his own style, and that of Charles Lamb and Charles Lloyd.[37] The interesting thing is that he uses parody, just as in the pseudo-Spenserian 'Effusion XXIV'. As Coleridge explains in a letter to Joseph Cottle, the parodies exaggerate stock figures and stylistic formulae in order to condemn the 'puny pathos' of the early sonnets as nothing more than rhetorical posture: 'the affectation of unaffectedness' (*CL*, I.357). This dissimulated, staged sincerity is something that this chapter has met time and again: it is yet another version of Longinus's concealed figure. However, the problem of the fabular, staged or rhetorical nature of emotion and the emotional self did not simply go away. Another important poetic speaking position that Coleridge adopted was also close to the Longinian tradition, and also demanded an exceptional subjectivity striking his auditors with a language of force. We find this in his political verse of the 1790s, and many of the same problems recur. When Coleridge began to doubt some of his former political convictions, he also began to realise that his speaking position had not automatically produced truth, despite being grounded in passions that seemed to be evidence of their own sincerity. A certain theatricality – a certain subtle performativity of self linked closely to the concept of enthusiasm – seemed to undermine him. This produced a crisis in his poetic authority, which we can trace in the 1798 quarto, *Fears in Solitude*.

2
'The Self-Watching Subtilizing Mind': the Impassioned Self in the 1798 *Fears in Solitude* Quarto

Strange as it may seem given the conventional understanding of Coleridge's poetic peak as 1796 to 1802, the *Poems* entered a third edition in 1803 with virtually the same contents, and prefatory material, as seven years before. Yet much had changed, not least the emergence of the so-called conversation poem and a severe chastening of Coleridge's poetic and political hopes. The slim 1798 quarto containing 'Fears in Solitude', 'France: An Ode' and 'Frost at Midnight' allows us to register a radically important event in the course of Coleridge's self-understanding as a poet. Whilst the quarto possesses no preface, the poems themselves are all concerned with the taking of a speaking position, and manifest a crisis of poetic voice that this chapter will chart. In the 1790s, Coleridge had often made political interventions from a prophetic outsider position that drew on the Longinian values of force, passion and a privileged poetic subjectivity, as in 1796's 'Ode to the Departing Year': 'with no unholy madness ... I raised the impetuous song, and solemnized his flight'.[1] The value of this 'impetuous song' (Latin, *impetere*, to rush upon, attack) became subject to anxiety as earlier political statements were reconsidered. The idea that one may stage one's emotions to oneself gained a political edge as Coleridge feared he had deceived himself.

In 'Fears in Solitude' and 'France: An Ode', powerful poetic subject positions – the ode and oratorical critique – become uneasily mixed with a necessity to justify oneself and one's past. A paradox emerges between the desire to stand outside society, and adopt a poetic idiom of force, and a contradictory desire to enter the public sphere, and to prove oneself before the reader. I argue that these paradoxes are inescapable, partially motivating the lyric turn of 'Frost at Midnight', which attempts to re-ground his poetry away from the public, in domestic, private space. Such re-grounding proves difficult: Coleridge is forced to turn to a fantasy of linguistic plenitude projected on to his own child. However, this fantasy screens an experience of emotion, language and subjecthood that is dispossessed and placeless. Drawing on Rei Terada's analysis of pathos, I argue that 'Frost at Midnight' marks one of the limit points for the Romantic lyric 'I'. Whilst this gestures forward to strange post-Romantic lyric sites, it also takes us full circle, to Longinus and the sublime, returning us to a Sapphic conception of lyric based not on power but loss.

'O forgive these dreams!': revoking sublime speech in 'France: An Ode'

Whilst the quarto opens with 'Fears in Solitude', the conclusions of the previous chapter make 'France: An Ode' a more pertinent starting point. As an ode, it appears to position Coleridge in an unambiguously sublime speaking position, being of the archetypally sublime lyric genre. Odes are typically irregular, highly performative, and linked to a particular moment. As emphasised by Paul Fry, they have the power to invoke what they describe, and suggest a certain poetic authority.[2] In addition, they have a long tradition as a public form, placing the ode-writer closer to the bardic or oratorical subjects normative in the Longinian tradition. As such, odes can be seen as a language of force of the type described in the previous chapter. However, although the genre would lead us to see Coleridge as occupying a position of sublime linguistic power, the Romantic Ode is not so simple. Fry notes that the *invocation* of the ode becomes entangled in the desires, and thus anxieties, of the poetic *vocation*, and that a 'burden of doubt' complicates the hymnal 'assertion of knowledge'.[3] Indeed, Fry goes so far as to argue that the ode might be opposed to the immediacy of poetry of the effusive kind: 'the turning of Wordsworth and Coleridge to ... ode writing is itself a farewell to the natural holiness of youth'.[4] Fry's privileging of the late odes, and specifically the dialogue between 'Dejection: An Ode' and the 'Intimations Ode', occludes the fact that Coleridge wrote a number of earlier odes. Nevertheless, his emphasis on the difficulties around the ode shows that the form was in no way an unproblematic inheritance for the Romantics.

Although the ode appears a genre of power, 'France: An Ode' involves a clear disavowal of such. Whilst Coleridge evokes a scene of inspired speech – familiar in its lineaments from his own self-fashioning in the effusions, and depictions of other favoured poets (e.g. Thomas Chatterton in the 'Monody on the Death of Chatterton') – it is rendered with the unmistakable tinge of nostalgia:

How oft, pursuing fancies holy,
My moonlight way o'er flow'ring weeds I wound,
Inspir'd beyond the guess of folly,
By each rude shape, and wild unconquerable sound.[5]

Like the memory of former poetic endowment in 'Effusion XXXVI: Written in Early Youth', this outpouring of voice seems to represent a receding possibility. However, in 'France: An Ode', this recession is more complex and more charged, bound with Coleridge's ardour for the French Revolution and anxiety about politico-prophetic stances he had previously taken.

Due to the political issues involved, the crisis in voice revolves particularly around justification. As explained previously, sublime utterance is self-authorising, both in the sense of compelling assent rather than submitting to judgement, and in being authenticated through its own origin in genius. However, in 'France: An Ode' the origin of the poetry in the individual's exceptional subjectivity becomes a matter of anxiety. On the one hand, Coleridge does continue to play on the privilege accorded to the exceptional individual: 'With what a joy my lofty gratulation / Unaw'd I sung amid a slavish band' (ll.26–7). Notably, the 'gratulation' of his songs of liberty is not *con*-gratulation. Coleridge avows that he had repudiated collective emotions, such as 'many friendships, many youthful loves / ... [and] the patriot emotion' (ll.33–4), in order to preserve the unique purity of his voice: 'still my voice unalter'd sang defeat' (l.36). Thus far, he conforms to Longinian values. A partition or limiting of voice – 'ne'er, O Liberty! with partial aim / I dimm'd thy light, or damp'd thy holy flame' (ll.39–40) – is always resisted, to maintain the fullness and sublimity of utterance.

Yet, with the invasion of Switzerland and Coleridge's sudden horror at his support for France, it is realised that the self-authorising nature of the sublime voice is not unerring. Now sharpened with severe political consequences, the self-staging aspect of emotion examined in the previous chapter threatens to void the liberal passions that had earlier motivated the poet. Note the fantastical vocabulary which tinges the second strophe, suggesting that his emotions had taken a dangerous detour through a deceptive literariness during their constitution: the European monarchs are described as 'like fiends embattled by a wizard's wand' (l.29), whilst Britain's hills are illuminated by a 'magic light' (l.35). As Coleridge's patriotism enters into tragic but openly theatrical strife with his pro-French instincts, a dangerous figural complex emerges around such self-deceit, both poetic and political: that of *enthusiasm*. The language used to describe revolutionary excess seems to double back on the language of inspiration that Coleridge has used to describe his own productivity: 'all the fierce and drunken passions wove / A dance more wild than ever maniac's dream' (ll.45–6). At worst, therefore, the Longinian emphasis on a language of force and a privileging of subjective passion as a guarantor of voice may create in the individual mind a loss of discipline akin to revolutionary terror. Coleridge describes the French as 'Slaves by their own compulsion!' (l.86), but poets too may become enslaved by a supposed freedom, i.e. their sublime voices. The spectre of enthusiasm runs throughout the ode, checking and qualifying the power of its voice, and suggesting – as before – a speaking subject which has staged itself to itself in a potentially damaging way in order to constitute its initial passion.

Yet, whilst Coleridge thus wishes to disavow certain previous assertions – 'forgive me, that I cherish'd / One thought, that ever bless'd your cruel foes!' (ll.70–1) – he also attempts to defend himself generally. To do this, he must present himself before the public. His poetic voice is openly partitioned, as Coleridge is forced to hold prior utterances in the grip of quotation marks. As such, the concentration of force that had characterised Longinian texts is dissipated. Previously the autonomy of the lone voice singing 'unaw'd' against society had been valorised; now that very voice is submitted for inspection. This careful display of past utterance moves Coleridge's poetic speaking position away from the single temporal blow associated with Longinian poetics. Not only does it divide the poetic voice into a ratio between past and present voices, it lays out the revoked utterances into typographical space: as emphasised by Longinus, spatiality is a medium of reflection in that an arranged structure invites judgement. Quotation marks allow Coleridge to reinscribe his discourse in a new context, distancing himself from what is disavowed and clarifying what is still confirmed. This examination – in which, of course, the reader is invited to share – complicates the single line of force running from sublime subjectivity to sublime discourse. The valorisation of the expressive moment so apparent in the effusion is called into question by the necessity for reflection, qualification and even revocation. The autonomous blow of the sublime voice no longer possesses self-assured and self-justifying mastery.

Indeed, the autonomy of the sublime voice becomes associated with a number of regrets and repudiations. Most prominently, Coleridge begs forgiveness for believing and asserting with quasi-prophetic force that 'France ... [shall] compel the nations to be free' (l.62). 'France: An Ode' proves in a political register what was lurking close to the surface in the treatment of fancy in the 1796 *Poems*: that an effusive ego might become a solipsistic victim to its own dreams. In distinct contrast to the sublimely individual tenacity of the prophetic voice are scenes of *listening* that open the poet to self-chastisement. The tone shifts from prophetic confidence to the sorrow of the penitent:

> Forgive me, Freedom! O forgive these dreams!
> I hear thy voice, I hear thy loud lament,
> From bleak Helvetia's icy caverns sent – (ll.64–6)

The space of reflection and inspection opened up by the public quotation of his prior utterance thus undermines the self-justifying quality of linguistic sublimity. As already suggested, the lineaments of the Longinian position have been reversed: instead of temporal force, there is spatial display; instead of appropriation of a speaking position, there is revocation; instead of an audience commanded, the poet submits – repents even. Indeed, I would hazard that the treatment of voice is by far a greater break with Coleridge's past than any shift in political convictions. In terms of revocation, it is the retreat from a certain self-authorising speaking position that is more important than a retreat from any particular political opinion. Indeed, as we shall see, the poem strives to maintain continuity in Coleridge's politics, based around an underlying fidelity to liberty. However, crucially, this fidelity is something that must now be proven; not forced home by the power of genius. By distancing himself from the self-authorising position of the lone poet-prophet, no longer can Coleridge's voice authorise itself: it requires exterior validation. A case must be presented, and a defence requires witness. Thus, Coleridge appeals:

> Yea, every thing that is and will be free,
> Bear witness for me wheresoe'er you be,
> With what deep worship I have still ador'd
> The spirit of divinest liberty. (ll.18–21)

Oath-making in 'Fears in Solitude'

This is where the place of 'France: An Ode' in the quarto as a whole becomes important. The crucial movement just identified is that Coleridge retreats from a self-justifying poetic – where passionate expression of the individual self is poetry's essence – to one which requires external justification, before and with witnesses. However, the ode's appeal to 'every thing that is and will be free' as guarantors should be read within context, for questions of justification and proof are extensively covered by the first poem in the quarto, 'Fears in Solitude'. To understand the witnesses of 'France: An Ode', then we must first understand the problematics of oath-making in 'Fears in Solitude'. As with the ode, certain stylistic cues suggest the possibility of a sublime speaking position, the poem described as 'perhaps not Poetry, – but rather a sort of middle thing between Poetry and Oratory – sermoni propriora'.[6] After an opening that recalls the calm and reflective Cowperian idiom of his recent conversation poems, the stillness is broken by external pressure:[7]

> My God! it is a melancholy thing
> For such a man, who would full fain preserve
> His soul in calmness, yet perforce must feel
> For all his human brethren.[8]

Tearing at the borders of the reflective retreat are voices: 'the thunder and the shout, / And all the crash of onset' (ll.37–8) brought by war and 'a groan of accusation' (l.45) piercing heaven itself. Against these voices, Coleridge must emerge from the 'small and silent dell' (l.2) and provide an answering voice.

The orator's position must be taken up. Although Coleridge is a little reticent in his notes, describing the poem as 'tame' in places and only *half*-oratorical, in fact the tone is strident and political, and could be seen as fully in the Longinian tradition:[9]

> We have offended, O my countrymen!
> We have offended very grievously,
> And have been tyrannous. (ll.42–4)

Compare Dionysius of Phoceaea's communal exhortation 'now, for our affairs are on the edge, men of Ionia' or Demosthenes' condemnatory 'vile flatterers, mutilators of their countries, who have given away liberty as a drinking present'.[10] It is a powerful, public voice that is needed. We might thus consider the oratorical stance of 'Fears in Solitude' as part of what Tim Fulford analyses as Coleridge's mounting ambition to find the 'authority to offer a public spiritual language'.[11]

Yet the taking of an oratorical voice will not be unproblematic. The paradox exerting continual pressure is that the public language of 'Fears in Solitude' conflicts with the poem's dogged condemnation of public languages generally. Almost as soon as the oratorical idiom is adopted,

'Fears in Solitude' turns to scenes of a linguistically corrupt public sphere, which would appear to threaten the very possibility of oratory:

> The sweet words
> Of christian promise, words that even yet
> Might stem destruction, were they wisely preach'd,
> Are mutter'd o'er by men, whose tones proclaim,
> How flat and wearisome they feel their trade.
> Rank scoffers some, but most too indolent,
> To deem them falsehoods, or to *know* their truth. (ll.60–6)

Dissimulation takes on a potentially structural pervasiveness. Some are active hypocrites, in contempt of the words they speak; for others, more frighteningly, epistemic issues are irrelevant. They mouth the words but skim over – o'er – their surfaces without the barest contact with their truth or falsity. 'O'er' also has the sense of *over and over* or *over again*, suggesting the blank, meaningless repetition of a 'flat and wearisome' trade. *Mutter* is tellingly onomatopoeic: the words are simply empty auditory forms, and the same combination of 'o'er' and onomatopoeia is repeated in the line: 'we gabble o'er the oaths we mean to break' (l.69).

The idea of a disincarnated language is the poem's major fear. Alongside the threat of deliberate abuse is a fear that language has become hollowed out, and structurally independent of a substantial base: 'mere abstractions, empty sounds' (l.112). As such, speakers do not so much consciously dissimulate, but are immersed within dissimulation. They participate in language through a kind of perpetual secondariness, as if speaking a language they do not really understand: in a later revision, Coleridge describes society as engulfed in 'vain, speech-mouthing, speech-reporting'.[12] When Coleridge attacks the war, his critique is based on its effect on language. The appetite for conflict is condemned as a hunger for spectacle, a virtual war vicariously enjoyed in print. The reader – 'fluent phraseman, absolute / And technical in victories and defeats / And all our dainty terms for fratricide' (ll.108–10) – does not ground the free-floating realm of media signifiers to violent reality. Coleridge's point is that language has been evacuated of sense. No longer a mirror in order to bring experience to articulacy, it is the prime layer of experience in itself, structurally enveloping its speakers:

> We join no feeling and attach no form,
> As if the soldier died without a wound;
> As if the fibres of this godlike frame

> Were gor'd without a pang: as if the wretch,
> Who fell in battle doing bloody deeds,
> Pass'd off to Heaven, *translated* and not kill'd. (ll.113-18, my emphasis)

Threatened by invasion, Coleridge describes providential punishment as the return of incarnation to a linguistically corrupt culture: to 'make us know / The meaning of our words' (ll.123–4).

Throughout, Coleridge has been holding two contradictory impulses together: to join public discourse, and yet to condemn public discourse at its root. This is obviously problematic: as Michael Simpson puts it, by abandoning the sequestered authorship of the rural poet for public intervention, 'the text becomes hypocritically susceptible to its own critique of hypocrisy'.[13] Coleridge's own stance must somehow allow for an uncorrupted speech-act outside of the structural corruption of the public sphere. He must ensure a distance between the ruined authority of public speech, and his own attempt at oratorical speech. If the poem is to work, we must believe Coleridge when he says

> I have told,
> O Britons! O my brethren! I have told
> Most bitter truth, but without bitterness. (ll.150–2)

As Mark Jones has argued, Coleridge's main strategy is to root his own public utterance in a dissenting religious tradition, suggesting a prophetic mantle.[14] Thus, whilst condemning others, he strives to create in his own discourse an exception to the rule, thus exemplifying 'the double character of the performative ... sociological fact and individualized fantasy'. This double character manifests the tension we have been treating all along, condemning public language within public language. Coleridge abhors the sociological fact of a public language debased by a debased society, but desires a position of individual power from which to exert critique. The paradox is ultimately inescapable. How can Coleridge's oratory escape a corruption of oratory that seems totally pervasive? Coleridge's attempt to exempt himself from his own searching analysis of the public sphere is, as Jones suggests, 'mystificatory'.[15]

We may take Jones's dichotomy between 'sociological fact and individualized fantasy' further, for this tension will show us precisely the fault-line within 'Fears in Solitude', and ultimately lead us back to 'France: An Ode'. We began with the idea of the speaker leaving sequestered silence to answer incoming voices of tumult and strife. Yet there is another important set of voices which 'Fears in Solitude' confronts: Coleridge's political critics. His reply to these voices is an oath:

> O my mother Isle!
> Needs must thou prove a name most dear and holy
> To me, a son, a brother, and a friend,
> A husband and a father! who revere
> All bonds of natural love, and find them all
> Within the limits of thy rocky shores. (ll.173–8)

Coleridge avers his patriotism, thus shoring up his public voice. Yet naturally this oath is vulnerable to the general paradox outlined above: the poem undermines the authority of all public speech-acts. Oaths are, in fact, one of Coleridge's main targets: 'college and wharf, council and justice-court, / All, all must swear, the briber and the brib'd' (ll.71–2). The gabbling of perjurious oaths disincarnates 'the very name of God' and makes it sound 'like a juggler's charm' (ll.76, 77).

As Jones correctly identifies, Coleridge must try to evade the corruption of the public sphere through 'the possibility of dissent by an exceptional individual'.[16] Yet our analysis of 'France: An Ode' (and, of course, the 1796 *Poems*) proves that the voice of the exceptional individual – especially the self-justifying utterance of the political or social prophet – is far from secure. By submitting to the necessity of avowing fidelity and patriotism, 'Fears in Solitude' is submitting to the necessity of exterior validation. Coleridge puts himself before the public: 'Nor deem my zeal or factious or mistim'd' (l.153), he pleads. Precisely because Coleridge appeals to the judgement of others and submits his voice to be assayed by them, the prophetic mantle that would be the escape from a corrupted public sphere is undermined. If Coleridge's oratorical position is that of the exceptional individual, it should be self-justifying, *pace* Longinus, because of its genealogy in his own inspired self, 'Unaw'd ... amid a slavish band' (l.27, 'France'). However, 'Fears in Solitude' shows that supposedly exceptional voice requiring the validation of the slavish band, for as long as Coleridge's politics remain suspect, he can be dismissed as a political enthusiast:

> Others, meanwhile,
> Dote with a mad idolatry; and all,
> Who will not fall before their images,
> And yield them worship, they are enemies
> Ev'n of their country! – *Such have I been deem'd.* (ll.168–72,
> my emphasis)

The making of an oath is an implicit admission that Coleridge's speaking position, despite its oratorical and prophetic elements, does not have sufficient intrinsic authority. Instead, it requires a granting of authority from the very social realm that it critiques.

This pattern comes into relief with particular clarity if we examine the linguistic structure of the oath. Even when it is not explicitly a formula to be assented to, the oath must partake in a certain citational structure; it cannot be self-originating, it must be *by* something recognised as a condition of oath-making (by God, Britain, kin, or brethren, for instance).[17] This citational structure is the purest example in the poem of the need to partake in a cultural language, but Coleridge holds such languages as hopelessly debased. Just as an oath must cite some commonly shared standard of promise-making, a public statement must adopt a commonly shared idiom: but such standards have been, for Coleridge, utterly violated. Hence, the poem is caught in a self-contradiction: it tries to cite from a discourse it regards as utterly corrupt. The fantasy of individual performativity that could somehow escape this corruption falls totally apart at the point of oath-making, for in trying to prove his political credentials across time (rather than making a prophetic intervention in a single sublime strike), his discourse shows its inevitable reliance on public languages and standards of authority. The oath shows us that Coleridge's speaking position is, inevitably, a 'sociological fact' born into languages and discourses it cannot transcend. The crisis in the authority of his speaking position has thus led to a severe limitation on the effectiveness and scope of his critique of society.

Bearing witness in 'France: An Ode'

This is where we can make a return to 'France: An Ode'. When the reader of the 1798 quarto finds Coleridge appealing for exterior validation and witness from 'every thing that is and will be free' (l.18), this is a type of speech already bearing a significant rhetorical load from 'Fears in Solitude'. When 'France: An Ode' begins the defence of Coleridge's political past – and his past political speech – then it re-engages the very problems that prompted 'Fears in Solitude' to attempt to supplement its own authority through a patriotic oath. Interestingly, however, the defence in the ode is not just prompted by attacks made by others, but by Coleridge's own anxieties. As the revocation of certain political dreams and the plea for forgiveness show, there is a definite anxiety about a political, and by extension, poetical position justified through inspiration, passion and sublime autonomy. These things, as suggested before, all run dangerously close to enthusiasm, and the subjection and overthrow of the self by passions that are conceptualised as theatrical, dreamlike and fabular. Jon Mee, who has written the authoritative account of enthusiasm in the period, shows that Coleridge regulated enthusiasm with *principle*. Speaking of the slightly earlier poem 'Religious Musings', Mee states that

> the acceptably regulated version of prophetic discourse that Coleridge articulates ... is one that presents itself as subjecting ecstasies of inspiration to the authority of 'fixed principles'.[18]

It is the matter of fixed principles that can reveal the most instructive relationship and contrast between 'Fears in Solitude' and 'France: An Ode'. In both cases, principles imply the setting and measuring of form and boundary. In both, Coleridge reassures his readers that despite his sometimes radical political voice, he was always grounded; he always maintained a fidelity to principle. However, in 'Fears in Solitude', the principles at stake are social. Coleridge commits himself patriotically to the nation conceived as a familial unit, extrapolating his own status as 'a son, a brother, and a friend, / A husband and a father!' (ll.175–6). As we have seen, however, he has severe doubts about the integrity of the public discourse that would constitute such a national family: 'May my fears, / My filial fears, be vain!' (ll.194–5). In the last instance, the public language of patriotic principles to which he binds himself is, by his own critique, already exploded.

In 'France: An Ode', conversely, he invokes no social principles, but binds himself to liberty conceived of as a *natural* or metaphysical principle, rather than a political one. In asking nature to bear witness for him, his ultimate goal is the same as the oath within 'Fears in Solitude': to prove and authenticate his voice before others. However, because liberty is a natural principle, the scene of proof enunciated *by* nature appears far more secure than any proof attempted through public or political discourses. Nature, being substance and not sign, should be technically invulnerable to degradation to 'mere abstractions, empty sounds' (l.112, 'Fears'). Thus, in 'France: An Ode', there is a concerted effort to impel the concept of liberty beyond any public discourse which might become compromised:

> O Liberty! with profitless endeavour
> Have I pursued thee many a weary hour:
> But thou nor swell'st the victor's strain, nor ever

> Didst breathe thy soul in *forms of human pow'r.* (ll.89–92, my emphasis)

It is notable that this crucial concluding moment of the ode revolves thematically around language and speech. Human speech – 'nor pray'r, nor boastful name delays thee' (l.94) – is rendered in opposition to the purer natural sounds of wind and sea. Liberty is pushed beyond the knotty difficulties of being attached to any human polity: no longer a word, it is a natural fact.

Hence, the avowal of principle – as a crucial justifying supplement to the speaking position of the lone, prophetic outsider – works differently in each poem. In 'Fears in Solitude', the public discourse of patriotic principle that Coleridge attempts to make an oath *within* is vulnerable to the critique of public discourse that the poem has already established. In 'France: An Ode', his fidelity to liberty is defined via the freedom of nature, thus avoiding the awkward negotiation of human, social discourse. Of course, although rhetorically satisfying, the problem with this approach is the same as its main benefit: nature is not part of discourse. As Angela Esterhammer notes, although the poem privileges 'the name [of liberty] which is inspired, in that it emerges from an encounter between the human spirit and the spirit of nature', this name must be publicly enunciated.[19] Nature is mute, thus we may justifiably ask: how can nature bear witness for Coleridge? How does nature speak? This problem collapses the poem back on its initial problematic. In order to bring the witness of nature before the readership, Coleridge turns towards a vocabulary of *touch*. Coleridge attempts to display his relation with his natural witnesses, and it is feeling that bears the weight of proof:

> Yes! while I stood and gaz'd, my temples bare,
> And shot my being thro' earth, sea, and air,
> Possessing all things with intensest love,
> O Liberty, my spirit felt thee there! (ll.102–5)

However, this avowal of a felt liberty lacks precisely what an oath made in public languages and discourses was designed to remedy: an external criterion of justification. The primacy of touch over speech and feeling over language at the ode's climax suggests internal affective intensity: the very heart of the sublime, prophetic speaking position which has been suspect all along. 'Shooting ... being' across the ranges of nature, and the seizing of possession, are the tropes of the Longinian sublime.

This is not a scene of principle, but of passion and of sublimity. The jury are not being courted by reason, but compelled by affect. The poem sets out avowing anxiety about the excesses of the prophetic mantle, and seeking external validation by setting forth a principled foundation that can be inspected and judged by others, i.e. fidelity to liberty. Now, that principled foundation – which supposedly stabilises and authorises Coleridge's prior utterances of sublime passion – turns out to itself be presented only through *another* utterance of sublime passion. Thus, although appearing to go beyond some of the difficulties of public speech tackled by 'Fears in Solitude', 'France: An Ode' is no less problematic, and in some ways even more contradictory.

'Frost at Midnight': the quarto's lyric turn

The first two poems of the quarto thus wrestle with the problems of a self-justifying voice. The authenticity of the feeling ego first embraced in the 1796 *Poems* becomes troublingly intertwined with the authority, or lack thereof, of the outsider, the prophet, the social or political critic. Previously, we saw how the effusions' true voice of feeling was threatened not only through the rhetorical presentation of the emotions to readers or auditors, but an internal differentiality: the presentation of the feeling ego to itself. The intertwining of emotion with a certain literariness meant that figurality and staging were not just problems involved in the expression of emotions in poetry, but in the constitution of emotion *per se*. The dangers of enthusiasm explored by Coleridge in 'France: An Ode' move this problem into a political register, as the elegant equation between passion and authority is undermined by the necessary intervention of exterior witness to validate the speaker. The supposedly self-justifying force of a Longinian voice – be it odal or oratorical – seeks the supplement of judgement and proof: the insertion of a more rational and legal moment into the subject's mental theatre of the passions. As I have argued above, this involved Coleridge in a series of difficulties: justification from the social sphere sought in 'Fears in Solitude' threatens to abolish the possibility of critique, whilst the appeal to nature's witness in 'France: An Ode' risks recapitulating the initial problematic by appealing, ultimately, to yet another scene of passion.

'Frost at Midnight' seems to mark a step away from such vexations. In the context of the quarto as a whole, it seeks to re-ground Coleridge's voice in a private, intimate space: it is a lyric turn. In arguing this, I would not want to play down the recent trend for readings which argue for the political resonance of 'Frost at Midnight', and interrogate the autonomy of its lyric form. After all, this poem appears first in its quarto form alongside the poems we have just examined, which are openly and undeniably political. Moreover, it has often been noted that Coleridge tried to model the political on more intimate groups of friends and family, Kelvin Everest describing such models as expressing 'values and activities [that] would embody resolution of the problems inherent in his social context'.[20] This is increasingly how 'Frost at Midnight' has been defined in historicist readings, the intimacy of the domestic signifying patriotism in a way that 'Fears in Solitude', with its more public idiom, could not.[21] The very retreat from a degraded public sphere makes a public statement through the negative. Yet, without wishing to detach the poem from its political context, I think the notion of a lyric turn, and concomitant attention to language and emotion, is still useful. The revisionary readings gain their purchase against a notion that the lyric somehow successfully transcends the political: an old-fashioned view that is quite rightly challenged. In my reading, however, I do not see lyric as something that seamlessly sublates political problems, but rather a haunting, difficult and dispossessed site for speech.

Given this focus, I want to begin with a prominent fantasy of linguistic fluency inset within the poem. In a scene posited in contradistinction to Coleridge's supposedly paralysing urban upbringing, his infant son Hartley is addressed as follows:

> But *thou*, my babe! shalt wander, like a breeze,
> By lakes and sandy shores, beneath the crags
> Of ancient mountain, and beneath the clouds,
> Which image in their bulk both lakes and shores
> And mountain crags: so shalt thou see and hear
> The lovely shapes and sounds intelligible
> Of that eternal language, which thy God
> Utters, who from eternity doth teach
> Himself in all, and all things in himself.
> Great universal Teacher! he shall mould
> Thy spirit, and by giving make it ask.[22]

Far from the inscrutability of an awesomely silent nature marked elsewhere in the poem (and to which we shall return), here a formulaically sublime landscape is envisaged with luminous clarity. The burst of speech that concludes the passage gathers together the linguistic motifs constituting the fantasy, and gesture forward to the shout of joy that ends this early version of the poem. What is happening here, then, is the ascription of a pure, emotionally rich and unproblematic relation to language which draws us right back to Coleridge's poetics of the effusion. As Susan Eilenberg notes, Hartley is given 'a voice to be used, in this fantasy ... in communion with God'.[23] Coleridge avers tellingly to William Godwin in 1800 that 'Solemn Looks & solemn Words have been hitherto connected in [Hartley's] mind with great & magnificent objects only – with lightning, with thunder, with the waterfall blazing in the Sunset–' (*CL*, I.625). This comment sums up precisely the kind of projection of sublime affect on to the child found at the very centre of 'Frost at Midnight'.

Yet, if there is justice in describing this linguistic fantasy as sublime – through its combination of well-established Longinian tropes for sublime speech (or indeed 'solemn Words') with a natural setting drawn from Burke and others (crags, lakes, and so forth) – it is undeniably a fantasy. Hartley's boundless potentiality is in sharp contradistinction to the 'self-watching subtilizing mind' (l.27) of the adult self. The question, therefore, is how to read the relationship between the speaker of 'Frost at Midnight', who finds it hard to speak, with the fantasy of Hartley, from whom authentic speech bursts forth. By orientating the poem around its address to Hartley, Tilottama Rajan and Susan Eilenberg have both produced fairly traditional deconstructive readings that see a rhetorical economy being initiated. Although this, like many conversation poems, claims dislocation from an ideal voice, it projects a *double*, an auditor, who can actually confirm the speaker's power: as Rajan puts it, 'the vicarious enjoyment of epiphany through a surrogate self'.[24] The power of blessing on the silent auditor, Hartley, is used to reclaim the original voice's potency. Eilenberg, who follows Rajan's reading closely, thus argues that one must in fact see Coleridge's 'self-sacrifices ... symbolically as acts of self-preservation, even self-exaltation'.[25]

Such readings would condemn any lyric turn found in 'Frost at Midnight' as suspect. Regardless of the political significations of the domestic, the idealisation of his son seems like a stark flight from political realities in the here and now. However, I would like to reorientate our reading around a different apostrophic structure that shows that the Hartley fantasy is not the only possible way into the poem. Coleridge writes the following note in the 1798 quarto concerning the flickering on the grate, which is mentioned prominently in the poem: 'in all parts of the kingdom these films are called *strangers* and supposed to portend the arrival of some absent friend'.[26] It is notable that this stranger never comes: Thomas Greene is one of the few critics to note this non-arrival and to suggest the absence underlies the turn to Hartley.[27] As a speech-act, we may consider 'Frost at Midnight' either as encompassing a determinate addressee (if we consider Hartley the auditor), or lying partially unrealised in expectation of its addressee (if we still, like Coleridge, wait for the stranger). The stranger is arguably a more fundamental addressee for the poem, and his or her non-arrival shadows the apostrophe to Hartley. After all, as Nicholas Royle points out, 'the putative addressee, the "babe so beautiful" could only become its reader in the future, after ceasing ... to be a babe', for the infant is *infans* – without speech.[28] Equally, the babe never wakes in the course of the poem. Although Hartley screens his solitude, the poem is constituted by a present when Coleridge is truly alone as a waking, and most pertinently a speaking, being.

Given this constant pressure of a radical solitude, it is interesting that the poem attests to a series of voids and absences, the 'interspersed vacancies / And momentary pauses of the thought' (ll.51–2). When Coleridge ceases to speak, inwardly or not, there is no one else there, just 'dead calm' (l.50). The addressee has not arrived. There is no intimacy of speech and the silences do not mark the brief cessation of lived exchange, as one person responds to another, for instance. There is quite literally *nothing* but 'strange / And extreme silentness' (ll.9–10) on to which the lyric voice seems to fall, opening up like an abyss before, in between and after utterance. The vacancies are to some extent traversed by the 'gentle breathings' (l.50) of Hartley: an entirely appropriate recourse in view of his function as poetic ideal. Yet, these unconscious breaths are only those of a baby, fragile and 'cradled by [Coleridge's] side' (l.49). Whilst they 'fill' the lonely silences that suffuse language (l.51) and heart (l.53) alike, they are clearly not the divine wind of inspiration, the influx of breath, *in-spirare*.

A depth of silence felt at every turn, in vacancy and pause, becomes a kind of constitutive absence for lyric utterance, the essence of a voice that is unsure of to whom it is speaking. The intimate, domestic point at which the narrator's 'abstruser musings' (l.6) begin, based around the countable dyad of parent and child, is enveloped by a dreamlike field with 'numberless' (l.12) scope. This is where I want to return to the crucial matter of emotion. The Longinian scene always involved the transfer of affect from an exceptional, feeling subject to a rapt audience, auditor or reader. It was one that Coleridge used as a model for his effusions and their bursts of feeling, and it recurred – albeit problematically, and edging dangerously close to enthusiasm – in the political passions of 'France: An Ode' and 'Fears in Solitude'. (It is perhaps telling, given the difficulties with audience in the quarto, that the fantasy with Hartley figures the linguistic exchange occurring with God and nature alone as auditors.)

Yet what happens to the emotional scene of the poem if the auditor is a stranger – a stranger, moreover, who never comes? It seems to me that 'Frost at Midnight' marks the disintegration of a poetic ideal based on the transfer of affect outward from a unitary lyric subjectivity, and a subsequent voiding of this lyric 'I' as it turns inward and interrogates the supposedly privileged space of its interiority. In doing so, Coleridge strips bare precisely what the effusions examined in the previous chapter are haunted by: that is, that the feeling self stages its own passions, and that it is self-divided in so far as it projects its own emotional states in a kind of mental fable. The dream motif found in the two effusions becomes a waking dream, or a dreamlike waking: 'all the numberless goings on of life / Inaudible as dreams!' (ll.12–13). The impassioned 'I' that had been so central to so much of Coleridge's self-fashioning as a poet is here turned uncanny and strange.

If interiority was always the privileged element of a Longinian poetics of feeling, here interiority is rendered hyperbolically into the *abstruse* (from the Latin, *abstrudere*, to thrust away, to conceal). We might identify both a time and a place of this ultimately self-dispossessing abstrusion. The time is midnight. As Matthew Vanwinkle notes, the morning will bring the first stirrings of Hartley's prophesised destiny as nature poet, shouting joyfully at the icicles.[29] Yet, at midnight Hartley still sleeps and the inscrutable 'secret ministry' (l.1) of frost is still at work: indeed, some icicles will disappear unheard and unknown, unless fallen, dreamlike, 'in the trances of the blast' (l.76). Where there is simple, instinctive joy in the daylight, midnight is a time of secrets, as the poem's gothic echoes of 'Christabel' suggest. All are asleep but one. Coleridge is suspended in this most intimate and yet lonely of times, between one day and another: it is little surprise that he is led to memories, regrets, hopes and prophecies. Language at midnight cannot be designated a time.

The spatial figure on which the scene centres is the film on the grate. Neither stranger nor friend, perhaps both, it foretells and thus offers a vatic promise: but Coleridge no longer credits the prophecy. The memory of what he once believed the film to mean is now succeeded by a signification purely of absence. As it flutters on an ebbing fire it seems to precisely suggest that time will run out before someone comes: the *OED* lists a guttering candle as another type of stranger. The thin film of ash, counterfeiting life and yet actually the consummation of flame (fire, like breath, a symbol of poetic inspiration), is the negative, the non-centre of Coleridge's lyric speaking position. Yet, the fire, even as a non-centre, remains central, drawing the poem's gaze. Although the poem has no addressee, Coleridge still speaks. Poetry remains, organised around this new strange experience of the film at midnight.

As Coleridge's poetic speaker turns inward, unable to face outward to an addressee, it finds an increasing sense of placelessness. Midnight is a time that is indeed abstruse, thrust away from the temporality and transparency of everyday life. Ben Brice appropriately speaks of the speaker's 'uncanny recognition that he is "unquiet" amidst the quietness and calm of the cottage'.[30] In the witching hour, proximate structures are dissolved and de-realized and the subject loses its bearings: 'Sea, hill and wood, / This populous village! ... inaudible as dreams' (ll.10–11, 13). The lyric 'I' struggles to feel: without an addressee, the self can only address its feelings to itself, but in doing so they become strange, and vex the self which is now out-of-place, 'self-watching' and disturbed:

> Only that film, which flutter'd on the grate,
> Still flutters there, the sole unquiet thing,
> Methinks, its motion in this hush of nature
> Gives it dim sympathies with me, who live,
> Making it a companionable form,
> With which I can hold commune. Idle thought!
> But still the living spirit in our frame,
> That loves not to behold a lifeless thing,
> Transfuses into all its own delights
> Its own volition, sometimes with deep faith,
> And sometimes with fantastic playfulness. (ll.15–25)[31]

Coleridge recognises, as he struggles to feel, that in matters of affect 'deep faith' lies close, perhaps indistinguishably close, to 'fantastic playfulness'. 'Frost at Midnight' lays bare in a starker, more radical and openly *conscious* fashion that which threatened 'Effusion XXXVI: Written in Early Youth'. The fantastical nature of emotion implicates the psyche as a mechanism which doubles (or transfuses) itself, able to stage scenes of affect even if the targets of those emotional intentions are fabular images veiling absences.

I would argue that Coleridge has here reached a limit of Romanticism: specifically, the limit of the voice of true feeling, and the point at which the lyric subject reaches an internal aporia (an aporia only softened by his clinging to his child, a movement that perhaps deserves further commentary which I cannot attempt here). In the absence of an addressee to which to stage its emotions, a turn inward leads not to an affirmation of the privileged space of interiority (the genius, or the effusive self), but rather the disintegration of that interiority into a series of simulacra, under the pressure of its own gaze. The idea is even stronger in Coleridge's later revisions to the poem:

> the idling Spirit
> By its own moods interprets, every where
> Echo or mirror seeking of itself,
> And makes a toy of Thought.[32]

It is a lonely, uncanny lyric ego, unable to even feel (itself) with assurance: dislocation runs right through its own centre, as it finds the experience of meditation to be vexatious and its perceptual being-in-the-world to be disturbing, inaudible and inscrutable. If the 1796 *Poems* grounds itself in an effusive, emotional authenticity, but is haunted by the dreamlike vertigo of a fabular self, then by contrast 'Frost at Midnight' knows itself to be grounded in a fabular self, but is haunted by the effusive, emotional authenticity it fantasises for Hartley and from which it knows itself to be infinitely removed.

Coleridge has broached something which we can further illumine via Terada's most important sub-thesis, the theorisation of *pathos* as a second-order emotion. What does one feel when one does not feel? Terada argues that when affective existence is itself undone, then one's own feelings grow strange and displaced, but there is nevertheless still a certain feeling of the sudden voiding of feeling: 'pathos bids to be the negative double of auto-affection'.[33] It is interesting that she cites Keats to illustrate what she calls the Planck length – the almost nothing – of emotion at this point of its own dissolution:

> the *economy of pathos*, the recirculating infinity of feeling living on. In the discourse of emotion, specific emotions appear and disappear ... but there is no such thing as the absence of emotion ... When we're aware of the second-order nature of emotion we call it 'pathos'.[34]

Whilst she also invokes a more obvious example from the postmodern, the Keats citation is a recognition that our most influential emotional discourse and inheritance – Romanticism – had almost inevitably interrogated the limits of its own concepts of feeling and interiority.

Coleridge was there too, I feel, probing the 'interspersed vacancies' (l.51) and 'fantastic playfulness' (l.25) of lyric subjectivity. 'Frost at Midnight' presents a psyche that watches itself suspiciously, straining for objects in which to root its own feelings and yet finding only images projected by itself. The minimal, hushed, unsure emotion of 'Frost at Midnight', I would argue, is what Terada identifies as pathos.

One final question remains: is this sublime? Critics have identified the poem as such before. Richard Berkeley, for instance, identifies a pantheistic sublime, founded partially on silence, where the subject is swallowed up the grand hush of nature.[35] 'Frost at Midnight' is invoked alongside 'The Eolian Harp' as part of an argument made by Markus Poetsch about the grounding of sublime visions in everyday domestic spaces.[36] Yet in so far as we are talking about a Longinian rhetorical or linguistic sublime, and indeed about the eighteenth-century neo-Longinian tradition of bursts of poetic feeling, it would seem 'Frost at Midnight' marks the end of the sublime, or at least the displacement of such extravagant desires. On the other hand, things are not necessarily so clear-cut. In a motif we shall meet on a number of occasions in this study, the limit or disintegration of one understanding of sublimity may find itself recapitulating a certain logic of the sublime – not least because sublimity has always included an understanding of limit and disintegration as one of its essential moments.

For example, as I have emphasised, the poem's 'strange / and extreme silentness' (ll.9–10) is very important. It is the dominant figure for the vexation of Coleridge's lyric subject and the suspension of its capacity for both language and feeling. Yet, of course, silence is identified by Burke as part of an array of sublime inscrutabilities (e.g. gloom, the indeterminate) based on the fact that what is vague is more affecting than what is clear. Moreover, we can find the same notion even in Longinus:

> It is natural inclination ... to admire not the little streams, *however pellucid* and useful, but the Nile, the Danube ... Nor do we feel so much awe before the little flame we kindle, because it keeps its light *clear and pure*, as before the fires of heaven, *though they are often obscured*. (p. 178, my emphases)

Given this, tropes such as the foreboding silence, the secrecy of the frost, the inaudibility of dreams, the vacancy of thought – not to mention the timelessness of midnight and the strange ontology of the film – suggest a certain sublime afterglow (like the film on a 'low-burnt fire' (l.14), we might say) permeating the poem.

It is thus appropriate that we might identify the effect of this text with various nominations that recall the sublime. The uncanny would certainly be one such name, and readings have been made on such terms by Anne Williams and, as previously noted, Ben Brice.[37] Pathos itself is another term with a history intertwined with the sublime, Terada arguing that 'the phenomenology of the sublime and the phenomenology of cogito are similar'.[38] One of her core readings, once again punctuated by a reference to Keats, is that of Kant's *apatheia*, a state of feeling feeling itself circulating emptily which is not so far away from the echoes and mirrors which Coleridge eventually inscribes into 'Frost at Midnight': 'the feeling of the failure of feeling – Keats's "feel of not to feel it"'.[39] In fact, the discourse on sublime feeling has always inscribed a certain *blockage* of feeling, as influential commentators such as Neil Hertz and Thomas Weiskel have noted.[40]

An analysis of such blockage, such *pathos*, as the emotion *par excellence* of a sceptical, reflexive, fragmented lyric subjectivity that follows Romanticism could certainly be mounted. Timothy Clark's recent work on lyric singularity, particularly his dialogue with the theories of Hans-Georg Gadamer, would be one route to justifying 'Frost at Midnight' as a fault-line between Romantic and post-Romantic feeling subjectivities: an indeterminate addressee, a struggle with the possibility of speech and an existential unsettledness are common to both 'Frost at Midnight' and what Gadamer calls *hermetic lyric*.[41] Yet there is a far older tradition of lyric negativity which takes us right back to the heart of the Longinian sublime and *Peri Hypsous*, where the following commentary is made on a Sapphic fragment:

> Do you not admire the way in which she brings everything together – mind and body, hearing and tongue, eyes and skin? She seems to have lost them all, and to be looking for them as though they were external to her. She is cold and hot, mad and sane, frightened and near death, all by turns. (p. 154)

As Yopie Prins notes, there is a complex tension in Longinus between positing Sappho as a beautifully articulated organic body and affirming a violence wreaked upon that body, a tension overdetermined by both gender issues and the fragmented state of Sappho's own textual corpus. Ultimately, Prins – in common with Suzanne Guerlac, among others – attests to the superior force of dismemberment.[42] There is an excessiveness in the fragment that unworks Longinus's drive towards rhetorical unity: 'rather than reintegrating a unified lyric subject,

Longinus ... perpetuates the fragmentation of Sappho. He reads the fragment as a living body, only to mutilate that bodily figure.'[43] I do not want to posit 'Frost at Midnight' as a Sapphic lyric *per se*, not least because the gendering in Coleridge's text (especially in the quarto version which includes the figure of Sara alongside the father–son bond) is complex. Yet I do want to note Sappho as a moment of fragile subjectivity within the Longinian tradition, and as a figure of dispersal and alienation: as Jonathan Culler puts it, a '[shift] away from Homeric moments of grandeur, of gods and heroes, to scenarios of self-loss'.[44]

This can read as much in terms of passions as bodies. Longinus interprets a 'complex of emotions' (p. 154) in Sappho, which encompasses a number of elemental dichotomies. Her identity seems to be cut up by heterogeneous passions, many of which – madness, trembling and dying – seem to imply further dissolution and dispersal. This is rather more hyperbolic than anything in 'Frost at Midnight', although something of its chaotic excess might be legible in the imagery of echoes and mirrors that proliferate in later versions of Coleridge's lyric. A more telling affinity is the estrangement of the self that Longinus identifies, which affects thought, sense and feeling alike: 'she seems to have lost them all, and to be looking for them as though they were external to her'. This is precisely the sort of uncanniness and dispossession that exists as a possibility in every *ekstasis*, and is intimately linked to the theories of emotion and *pathos* examined above. Coleridge's speaker too seems to find feeling outside of himself, and is searching for it. Coleridge's speaker too is estranged: not least by the stranger's mark made in the grate.

In conclusion, if we attend to the linguistic and affective condition into which the fantasy of Hartley is embedded, rather than the fantasy itself, we find a different picture of Coleridge's turn to lyric. It is a haunting one, where the 'I' has no addressee, is dislocated, and finds the spaces of its own interiority to be disturbingly subject to a kind of emptiness, hollowed out as affect plays fabular games with transfused images. Coleridge has reached the edge of a set of possibilities, first inscribed in his youthful effusions, for a poetic subjecthood based on passion and a privileged interiority. The Longinian tradition primarily tries to assert realisation and possession, from the orator seizing the passions of his audience to Coleridge's speaker in 'France: An Ode' 'possessing all things with intensest love' (l.104). 'Frost at Midnight', however, involves dispossession and non-realisation. Coleridge engages a distinctively finite kind of self, one that loses hold of its passions, and itself. In doing so, I think Coleridge looks forward to the kind of strange lyric sites of post-Romanticism: of Mallarmé, of Rilke, of Celan. Yet, he is also subject to a much older impulse, the Sapphic loss inscribed right there in Longinus:

> all the numberless goings on of life,
> Inaudible as dreams! The thin blue flame
> Lies on my low-burnt fire, and quivers not. (ll.12–14)

> my tongue is broken, a subtle fire runs under my skin; my eyes cannot see, my ears hum
> ...
> I am paler than grass; I seem near to dying.[45]

Part II
Terror, Burke, Ethics

3
'Cruel Wrongs and Strange Distress': an Ethical Terror-Sublime in 'The Destiny of Nations'

John Axcelson has recently identified a series of Coleridge's long politico-prophetic poems – 'The Destiny of Nations', 'Religious Musings' and 'Ode to the Departing Year' – as exemplary of a sublime mode in his early poetic output. Stylistically, Axcelson emphasises the 'grand, world historical approach ... [and] extravagant rhetoric' of these texts, a set of characteristics echoed by Peter Kitson in singling out 'The Destiny of Nations' as articulating a so-called Unitarian sublime.[1] However, in this chapter I shall identify a different kind of sublimity found not in the poem's rhetorical and visionary flights but in the tragic, naturalistic narrative that lies at its centre. This describes the heroine, Joan of Arc, coming across a dying family of refugees caught up in the turmoil of war.[2] Consider the following passage:

> The foremost horse
> Lay with stretched limbs; the others, yet alive
> But stiff and cold, stood motionless, their manes
> Hoar with the frozen night dews. Dismally
> The dark-red dawn now glimmered; but its gleams
> Disclosed no face of man.[3]

The writing is realistic and largely non-figural, embellished with disturbing gothic touches and a foreboding sense of hostility and danger.[4] If we were to look for literary analogues, it would not be in the fantastic excess of Milton (invoked by Kitson), but rather something like Friedrich Schiller's *The Robbers*. As a young Coleridge wrote in 1794, in a note appended to an admiring poem dedicated to the German playwright, 'SCHILLER introduces no supernatural beings; yet his human beings agitate and astonish more than all the *goblin* rout – even of Shakespeare.'[5]

In this chapter, I explore the nature and function of this sublime of terror, and its roots in a purely human experience of suffering, injustice and horror. This involves a crucial ethical, social and political dimension. Unlike Burke's sublime, which was the dominant contemporary theory of an aesthetics of terror, 'The Destiny of Nations' is a poem in which terror is deliberately and forcefully intertwined with a consuming experience of sympathy, exemplified by its heroine and in which the reader is impelled to share. Thus, where the *Philosophical Enquiry* identifies the sublime as a passion of self-preservation grounded in the immediacy of one's own physiological stimulation, I will show that Coleridge, with the aid of David Hartley's philosophical system, conceived of a powerfully ethical response to terror, based on feeling *alongside* others. However, as I argue in the second half of the chapter, the very intensity of this sympathetic passion creates problems of its own. 'The Destiny of Nations' enacts a series of compelling demands made by the innocent dead that cannot be easily satisfied by standard Unitarian ethics but only by more archaic forms of retribution: a bloody, divine counter-violence. The intensity of sympathy that Coleridge draws forth for radical ends is born in the crucible of sublime terror: in so far as sympathy in turn creates a demand for justice, this sublime, intensifying context seems to produce a desire for an equally terrifying justice.

Two empiricisms: Edmund Burke and David Hartley

There is little doubt that Edmund Burke's 1757 *A Philosophical Enquiry into the Origin of Our Ideas of the Sublime and Beautiful* eclipses every other modern theorisation of the sublime with the exception of Immanuel Kant's *Critique of Judgment*. For the Coleridge of the 1790s, yet to engage with the German tradition, he would certainly have been the dominant voice. Moreover, if we are thinking in terms of terror, it was Burke who placed it unambiguously at the centre of sublimity and provided explicit theoretical rationale for doing so:

> Whatever is fitted in any sort to excite the ideas of pain, and danger, that is to say, whatever is in any sort terrible, or is conversant about terrible objects, or operates in a manner analogous to terror, is a source of the *sublime*; that is, it is productive of the strongest emotion which the mind is capable of feeling.[6]

The theoretical rationale in question was firmly empiricist. It is thus with Burke's distinctive model of the human subject that I want to begin, showing how a highly parsimonious analysis of consciousness led, firstly, to a physiological definition of aesthetic affects and, secondly, to an important identification of the sublime as a passion of self-preservation.

The topic with which the *Enquiry* opens is pleasure and pain, which exemplifies Burke's tendency to start with the most basic terms of analysis, drawn from immediate experience. However, the sublime is something of an anomaly within this initially simple schema since although the text is insistent in making sublimity a function of terror – and thus of pain – there is no doubt that it is also a kind of pleasure. Burke is thus led to 'enquire how any species of delight can be derived from a cause so apparently contrary to it' (p. 122). The answer is rigorously empirical, returning to the sense organs themselves: the terrors of sublimity are conceptualised 'as producing an unnatural tension and certain violent emotions of the nerves' (p. 121). Thus, the idea of something dangerous produces a fearful physiological reaction, anything obscure strains the faculties of perception, a grand colonnade subjects the eyes to an agitated repetition, darkness strains the fibres of the iris beyond their natural state, a loud sound strikes the ear forcefully, and so on.[7] It is suggested that this exercise of the fibres – particularly in the finer sense-organs of the eye and ear – is pleasurable, or rather 'not pleasure, but a sort of delightful horror, a sort of tranquillity tinged with terror' (p. 123).

Burke's level of analysis is thus resolutely determined to root itself in the simplest, empirical levels of human existence: basic sensory responses, pain and pleasure, the body. His ultimate datum was physiological, and his final explanations of aesthetic passions refer to the nervous system. This explanatory framework is also crucial in determining perhaps Burke's central analytic distinction: that between beauty as a social passion and the sublime as a passion of self-preservation. Supposedly, all experiences of the beautiful stem from the pleasures of sex and generation, whilst the sublime derives from the threat of physical destruction. One can see a starkly but elegantly reductionist picture of the human animal lying behind this binary, and the many others (such as the masculinity of sublimity versus the femininity of the beautiful) derived from it. The human subject, analysed through a certain form of empiricism, becomes something whose fundamental functions are to survive and to reproduce. As Burke notes, he wishes to root his study of taste in the most basic things – 'the most common, sometimes ... the meanest things in nature' – and condemns others for seeking 'the rule of the arts in the wrong place ... among poems, pictures, engravings, statues and buildings' (p. 49).

Sublimity, linked to the empirical survival of the self and basic threats to its body, is thus a resolutely individualistic experience: 'conversant about the preservation of the individual ... [as such] the most powerful of all the passions' (p. 36). Indeed, as Frances Ferguson notes, Burke's sublime is in underlying conflict with social relation and communication, since the latter inevitably departs from the immediacy of sensate data that is the privilege of the individual and the basis of Burke's theory. Thus, as Ferguson argues, 'one can relate [i.e. communicate] one's feelings to another ... but without any guarantee that those feelings remain reliable indexes to current sensation'.[8] Moreover, the physiological reductionism of the *Enquiry* means that when the sublime becomes a social rather than an individual experience, it becomes customary and thus loses the stimulating force that resides in novelty and shock.[9]

Burke does admittedly make an attempt as part of his discussion of tragedy to incorporate sympathy – and thus a certain sociality – into the analysis of the sublime. Sympathy is introduced into the *Philosophical Enquiry* because the dichotomy between social passions and passions of self-preservation has been so strongly drawn that Burke must struggle to distance himself from the notion that we take pleasure in suffering because we are safe ourselves:

> It is absolutely necessary my life should be out of any imminent hazard before I can take a delight in the suffering of others ... but then it is a sophism to argue from thence, that this immunity is the cause of my delight. (p. 44)

Nevertheless, the position that we enjoy the sufferings of others because of the thrill of our own self-preservation is a logical consequence of Burke's own theory. Sympathy – which is a social passion, and should arguably be part of the beautiful – is to some extent grafted artificially on to the argument at this point. Burke's case is not helped by his famous illustration that an audience would abandon a theatre for an execution: although his point is to illustrate the superiority of real sympathies, the element of spectacle in both examples suggests the alternative that the audience seek the execution merely as voyeurs.

What I want to argue is that if we look at Coleridge's use of terror in his early poems – specifically in 'The Destiny of Nations', although I think parallel readings could be made elsewhere – we find it diametrically opposed to Burke. Where the *Enquiry* sees sublimity as an individualistic passion, Coleridge posits it as a social and ethical one;

where the *Enquiry* includes sublimity within an analysis of the barest levels of human existence, Coleridge invokes a narrative of human self-transcendence; and where sympathy is an awkward addendum to Burke's theory, in Coleridge's poetry it is fundamental and central. These differences have an intellectual (and ultimately a political) backdrop, which can be revealed by referring to Coleridge's greatest intellectual influence before Kant: English associationist philosopher, David Hartley.

Hartley and Burke do not start from radically different places. Both are predominantly empiricists, working out of a Lockean tradition, and both root their empiricism in an analysis of the nervous system. Indeed, the account of stretched fibres in the *Enquiry* seems very similar to the famous theory of vibrations articulated in the *Observations on Man*. Objects impress infinitesimally small vibratory motions on to the sense organs, vibrations which carry up the nerve and to the brain.[10] Oft-repeated impressions supposedly leave miniature traces known as *vibratiuncles*, which correspond to Locke's simple ideas.[11] When Hartley turns to the passions, his analysis of aggregates of ideas provoked by vibrations, and split into two basic classes (attraction and repulsion), hardly seems to suggest Hartley and the *Enquiry* have vastly different understandings of human subjectivity.

Yet, due to Hartley's doctrine of association, the models diverge radically after this point.[12] Whereas Burke tends to remain on the minimal, physiological level of analysis, Hartley describes the association of ideas as constructing ever more complex levels of human subjectivity, based around more and more sophisticated aggregates of ideas. Mirrored in the structure of his own treatise, the human subject rises from its basic sensory starting point through six ascending classes: imagination, ambition, self-interest, sympathy, theopathy and the moral sense. Richard Allen, who has written the most detailed account of Hartley, describes this as 'a psychological epic ... the reintegration of a fallen, fragmented, and self-alienated humanity'.[13] This *narrative* of subjectivity would make Hartley among the most attractive influences to dissenting radicals, such as Coleridge himself, who wanted to envisage a perfectible humanity which could overcome its tendency towards evil and conflict to create an ultimately just society. Whereas Burke stripped the human being down to its most basic level, Hartley worked on the principle of what the human being could develop into.

One place where this difference between Burke and Hartley becomes particularly important for our reading of 'The Destiny of Nations' is sympathy. We have already seen how sympathy held an awkward and problematic place in Burke's schema, complicating the clear distinction between passions of self-preservation and passions of social intercourse.

By contrast, sympathy possesses a pivotal position in the teleological narrative set out in the *Observations*:

> the Pleasures of Sympathy improve those of Sensation, Imagination, Ambition, and Self-interest, by limiting and regulating them ... Their Union and intire [sic] Coincidence with those of Theopathy are evident, inasmuch as we are led by the Love of good Men to that of God, and back again ... In like manner, they may be proved to unite and coincide with the Pleasures of the Moral Sense, both because they are one principal Source of the Moral Sense, and because this, in its turn, approves of and enforces them intirely [sic].[14]

The very division that animates Burke's treatise – between the individual and the social – is the one carefully bridged here. The ability to not only feel one's own passions, but to feel the passions of others, is the point which opens up the human subject to the possibility of even higher cognitive levels – the religious and the ethical. It is this conception of the nature and overall function of sympathy which I shall now take forward to 'The Destiny of Nations', for it is fundamental to how Coleridge reorientates the terror-sublime away from the Burkean understanding, and towards an ethical and social one.

Sublimity and sympathy: Joan of Arc as Unitarian heroine

As mentioned above, critics such as Axcelson and Kitson have identified 'The Destiny of Nations' with a rhetorical, epic, visionary kind of sublimity, drawing largely on the oldest textual material – that contributed to Robert Southey's *Joan of Arc* – as their evidence. However, the tragic tale which is at the structural heart of Coleridge's rewriting of the poem evinces a rather different kind of sublime based on purely quotidian terrors: those of war, injustice, famine and death. As suggested above, it is more Schillerian than Miltonic, in the sense that a young Coleridge responded to *The Robbers* by writing to Southey, 'who is this Schiller? This convulser of the Heart? Did he write his tragedy amid the yelling of Fiends? ... Why have we ever called Milton sublime?' (*CL*, I.122). As he wrote in a sonnet dedicated to the German author, the 'goblin rout' (l.7) of supernatural terrors is forced to withdraw in the face of a 'famished Father's cry' (l.4), ceding true horror to 'the more withering scene' (l.8) of human suffering.[15] It is this kind of sublimity on which Coleridge plays in 'The Destiny of Nations':

> The village, where he dwelt a husbandman,
> By sudden inroad had been seized and fired

Late on the yester-evening. With his wife
And little ones he hurried his escape.
They saw the neighbouring hamlets flame, they heard
Uproar and shrieks! and terror-struck drove on
Through unfrequented roads, a weary way!
But saw nor house nor cottage. All had quenched
Their evening hearth-fire: for the alarm had spread.
The air was clipped keen, the night was fanged with frost,
And they provisionless! The weeping wife
Ill hushed her children's moans; and still they moaned,
Till fright and cold and hunger drank their life. (ll.233–45)

The combination of savagery, pathos and political injustice is characteristic of this stretch of the poem. The pathos of the familial is repeatedly invoked. Coleridge works with an economical poetic palette of frost and fire, evoking a forebodingly hostile nature, which seems as brutal as the soldiers who fire the village. Subtle touches such as the fanged frost create a gothic atmosphere: indeed, the minute observation Coleridge devotes to the bodies of the dead elsewhere in the section would not be out of place in a gothic novel.

Joan of Arc's response is, quite simply, to feel. She tends the husbandman, weeps, prays and listens to his tragic tale. 'The Destiny of Nations' takes great pains to establish sympathy as the defining quality of its heroine:

the Maid
Learnt more than schools could teach: Man's shifting mind,
His vices and his sorrows! And full oft
At tales of cruel wrong and strange distress
Had wept and shivered. (ll.153–7)

Her face is said to reveal 'That pity there had oft and strongly worked' (l.169), whilst she is also described 'suffering to the height of what was suffered, / Stung with too keen a sympathy' (ll.253–4). Her intense, almost ecstatic, response to witnessing suffering is an overthrow of the subject, in the sense that she mingles her own passions with those of others. As heroine, Joan is an exemplary surrogate for the reader also: given the wrenching portrayal of the innocent family's suffering, we too are invited to feel. Unlike for Burke, then, the experience of terror here incorporates sympathy as one of its central aspects: it is a social and ethical terror-sublime.

It is also a political one. As Robert Southey's *Joan of Arc* had done a few years before, with its provocatively pro-French presentation of history covered canonically but nationalistically by Shakespeare, 'The Destiny of Nations' was drawing attention to recent events in Europe in which Coleridge had deep radical investments. The terrors of his poem were, as their similarity to the war reportage of *The Watchman* also proves, meant to invoke the terrors of contemporary Europe. This allows us to see another crucial link back to the Hartleian context. Joan's ability to be moved by the terror of war makes her a heroine in terms of Coleridge's Unitarian radicalism, underwritten by the theories of the *Observations of Man*. As mentioned above, sympathy – as the point where the self begins to feel for others, and thus transcend its self-interest – was a crucial moment in the perfectibility of humankind. In 'Religious Musings', correctly described by Nicola Trott as depicting the 'ascent to the Unitarian God ... [drawn from the] psychology of transcendence from the *Observations on Man*', he is more explicit about this progress of the human subject:[16]

> 'Tis the sublime of man,
> Our noontide majesty, to know ourselves
> Parts and proportions of one wondrous whole!
> This fraternizes man, this constitutes
> Our charities and bearings.[17]

It is Joan's exemplary capacity to share feeling and to participate, affectively, in the 'one wondrous whole' that makes her the heroine of 'The Destiny of Nations'.[18] In so far as the poem invokes a terror-sublime, it is one which is not rooted in self-preservation, but rather in the self's ability to feel alongside others. Coleridge's sublime carries a moral and ultimately political content – charity, sympathy, fraternity – which lies beyond the scope of Burke's account.

To return to Frances Ferguson's point, noted earlier, the Burkean sublime is based on raw physiological stimulation, grounded in an immediacy which cannot be shared. Coleridge's turn to a more ethical sublime, underwritten by Hartley's model of a human subject whose initial physiological states develop into ever more complex layers of selfhood, demands precisely a mediated experience, *sym-pathy*, or feeling together. Part of the problem with Burke's discussions of tragedy and sympathy is that his theory does not find a ready home for them, because they demand a shift away from his privileging of the sense-data of the individual. Indeed, in sharp contrast to Hartley's discussion of how sympathy emerges from the association of ideas, the *Enquiry* must simply invoke God to explain it: 'our Creator has designed we should be united by the bond of sympathy' (p. 42). It also worth noting that Burke's definition of the sublime as physiological shock, which loses its force over time, is diametrically opposed to the Hartleian grounding of Coleridge's terror-sublime, which treats Joan's repeated exposure to suffering as a kind of schooling: 'she was quick to mark / The good and evil thing' (ll.141–2). Indeed, this is exactly what associationism would predict: the building of lasting associations (or marks, one might suggest) between impressions is the principle on which Hartley's higher levels of subjectivity are constructed. It is the same kind of ethical schooling, and firming of sympathetic associations, that by extension lies behind Coleridge's hope for humanity's perfectibility.

Before moving on, I would like to note how this reading of 'The Destiny of Nations' and its ethical terror-sublime might alter current critical understanding of the poem. The two most detailed interpretations thus far have been made by Robert Sternbach and William Ulmer. Sternbach opens a reading in which the style of the refugee episode, in its contrast to the more visionary material, expresses a political tension between optimism and realism. He describes the move from the allegorical scenes to 'a fresher, more literal approach to the story of Joan's life and inspiration' as precipitating a confrontation with a more realistic perspective on history and 'the intractability of some evils ... a poetic impasse'.[19] William Ulmer refines Sternbach's perspective in re-reading the allegorical, visionary scenes as themselves exposing certain problems within the ideology of political and historical optimism (notably their tendency towards the apocalyptic – a theme I shall return to below). Nevertheless, he assents to Sternbach's judgement that the scene with the dying family represents the intrusion of concrete, historical suffering and 'the suspension of Joan's power of historical agency ... the familiar Coleridgean impasse'.[20]

By invoking the sublime, my interpretation supplements these readings in two ways. Firstly, it highlights the aesthetic aims of the passage, which Ulmer and Sternbach largely overlook. Both critics appear to see the refugee episode as little more than a mimesis of the real, directly portraying the problematic 'goings-on of the historical process'.[21] Whilst it is clearly naturalistic, and in sharp stylistic contrast to rhetorical flights found elsewhere in the poem, it also evokes a very specific aesthetic effect – a terror-sublime with the gothic and pathetic elements we have just examined, with sympathy as the implicated affect. Secondly, by revealing the ethical and political importance of sympathy, one can suggest that whilst posing certain problems to Coleridge's Unitarian radicalism in the shape of contemporary suffering, the refugee narrative also tries to negotiate the horror of this suffering in a specifically Unitarian way, i.e. through the necessity of compassion and charity. Whilst Ulmer and Sternbach are correct to identify concrete suffering as something which disrupts one element of Unitarian radicalism – its progressivist faith in an ever-improving humanity – the other side of the story is that that very suffering may be the spur to improve humanity. The everyday horror of oppression and war may lead the radical reader to question their idealism; on the other hand, it may drive them towards working for a more just society.

Nevertheless, Ulmer and Sternbach are correct in identifying a potentially critical fault-line in Coleridge's politics here. There is a problem in courting such terrible sufferings. Although Joan of Arc possesses radical sympathy, Coleridge struggles to muster an appropriate response on her behalf. It is impossible to deny that Joan's experience of 'troublous ecstasy' (l.272) presents an impasse for Coleridge: the fractured state of the poem, which breaks off at the moment of Joan's greatest sympathy, offers structural proof. Having reached an intense apex, 'The Destiny of Nations' appears fearful of thinking through this moment. Although Joan's psyche has reached an exemplary ethical height, in the face of the refugee family's sufferings there seems no rationale – at least no rationale within the psychological, naturalistic mode of the episode itself – that can pass beyond it. As Ulmer emphasises, although Coleridge could frame epic theodicies, they seemed to offer little in the context of concrete suffering and identification with those who suffered: 'due to his inability to mediate vision and action – his inability to show visionary enlightenment actually moving history forward – Coleridge the Unitarian can seemingly portray visionary spectacle or real political action, but not both at once'.[22] However, given that we have identified an ethical terror-sublime founded on sympathy, we also possess a new framework with which to re-examine the point of crisis to which Joan of Arc is brought. Certainly, it is a matter of the intractability of suffering, and a response to that suffering – and thus, as Sternbach and Ulmer both point out, political agency. But now we have the Hartleian psychology of transcendence to aid a more exact analysis of the failure of what Coleridge was attempting with the refugee narrative.

As already noted, Coleridge felt universal benevolence was to be sought in an affective movement transcending the boundaries of the self and encompassing circles of others, and sympathy was the crux of this. In short, the possibility of a just society is inseparable from the realisation of participation in a whole, of *sym-pathos*. This can be seen in the 'noontide majesty' passage of 'Religious Musings', given above, but also in the early sections of 'The Destiny of Nations' where Coleridge considers the hypothesis that 'Infinite myriads of self-conscious minds / Are one all-conscious Spirit' (ll.43–4). As he would also do in the famous conclusion to 'The Eolian Harp', Coleridge retreats before these monist metaphysical speculations, but there is no hesitation in maintaining them in an ethical and political register, as when Joan laments:

> Ah! why, uninjured and unprofited,
> Should multitudes against their brethren rush?
> Why sow they guilt, still reaping misery? (ll.381–3)

In short, the idea of binding together individuals in recognition of their common participation in a providential order is a major element of Coleridge's Unitarian radicalism, and it is recognition of one's ties outside the self that makes sympathy such a potent and fundamental passion. As 'Religious Musings' notes, once more invoking the family:

> in his [God's] vast family no Cain
> Injures uninjured (in her best-aimed blow
> Victorious murder a blind suicide).[23]

It is this binding and uniting aspect of sympathy, I will argue, that appears most under stress in 'The Destiny of Nations'. After Joan of Arc has heard the tragic tale of the husbandman, we see not an expansion out of the self, but a turn inward. Thomas de Quincey's *Suspiria de Profundis* describes a crisis of sympathy in the face of absolute ruin that could easily be applied here: 'the voice perishes, the gestures are frozen; and the spirit of man flies back upon its own centre'.[24] Joan's immediate reaction, on seeing the last of the family die, is flight to the solitude of a hilltop. Coleridge transfigures her face, making the very locus of communication with others uncanny and impenetrable: her eyes are filled with 'strange vivacity' (l.257), and she mutters unintelligible speech to herself: 'the Maid / Brooded with moving lips, mute, startful, dark!' (ll.254–5). (Compare ll.164–74, where virtue is said to be easily and transparently read in her features.) Instead of ascent and expansion, there is collapse; far from creating bonds with other selves, the integrity of her own selfhood seems to crumble: 'Naked, and void, and fixed, and all within / The unquiet silence of confusèd thought / And shapeless feelings' (ll.259–61).

With the associationist context of sympathy guiding our reading, the origin of this traumatic turn inward can be explicated in more detailed terms than just identifying it as an impasse of agency in the real world.

Those in whom Joan makes affective investments are the dead and dying. Far from creating an ethical community of individuals bonded together by sympathy, Joan's identifications are with those destroyed by war and poverty. As bonds with others, they are sheared off even as they are first made. The community of sympathy that 'The Destiny of Nations' erects is one of ghosts: a distorted counterpart, to some extent, of the ethical community that Unitarian radicalism aimed to create. Binding oneself to the memory of the dead does not achieve the positive movement outward that sympathy with the living can, but rather marks the self with wounds of loss that it must struggle to assimilate. If one feels alongside others, what happens when their passions are dead? There is a trauma of mourning for Joan to face. As Freud's famous account of mourning suggests, the so-called *hypercathexis* of the lost object leads to a turning away from reality, a suspension of agency and even – interestingly, given the visionary content of 'The Destiny of Nations' – hallucination: 'this inhibition and circumscription of the ego [in mourning] is the expression of an exclusive devotion to mourning which leaves nothing over for other purposes or other interests'.[25]

Marked by suddenness and suffering, there is a convulsive necessity to assimilate the facts of the deaths. Joan, in fleeing the scene, seems to relive the sufferings of the refugees, as we can see through a pattern of subtle reflections between her trance and the husbandman's tale. They are 'terror-struck' (l.238), she is 'fancy-crazed' (l.258); where they flee along hauntingly abandoned roads, she is driven up a desolate hillside by a 'mighty hand' (l.261); where the family finds shelter under the coverture, she huddles beside the hilltop beacon. The weeping of the mother and her children is echoed by her 'pant and sob' (l.269), and just as 'fright and cold and hunger *drank* their life' (l.245), she is '*swallowed* up in the ominous dream' (l.267, my emphases). Yet if this is a form of introjection – an attempt to suffer in their place – it fails. Crucially, the trauma proves inassimilable: instead of the psyche incorporating the terror of what she has witnessed, this terror threatens to engulf her: 'she toiled in troublous ecstasy, / A horror of great darkness wrapt her round' (ll.272–3).

It is at this point that Coleridge desired to shift into the visionary mode, and return to the material that he had contributed to Southey's *Joan of Arc*. The literary dilemma for Coleridge is thus somewhat analogous to the psychic dilemma. Joan is seeking to integrate the traumatic facts of loss and death into her psyche. Coleridge is seeking to integrate the sublime terror that he has invoked in the refugee episode: it too is a kind of trauma, one that the Unitarian optimism structuring the poem struggles to incorporate. In fact, we know that Coleridge failed: as mentioned before, the poem is cut off just after the trance, and apparently Coleridge never managed to find a satisfactory way to bring the fragments of allegorical and apocalyptic vision into a coherent relationship with the episode with the abandoned coach. Nevertheless, these fragments do present interesting linkages with the truncated main body of the poem, and we can use these links to analyse what Coleridge was attempting.

For instance, given that Joan's psyche is greatly disturbed and disunified after she witnesses the death of the refugees, it is interesting that a key figure in her visions is an idealised double of herself: Peace. A number of parallels are apparent. Just as Joan's brow is said to be a 'sublime and broad' (l.164) icon of pity, the 'power of Justice like a name all light' (l.378) shines forth from the brow of Peace. She is said to live in the world 'as in a place of tombs' (l.177) whilst Peace is described as fleeing to 'a place of tombs' (l.373) during a time of war. Both are ministering, angelic female figures, who pour out the balm of compassion in a time of strife, but are limited by providential imperatives demanding they await a millennial time. However, unlike Joan, Peace is placed within an authoritative narration. She can see, in Peace, a version of her own plight, but one structured in an explanatory way – a contrast to the arbitrary trauma dominating her own experience of terror and suffering. Note the measured rhetorical antithesis of:

> And hence, for times and seasons bloody and dark,
> Short Peace shall skin the wounds of causeless War,
> And War, his strained sinews knit anew,
> Shall violate the unfinished works of Peace. (ll.416–19)

In identifying with Peace, a semi-divine figure, Joan can shore up the integrity of her own self, which had been threatening collapse.

Peace's place in a coherent theodicy is absolutely characteristic of the visionary fragments, which are very much a justification of suffering. They fulfilled this function as part of Southey's poem, but in the 1796 text take on the added burden of answering directly to the suffering witnessed in the refugee episode. In describing the mourning process thus far, we have concentrated on the assimilation of trauma. However, there is another equally important aspect of mourning: in carrying the memory of the murdered, Joan is haunted by the ethical demands made by the dead. Because of her radical capacity for sympathy, she bears within herself the voices of the now voiceless and part of her trauma is quite simply the necessity – and yet the apparent impossibility – of rendering justice for those she mourns. By provoking intense pity for suffering,

Coleridge also invites an affective desire for recompense in Joan and, of course, the reader. It is with this aspect of the poem that I wish to conclude, showing that the justice promised in the visionary fragments may well answer the demands of the dead, but in a way that offers a logic of punishment, vengeance and purification entirely at odds with Unitarian beliefs. By invoking a terror-sublime, Coleridge appears to set into motion a logic of force and violence – not least in the shape of an awe-inspiring, Old Testament deity – which overruns the very ethical commitments that motivated the turn to the sublime in the first place. One regresses, in fact, to a sublime of pure force which is more Burkean than Unitarian.

Blood and pollution: ritual morality in 'The Destiny of Nations'

To see how the claims of the innocent dead begin to undermine Coleridge's ethical views, we should first consider the treatment of punishment in contemporary radical theory. Coleridge ascribed at the time, under the influence of David Hartley, Joseph Priestley and – to a lesser extent – Godwin, to necessitarianism. This, of course, posed a challenge to ethics and law in that a notion of culpability and responsibility based around the intuitive belief one could have acted otherwise was no longer tenable. As Priestley states it, put a given man in a given situation, and 'he would always, voluntarily, make the same choice, and come to the same determination'.[26] In much the same way as with twentieth-century analytic philosophers, the possibility of free will is maintained with a compatibilist analysis that holds that an action motivated by one's own inclinations is evidence of agency, even if one could not have done otherwise.[27] However, this commitment to necessitarianism does lead to a very specific view of punishment.

Chiefly, it must become future-orientated. Punishment must become part of the array of causes that affect prospective events, subservient to the wider goal of perfecting society. Priestley thus states that 'punishment is proper to ... reform the sinner, and warn others, [these] are all the just ends of punishment; everything else deserving no other name than vengeance, and being manifestly absurd, because answering no good purpose'.[28] Indeed, in his *Lectures on History*, Priestley suggests that could these functions of reform and deterrent be enacted without actually punishing anybody, then that would be the ideal course of action:

> The object of criminal law is to lessen the number of crimes in future ... if this could be done without the actual punishment of any

> criminal, so much evil would be prevented as his punishment implies. Consequently, punishment has no reference to the degree of moral turpitude in the criminal. It has been justly observed that, properly speaking, a man is not hanged for stealing a sheep in this country, but that by the terror of his punishment sheep may not be stolen.[29]

An analogous position, perhaps even more dramatically driven home, is taken by William Godwin, who holds that 'the justice of punishment ... can only be a deduction from the hypothesis of free-will, and must be false, if human actions be necessary'.[30] Once again, punishment itself becomes merely a lever in a forward-looking calculation designed to encourage progression to a just society. For Godwin, as for Priestley then, the notion of rendering punishment on to the criminal himself – *retributive* rather than *utilitarian* justice – is incoherent because it depends on a fallacious understanding of agency.

However, if we return to 'The Destiny of Nations', the understanding of justice and punishment seems more complex. We have suggested that the arrangement of the visionary drafts after the refugee episode means that the theodicies of the former act as answers to the ethical demands of the latter: underlying Joan's vision is her desire to repair the injustice of the deaths of the innocent, when her radical sympathy turns into the trauma of mourning. However, if we look at the prominent punitive vocabulary in the visionary fragments, then it is not the rational, forward-looking vocabulary of Unitarian theory. Admittedly the explanations for the *crimes* of war given by the tutelary spirit are in a psychological, empirical vein entirely consonant with necessitarian theory. For example, Coleridge holds that war is the last stimulant for the jaded appetites of kings, calling to mind two major Godwinian positions in *Political Justice*: his emphasis on the psychological abnormality of kingship, and his trenchant opposition to wars fought where 'men deliberately destroy each other by thousands without any resentment against or even knowledge of each other'.[31] On the other hand, the description of the *punishment* wreaked on those who fan the flames of war moves into a different register.

The apocalyptic, punitive climax of 'The Destiny of Nations' deserves to be cited at length:

> Shriek'd Ambition's giant throng,
> And with them hissed the locust-fiends that crawled
> And glittered in Corruption's slimy track.
> Great was their wrath, for short they knew their reign;

And such commotion made they, and uproar,
As when the mad tornado bellows through
The guilty islands of the western main,
What time departing from their native shores,
Eboe, or Koromantyn's plain of palms,
The infurate spirits of the murdered make
Fierce merriment, and vengeance ask of Heaven.
Warmed with new influence, the unwholesome plain
Sent up its foulest fogs to meet the morn:
The Sun that rose on Freedom, rose in blood! (ll.437–50)

Although it appears that the storm is meant to describe the 'uproar' *of* Ambition and Corruption, in fact it seems impossible to avoid conceiving of the 'mad tornado' as providential violence wreaked *upon* the forces of evil, given that Coleridge draws in the context of slavery and the 'guilty islands' of the Caribbean. Moreover, the entire passage calls up rhetoric of plague (the locusts, and the Egyptian pestilence used as a simile in l.423) that recalls the divine inflictions visited on the Pharaoh in Exodus 7–11.

The 'infurate spirits' make an ethical demand which, in terms of necessitarian radicalism, is utterly irrational: they ask to be avenged. And it appears that God provides for this vengeance, fulfilling a blood debt in a sacrificial rite: 'The Sun that rose on Freedom, rose in blood!' This providential constellation of storm, sky and blood, in fact, seems to recall Coleridge's description of the coming of the evils of war:

Black rose the clouds, and now (as in a dream)
Their reddening shapes, transformed to warrior-hosts,
Coursed o'er the sky, and battled in mid-air.
Nor did not the large blood-drops fall from heaven
Portentous! (ll.364–8)

Providence, far from being a process of enlightenment based around 'Mind['s] ... perpetual tendency to rise', is now the clash of two types of barely distinguishable bloodshed.[32] A sacred counter-violence expunges the original violence of transgression. Although Coleridge has previously opposed Peace's 'grassy altar piled with fruits' (l.387) to the 'shrine of demon War' (l.388), the apocalyptic plain over which the sun of freedom rises seems more sacrificial than votive. Peter Kitson's reference to a collective guilt 'purged by a national disaster created by external, geological violence' refers to later poetry than this, but seems entirely apt.[33]

Whilst all this rhetoric had been in place when Coleridge had contributed the lines to Book Two of Robert Southey's *Joan of Arc*, the new juxtaposition with the refugee episode brings new intensity. 'The Destiny of Nations' presents us with several deaths, inviting and demanding our intense sympathy with the dead through the force of its ethical terror-sublime. But these are not the deaths of Brutus and Leonidas (who Coleridge mentions in his opening invocation), the martyrdoms of whom one might potentially justify as a necessary sacrifice in the march towards liberty. They are the deaths of the innocent and forgotten, history's cast off victims. The ethical demand to respond to the deaths of these innocent dead does not seem fully answered in stating acts shall be framed to discourage war in future (the Unitarian approach to punishment), or by claiming that they were a necessary event in the providential chain of cause-and-effect (the Unitarian approach to evil). Rather, they seem – like the slaves – to demand vengeance. The sublime terror that had provoked the radically sympathetic response to injustice now seems to determine a similar context of sublime terror for the realisation of justice.

Indeed, it is interesting to note – given that Coleridge's *ethical* understanding of the terror-sublime departs fundamentally from Edmund Burke – that the presentation of the divine here seems to return to the terms of the *Enquiry*. Burke's insistence on grounding his analysis in the immediacy of basic sense-data means that he privileges power above all else when considering religious sublimity:

> whilst we consider the Godhead merely as he is an object of the understanding, which forms a complex idea of power, wisdom, justice, goodness ... in this refined and abstracted light, the imagination and passions are little or nothing affected ... some reflection, some comparing is necessary to satisfy us of his wisdom, his justice, and his goodness; to be struck with his power, it is only necessary that we should open our eyes. (pp. 62–3)

Burke goes on to cite from the Old Testament and emphasise the 'salutary fear' (p. 64) in religious belief. We see that the *Enquiry* places raw power and potential violence as the most immediate, most obviously sensuous – and thus the most sublime – qualities of the Godhead. By contrast, Hartley's system – with its insistence on the ability of the self to raise itself up to ethical and theopathic levels of existence – would seem to have a richer conception of God, and more confidence that the human being can participate harmoniously in a providential order. It is thus not entirely coincidental that when Coleridge seems to reach a crisis point in this Hartleian conception of humanity, he also seems to revert to an understanding of God which sees him in his rawest, Burkean form: as an awesome force, power and violence that may be unleashed against the world.

The sublime intimated by the 'noontide majesty' of a perfectible humanity, drawn together in sympathy and against suffering, is hence displaced by the sublimity of a furious Jewish God, an infinity of physical force alone, rather than the complex idea which includes wisdom and love. Having raised sympathy to a tragic pitch in both the reader and Joan, the instinct – perhaps because affective rather than rational – is for truly *retributive* justice: backward-looking, compensatory justice grounded in the blood-debt, a counter-violence. And in his visionary fragments, Coleridge had such a rhetoric of counter-violence to hand. If Joan's vision appears as a response to the deaths of the refugees, the tutelary spirit's ultimate response to her is a promise of sacrificial justice. Previously, in the context of Southey's *Joan of Arc*, it was merely allegory, and could be treated as such. Yet in being brought into contact with a naturalistic scene, bloody atonement now seems to answer to a very real historical situation, threatening to undermine all the rationalism of Unitarian ethics on which the poem is built.

Moreover, if the apocalyptic justice meted out at the end of 'The Destiny of Nations' appears to create a regressive understanding of the ethical, this is not the only time that an archaic, ritual language belies the utilitarian, rationalist commitments of Coleridge's theory. In the sections preceding the refugee episode, the narrator says of Joan of Arc:

> Guilt was a thing impossible in her!
> Nor idly would have said – for she had lived
> In this bad World, as in a place of tombs,
> And touched not the pollutions of the dead. (ll.175–8)

Given the prominence of guilt in setting up the metaphor, Coleridge is suggesting a stain of moral depravity tainting the world, which the guiltless Joan refuses to touch. And in associating moral guilt with pollution, he is skirting a doctrine that he refused as a Unitarian: that of original sin. Indeed, as Julia Kristeva argues, Christianity's conception of sin can be read as bringing the abject inside the subject; 'the interiorization of impurity'.[34] Kristeva's analysis depends on Lacanian psychoanalysis, suggesting that taboo works to separate the legal, rational subject from all traces of its roots in an irrational, organic body, and that Christianity refines this process by internalising pollution. Yet as

Coleridge's use of the same association suggests, the link between pollution and sin had long been noted. Indeed, Jesus himself had played on it in a rebuke to Jewish elders: 'not that which goeth into the mouth defileth a man; but that which cometh out of the mouth, this defileth a man' (Matthew 15:11).

Yet this whole vocabulary of guilt, sin and pollution – like the vocabulary of sacrifice – was resisted by Unitarianism. In Priestley's polemics against original sin, there is a strong desire to cleanse Christianity of an archaic, ritualised element, of which the association of morality with the unclean is one major part. For instance, in his commentary on Job 14:4 ('who can bring a clean thing out an unclean?'), he is at pains to foreclose any moral aspect to the Judaic language of taboo: 'This is a proverbial expression ... Job is not speaking in this place of the guilt and pollution of man, but of his sorrows and mortality'.[35] And when he considers penances in a later work of 1799, he firmly distinguishes the sophisticated, moral idiom of Judaism from the rituals and superstition of Hinduism:

> It is in vain ... to look for any thing parallel to this doctrine of purification and expiation in the institutions of Moses ... All the modes of purification prescribed there are for involuntary offences, or impurities that are not of a moral nature.[36]

Original sin itself, he suggests, is a 'strange doctrine ... injurious both to our maker and ourselves'.[37] By refusing the idea of a stain on human nature (Kristeva's internalised abject), he is denying the need for a ritual expiation such as that effected by Jesus's death on the cross: a doctrine that the young Coleridge also inveighed against as confusing metaphors of sacrifice with realities.[38] Instead, just like the future-orientated cast of Unitarian views on crime and punishment, 'the only atonement for sin' is forward-looking, and based on 'repentance and reformation'.[39] By repudiating the doctrine of original sin, Unitarianism can embrace the perfectibility of humanity, which is precisely why so many Unitarians became political radicals.

We know that the young Coleridge was deeply guided by this enlightened form of religion, and in his first 'Lecture on Revealed Religion' there is a similar rationalisation of apparently ritualistic elements of Judaism.[40] Yet as we have seen, Coleridge's 'The Destiny of Nations' includes a distinctive vocabulary of taboo. In the poem, there is repugnance at the state of the world's sufferings that seems to run deeper than Coleridge's rational commitments to Unitarian positions on suffering and evil. Just as with blood sacrifice, the rhetoric of guilt and stain seems to be made more concrete by being juxtaposed with the refugee episode. It was one thing to use such dark views of human nature and history as poetic materials: but when Coleridge began to explore a sublime of human pathos, the intensity of suffering thereby evoked seemed to demand that such darkness be taken literally. Sympathy and pity were supposed to be elements in the service of an optimistic world-view, but if one is to feel the suffering of history's abandoned victims, then such a world-view is put under great pressure. In short, in attempting to feel alongside history's victims, perhaps Coleridge began to feel that there always would be victims, that humankind was indeed burdened with evil.

William Ulmer has claimed that Coleridge's growing realisation of evil remained articulable *within* his Unitarianism and presented no great conflict. Even when Coleridge acknowledges the reality of original sin in 1798, Ulmer reads this as stating 'merely a form of imperfection rather than of criminality ... leaving us no debt to discharge'.[41] Ulmer is right to look at the complexities of Coleridge's later understanding, not least because Coleridge separates matters of guilt and sin in an oft-cited letter to his brother, George (*CL*, I.396). Nevertheless, I hope I have shown that, as early as 1796, there is a narrative of debt and discharge dangerously close to the surface, one that appears to be the only adequate moral response to the sufferings invoked by Coleridge's terror-sublime. If humanity was truly corrupted with a tendency to evil, then only a violent purification – rather than a gradual enlightenment – could open the way for the millennial age that Coleridge desired. The radical sympathy that 'The Destiny of Nations' idealises and invites aims at universal benevolence (*bene-volens*, good wishing) but it appeared one could not feel the wounds of the world without being drawn to wishing some evil upon the perpetrators of those wounds. Unlike Ulmer, I believe that there is a growing conflict within Coleridge's moral universe, one that will return with renewed intensity in perhaps Coleridge's most famous poem: 'The Rime of the Ancient Mariner'. It will be one that will wreck, once and for all, the Unitarian desire for perfectibility, and one which will, most disturbingly of all, bring terror and evil inside the subject itself. The ethical terror-sublime was about to take a shocking turn, breaking its association with transcendence and stretching the bounds of eighteenth-century taste.

4
'My Soul in Agony': the Terrors of Subjectivity in 'The Rime of the Ancient Mariner'

This chapter[1] bases its central argument on the fact that 'The Rime of the Ancient Mariner' is different in *type* rather than *degree* when compared to the standard eighteenth-century terror-sublime. We may see this by beginning with obscurity. Obscurity had an established affinity with the sublime, as we find, for example, in Burke's preference for perceptions that were dim, indeterminate or irregular. However, in turning to Coleridge's 'The Rime of the Ancient Mariner' it seems as if we confront a deeper and more disturbing sense of obscurity, obscurity that threatens to outstrip the bounds of eighteenth-century taste altogether. This is particularly evident in perhaps the most famous judgement on the text, Robert Southey's pronouncement that it was 'a Dutch attempt at German sublimity'.[2] Redoubling the associations of excess and irrationality associated with German literature, Southey measures the poem not just fundamentally incoherent, but exorbitantly so.[3] We might read the phrase as a kind of self-multiplying and self-deepening tautology: more obscure (Dutch) than obscure (German) obscurity (sublimity). Yet as we see in a fulsome review by John Gibson Lockhart for *Blackwood's Magazine* in 1819, this deep-lying sense of the strange was for others precisely the source of its greatness:

> it is a poem to be felt, cherished, mused upon, not to be talked about, *not capable of being described, analyzed, or criticised*. It is the wildest of all the creations of genius ... its images have *the beauty, the grandeur, the incoherence* of some mighty vision. The loveliness and the terror glide before us in turns.[4]

In this chapter, I argue that the poem's terrors are indeed more disturbing and more obscure (in *kind*, rather than *degree*) than anything theorised in conventional eighteenth-century thought, particularly Burke. There is a definite reason for this: because the 'Rime' shifts the terrors from *outside* a perceiving subject, as they are in Burke and indeed Coleridge's Hartleian schema, and relocates them *inside* the subject. The psychological discourse that Burke and others use to regulate, define and understand the experience of the sublime is itself overrun *by* the sublime.

As a result, the subject terrifies itself, it struggles to comprehend itself, it finds an abyss within. It becomes sublime. To trace the emergence of this distinctive new turn in the terror-sublime, I believe that one needs to interrogate Coleridge's shifting theological positions on original sin, continuing the analysis of guilt and evil that was begun in the previous chapter. For although the haunted, guilty subjectivity that dominates Coleridge's poem is strikingly contemporary in one way – and I shall draw out some contemporary resonances at the end of the chapter – it is also deeply rooted in a Christian thought of ethics, evil and theodicy. Our interpretation thus also, as it moves forward, departs from a modern critical consensus which I believe has persistently misidentified a Christian reading of the poem as implying or demanding its explicability and harmony. I would hold that Coleridge's religious thought is more disturbing, more complex and more profound.

The cross and the albatross: Christianity, irrationality and ethics

Given the characteristic reactions of Lockhart and Southey, the sublimity of the 'Rime' lies with its ability to compel and disturb in the same movement, possibly to excess. What is the root cause of this obscurity or unintelligibility, this 'Dutching' of the terror-sublime, that threatens to move the poem out of the orbit of eighteenth-century taste – but in doing so also makes it utterly singular? Here, I think our analysis of the earlier poem, 'The Destiny of Nations', marries very well with existing critical discussion of the 'Rime'. In the previous chapter, I argued that Coleridge departed from Burke by making sympathy (feeling-with-others or mediated feeling) rather than self-preservation (the immediacy of physiological stimulation) central to his terror-sublime: in short, he made it *ethical*. This seems an appropriate point of departure, because one of the dominant issues in critical debates about the 'Rime' has always been the coherence or otherwise of its ethical signification. In reviewing a long-running debate on the poem, I am going to show that the sense of inscrutability that permeates the poem's 'loveliness and terror' is rooted in the inability of readers to fully rationalise its ethical order. This then is where we must begin, I feel, to unwrap the disturbingly obscure sublimity that seems to characterise the 'Rime'.

If there is an enigma that could stand, synecdochally, for the way that the poem seems to outstrip even the eighteenth-century taste for the obscure and creates a disturbing 'Dutch' atmosphere, it is surely the slaying of the albatross, the poem's narrative, ethical and imaginative heart. There are two especially strange elements to the killing. Firstly, as many critics have pointed out, it happens without any apparent foresight or motive. In one stanza, the Mariner is describing vespers in the moonlight; in the next, the Wedding Guest is shocked by the terror in the Mariner's face: the killing simply happens. This is particularly interesting given the weight that Unitarian moral theory placed upon motives, since the determinative effects of motives were, in their compatibilist analysis of volition, the only marks of responsibility. Moreover, after the killing, it seems that barely anything has been changed. Coleridge begins the next segment of the poem by repeating an already met image of the sun metronomically rising and falling, whilst 'the good south wind *still* blew behind' (l.85, my emphasis). Nature seems curiously unmoved by something that has been often read as a crime against it. This is entirely appropriate for – in the original 1798 version, unaided by Coleridge's glosses – there is no initial reason to believe that the killing of the albatross has set in motion any clear sequence of events whatsoever.[5] Moreover, apart from its haunting presence at vespers, which itself could be protective, malign or perhaps even arbitrary depending on the whim of one's reading, the bird seems to have no obvious or lucid moral or religious significance.

Thus, the death of the albatross is a powerful but initially unintelligible event. It refuses to fit into the narrative immediately before and after: we do not know why the Mariner killed it, and, certainly at this point, we do not know what such a killing meant. Nevertheless, it becomes rapidly apparent that, although the import of the crime is confused, it *is* a crime:

> Ah wel-a-day! what evil looks
>   Had I from old and young;
> Instead of the Cross the Albatross
>   About my neck was hung. (ll.135–8)

Yet even this image seems massively overdetermined. Is the Mariner a Christ-like figure, and if so in what sense? Or, perhaps, the Mariner and the albatross are involved in a disturbing inversion of the crucifixion?

The allusive internal rhyme that links the cross and the albatross creates an enigmatic pattern of significance, but not one that is easily deciphered.

If the relationship between the cross and albatross is unreadable, this reflects a wider ambiguity in the relations between the supernatural events of the poem and orthodox religion: a liminality tracing a sublimity which flickers between the religious and the gothic. The order against which the Mariner has offended does seem to be encompassed by a broadly theistic ontology. Certainly, the Mariner interprets events through his Roman Catholic faith and appeals insistently to Christ, the cross, Mary and so forth. One could speculate that the archaic diction might be a way of suggesting that the Mariner is an unsophisticated, unreliable narrator, e.g. 'To Mary-queen the praise be yeven' (l.286), and some critics have suggested he is unfit to interpret his own experience.[6] Nevertheless, in so far as the events of the poem can be trusted at all, they do seem to suggest a broad Christian framework.

For example, the sleepless agony – one of the central trials undergone by the Mariner – is broken by the ability to pray. Whilst one may query the Mariner's interpretation of the event – 'sure my kind saint took pity on me' (l.278) – the fact that the curse involves an inability to pray, and is lifted by the making of prayer, is incontrovertible. Similarly, unless we are to dismiss the coming of the two spirits merely as hallucination, they also seem to confirm a Christian context, defining the Mariner's experience as penance and identifying the Mariner 'By him who died on cross' (l.404). Finally, the demand made by the Christian hermit to 'say / What manner man art thou?' (ll.609–10) seems to have an indisputable effect on the narrative by setting up the strange catharsis of the tale-telling. This would also suggest that Christian ministry, and the authority invested in Christian holy men, have a certain privilege within the poem.

Nevertheless, although the broad context of the Mariner's ordeal seems framed in Christian terms, much of the detail is ominously ambiguous. The fearsome sun could be a providential sign, in the same way that the sun of freedom rises in blood at the end of 'The Destiny of Nations'. On the other hand, the ambiguous *like* could be read so as to displace theistic forces, rendering the monstrous sun as an alternative godhead, i.e. like a deity, but not the Christian one: 'Nor dim nor red, like God's own head, / The glorious sun uprist' (ll.93–4). Similarly, the horrifying animation of the waters provokes a Christian oath in l.119, and yet seems to belong to a non-Christian, pagan mythology:

> About, about, in reel and rout
>   The Death-fires danc'd at night;

The water, like a witch's oils,
    Burnt green and blue and white. (ll.123–6)

These portents of a less-than-Christian world are merely preparatory, however, when compared to the poem's gothic centrepiece: the appearance of the spectral ship. The sun, previously compared to God's head, is now transfigured into a ghastly face:

And strait the Sun was fleck'd with bars
  (Heaven's mother send us grace)
As if thro' a dungeon grate he peer'd
  With broad and burning face. (ll.169–72)

Out of this chilling optical illusion comes the eerie vessel itself, manned by two hideous, spectral figures. Raimonda Modiano has suggested that Coleridge's inventive gothic imagery often seems to overpower the Christian backdrop of the poem, and this would surely be the central example of this.[7] Yet the episode is not only troubling in its imagery, gothically sublime though it is. Given the references to hulks and dungeons, the mood of the passage is suitably punitive, but if the spectral ship does represent the coming of a judgement, it is an irrational and apparently capricious one. The dice game hardly seems appropriate as an instrument of Christian providence:

The naked Hulk alongside came
    And the Twain were playing dice;
'The Game is done! I've won, I've won!'
    Quoth she, and whistled thrice. (ll.191–4)

What kind of game is this? The victory of this enigmatic female figure, mysteriously described as 'far liker Death' (l.189) than her skeletal, male companion, is claimed under a 'hornèd Moon' (l.202). Moreover, the curses rendered by the Mariner's ship-mates – which seem to be the result of the outcome of the dice game – are made *by* this sign. This would suggest it holds a central place in explicating the signification of what is going on in this part of the narrative. Unfortunately, like so many of the apparently sense-bearing objects already discussed, the horned moon is yet another enigma. In the rest of the poem, moonlight seems to accompany God's possible presence, as in the vespers service (l.76) or when the Mariner returns home (l.479). By contrast, it here seems diabolical, once again raising questions about the relations between these weird forces and those of the Christian God.

A final irrationality, and challenge to any Christian reading, lies in the apparently inexpiable nature of the crime. It appears on numerous occasions as if the Mariner may have finally fulfilled the terms of his punishment. Most notably, he blesses the water-snakes and the terrors of his persecution seem replaced and absolved by a sudden apprehension of beauty. This is certainly interpreted by the Mariner as a moment of release:

> Oh happy living things! no tongue
> Their beauty might declare:
> A spring of love gusht from my heart,
> And I bless'd them unaware! (ll.274–7)

This passage is often cited in *one life* interpretations that believe the killing of the albatross was an act of hostility to nature, and the blessing is an act of reconciliation with nature.[8] However, it is barely halfway through the poem, and it is not long before the Mariner is overcome by stifling fear yet again, '[quaking] to think of my own voice / How frightful it would be' (ll.337–8). Like other passages of beauty (e.g. the pastoral music of ll.339–61, and the homecoming of ll.457–80) it seems to offer only temporary relief, and is menaced by a juxtaposition with terror.

The homecoming, in particular, seems to provide a problematic lack of resolution if the poem is to be Christianised. The sweet 'meadow-gale' (l.462) blowing from the Mariner's homeland immediately follows a vivid, paranoiac stanza describing

> one, that on a lonely road
> Doth walk in fear and dread,
> And having once turn'd round, walks on
> And turns no more his head:
> Because he knows, a frightful fiend
> Doth close behind him tread. (ll.451–6)

These are hardly the words of a man who has been fully released from guilt and debt. As the Mariner himself remarks of the breeze: 'it mingled strangely with my fears' (l.463). Those fears never leave him, and insistently throughout the poem terror cannot be exorcised. Red light, initially associated with the bloody sun, recurs a number of times through the poem as an image of guilt and terror. As late as the return to the harbour, the vision of a beautiful moonlit sea is broken by rising crimson flames, and Coleridge adds a typically ghastly touch as the Mariner is suddenly horrified by the blood-red gleam on his own skin:

> A little distance from the prow
> Those dark-red shadows were;
> But soon I saw that my own flesh
> Was red as in a glare. (ll.485–8)

The dark-red shadows cannot be escaped, any more than the repeated reanimations of the crew, or the curse of their dead eyes which prevents his prayer: 'the pang, the curse, with which they died, / Had never pass'd away' (ll.443–4).

If the sudden return of the sinister red light suggests that guilt has followed the Mariner even to his homeland, neither does the poem finish on a note of absolution. As the Mariner returns to shore, we are presented with a mediator and confessor in the figure of the Hermit. Yet instead of shriving the Mariner, the Hermit can only set in motion an endless penance: '"Say quick," quoth he, "I bid thee say / What manner man art thou?"' (ll.609–10). The poem turns upon itself, and we find that the narrative that we have overheard – which is rationalised in Christian readings as describing a man who comes to knowledge through suffering – *is* the continuance of that very suffering. Thus ends – or rather fails to end – the Mariner's tale: not with an absolved and reconciled Christian, but with a deeply ambiguous character, potentially possessing daemonic characteristics. (This very ambiguity disturbs the Wedding Guest during the tale itself, as he fears the Mariner may himself be one of the dead.) The strangeness of the Mariner and his experiences has not in any way been reincorporated into a Christian community: if anything, the Mariner lies in the tradition of Ahasuerus, the Wandering Jew, as an outcast. He passes 'like night, from land to land' (l.619), still unable to reach the daybreak of redemption, unable to expiate his sin, but only to relive it in the telling.

These points – the ambiguity of the moral action, the dominance of the daemonic, and the inexpiability of the crime – have been noted throughout the history of criticism of the 'Rime'. They are, after all, surely the spurs for the original judgements of irrationality made by Coleridge's contemporaries. Modern criticism has often organised them in a broadly similar interpretive fashion. As we have noted, the poem does suggest something of a Christian moral order on which classic Christian readings such as those made by Robert Penn Warren and G. Wilson Knight relied.[9] However, the counter-tradition is to suggest that this moral order is not sufficient to contain the dark forces represented within the poem. For instance, Edward Bostetter holds that readings of the poem that see a coherent Christian narrative can only function

> by rationalising those portions of the poem in which the powers of the universe are presented as sternly authoritarian and punitive, and ignoring those in which they are revealed as capricious and irrational.[10]

Similarly, Raimonda Modiano claims that whilst 'the Mariner conspicuously relies on Christian rituals and beliefs ... the Christian doctrine fails to explain his world of excessive suffering and irrational events'.[11] David Miall, attributing the poem's irrationality to irreparable childhood guilt, confirms that 'behind the moral concepts of the poem lies some other, more intractable experience which resists the moral reading'.[12]

This tradition reaches right into recent criticism. For instance, Anne Williams contends that 'the concept of crime and punishment rushes in as a way of ensuring order in the universe'.[13] Williams's Kristevan reading sees the poem's ethical side as a symbolic order striving to contain 'the semiotic pre-history of the speaking subject ... the primal break' which offers up a 'horrifying vacancy'.[14] And Leah Richards-Fisher takes the 'lack of reason in the universe and the capriciousness of providence' as her starting point in arguing that the Wedding Guest has a more tragic appreciation of the world than the Mariner, the latter using providential categories to try to make sense of a senseless world.[15] Whilst these five readings range over different approaches and emphases, they all suggest that Christianity represents a rational moral order in the poem, which is overcome by irrational forces stemming from a darker apprehension of the world. I am going to argue that this common reading – which we might gloss as the counter-moral tradition – creates a false opposition between Christianity and the irrational, and thus misidentifies the source of the poem's obscurity and hence (ultimately) its terrifying sublimity. We shall see that the disturbing nature of the poem's terrors lies in a specifically Christian subjectivity, haunted by its own evil. To argue this will require a detour through the theology of sin, guilt and evil, beginning by returning to points made in the previous chapter, where we saw a Unitarian optimism about human nature and perfectibility under growing strain. What will eventually emerge, in excess of the eighteenth-century terror-sublime and its related gothic tropes, is a subject that is terrified to look not at earthquakes or ghosts, storms or tragedies, but at itself.

Original sin and originary guilt

The young Coleridge, in line with the position of contemporary Unitarianism, had accepted that whilst moral responses and judgements are entirely fitting at the human level, at the metaphysical level all apparent evil is subordinated to a higher, providential scheme. 'Reasoning strictly and with logical Accuracy', Coleridge writes, 'I should deny the existence of any Evil, inasmuch as the end determines the nature of the means and I have been able to discover nothing of which the end is not good.'[16] When combined with a few other theodical commonplaces – suggesting that we are only happy if we progress to a better state, and that ultimately God's ways cannot be questioned by human reasoning – Coleridge in his first 'Lecture on Revealed Religion' (1795) holds a broadly optimistic view of the world. In this view, as he confides to John Thelwall in 1796, '*Guilt* is out of the Question' (*CL*, I.213). Crucially, therefore, we have an optimistic model of the subject, the very same one we saw underwriting the sublimity of 'The Destiny of Nations' in the previous chapter. In his journey towards Anglicanism, a constellation of related shifts appeared in his thinking: from Socinianism to Trinitarianism, from confidence in perfectibility to a need for redemption, and, crucially, from a view that evil is actually part of divine benevolence to an acceptance of original sin.[17] As I argued in the previous chapter, some of the initial positions in this constellation were already being troubled as early as 1796, in response to the violence of the French Revolution and the dashing of utopian hopes.

It is the two-year period between 'The Destiny of Nations' and the 'Ancient Mariner' that marks the beginning of the end of his Unitarian faith. In March 1798 – the very month that the 'Rime' was finished – Coleridge wrote to his brother, George:

> I believe most stedfastly [sic] in Original Sin; that from our mothers' wombs our understandings are darkened; and even where our understandings are in the Light, that our organization is depraved, & our volitions imperfect. (*CL*, I.396)

What is striking about this passage is not only the admission of human imperfection, but the identification of an *inherent* depravity which appears prior to the reception of sense-data and the formation of associations. Although the reference to 'organization' might suggest Coleridge is still thinking in terms of the empirical psychology bequeathed to him by Hartley, this notion of innate corruption is in clear tension with such a psychology and the ethics derived from it. There is a tendency to evil; a stain on human nature: something that we saw close to the surface of 'The Destiny of Nations' and now explicitly avowed.

On the other hand, we must note that Coleridge also remarks in the same letter, 'Of GUILT I say nothing'. In William Ulmer's words, the '1798 profession seems Janus-faced ... mediately between the poet's Unitarian and Anglican phases'.[18] Whilst Coleridge is forced towards acknowledging a darker view of human nature, he is clearly still uncomfortable with the aspect of culpability. Ulmer attempts to maintain a continuity and stability in Coleridge's beliefs ('surely he knew his own mind?'), claiming that the letter denies guilt and maintains the view that original sin is imperfection but not criminality.[19] Yet, I would hazard that the matter is more complex than this. For it is certainly difficult to invoke the doctrine of *peccatum originale* without calling up the idea of guilt. Indeed, Coleridge does not actually *deny* guilt as such, but rather abstains from comment (in contrast to his steadfast avowal of original sin).

Thus, we know that in 1798 Coleridge accepted original sin, but was hesitant – and perhaps uncertain – over the notion of what we might term originary guilt. Yet, of course, the 'Ancient Mariner' is a poem that revolves precisely around guilt. If Coleridge says nothing of guilt in the letter to George Coleridge, then the 'Rime' is positively obsessed with it. The poem is filled with religious motifs that demand a view of sin as criminality: blessing, shriving, penance, confession and intercession, for instance. These are all practices alien to Unitarianism, in that they look backwards to expiate deeds, rather than forward to reform future conduct. Even if these practices are directed at sins committed in life – *personal* rather than original sin – they imply a theological framework based around purification and corruption, of which original sin and the atonement are the doctrinal archetypes. Equally, as ceremonies that recur, they suggest an inevitable tendency to transgression on the part of human beings who thus require outside aid to overcome their moral failings.

William Ulmer, attempting to reconcile the poem with Unitarianism, claims that the trials of the Mariner are simply an ongoing moral education through suffering, and that the poem 'defers the entire issue of an achieved salvation'.[20] Yet his focus on providentially justified suffering ignores the fundamental desire for purification and release that accompanies the distinctly penitential motifs like those mentioned above. We cannot but think about the questions of ultimate release from guilt and whether humans can achieve this themselves, questions that Ulmer claims are bracketed out, not least because the poem itself borrows the language of atonement: 'He'll shrieve my soul, he'll wash away / The

Albatross's blood' (ll.545–6). Even Ulmer must query, 'why should his anguish and alienation continue?'[21] This obsession with guilt and its expiation, I feel, suggests that the poem expresses a darker feeling for culpability attached to original sin than that to which Coleridge would explicitly attest at the time. This feeling for culpability strongly suggests that the poem is exploring ground *outside* of Unitarianism.

Yet in reading the 'Rime' in this way, I am not simply overlooking Coleridge's doubts about the doctrine and interpreting the poem as what Ulmer critically terms 'an occluded Anglicanism unable to recognize itself as such'.[22] Coleridge's doubts over originary guilt *also* stamp their mark powerfully on the character of the poem; indeed they are, I believe, the initial source for the poem's intractable irrationality. If the 'Ancient Mariner' is at one moment a powerful ethical narrative and at the next a horrifying irrational one, I would derive this divided tone, in the first instance, from Coleridge's difficult passage *between* Unitarianism and Anglicanism. He was drawn towards the mainstream position he would ultimately adopt – 'My faith is simply this – that there is an original corruption in our nature ... from the consequences of which, we may be redeemed by Christ' (*CL*, II.807) – from a Unitarian position that saw original sin as unjust, superstitious and unintelligible. The 'Ancient Mariner' reflects its time of writing by involving both: like the 1798 letter, it is 'Janus-faced'. It reflects both the power and the terror of the doctrine.

On this basis, I am going to argue for a radical modification of the counter-moral tradition of readings. Such readings see non-Christian irrationality, such as the unconscious, gothic or simply a morally tragic world, troubling a rational order presented in Christian moral categories. Conversely, I would argue that the irrationality comes from *within* the Christian tradition, in so far as Unitarianism had characterised original sin as a strange and injurious superstition. Whilst Coleridge, in the 'Rime', is clearly drawn to the moral narrative set up around original sin, he also attests to the horror he still feels at such a narrative, a horror deriving from Unitarian optimism and rationalism. The strongest evidence for this is that the character of the irrationalities that we have identified in the 'Ancient Mariner' can be traced back to specific Unitarian polemics against originary guilt. The force of these objections still seemed to affect Coleridge even as he explored the possibility of a depraved or guilty humanity.

Thus, for instance, we earlier identified the Mariner's transgression as being a moral non-event: there was no evil motive adduced for it, and it was initially unclear whether the albatross's life had any moral significance.[23] The Mariner transgressed a moral rule without realising; as such, it is hard to know how guilt could or should be incurred. Whilst the Mariner's punishment is at least related to one of his own acts, thus foreclosing a direct analogy with original sin, there is the same atmosphere of existential persecution so ably communicated in Unitarian polemics. As Priestley writes with disapproval: 'And they say ... it would have been just in God to have made us all suffer the most exquisite and endless torments in hell, even though we have never sinned in our persons.'[24] Original sin dislocates the moral calculus from its roots in actual motive or agency: guilt is simply something that befalls us, and this is something reflected in the Mariner's tale.

It was also noted that the poem's imagery often seemed unaccountably daemonic given the supposedly theistic framework. Yet this too seems to have a source in Unitarian objections to conventional Christianity. As shown in the previous chapter, Unitarianism held the constellation of doctrines around original sin and its expiation to be ritualistic superstitions: 'unmeaning and even base and mischievous', in Priestley's words.[25] Coleridge, in 1795, had described the orthodox Christian view of punishment to be 'this dreadful Equity, this Tartarean Justice'.[26] The crucial word here is 'Tartarean'. Just as Priestley endeavoured to separate the sacrifices of the Hindus from the morality of the Jews, here Coleridge is trying to separate Christianity from the pagan belief in a fearsome underworld such as Tartarus (Hades). What the 'Rime' inherits from such polemic is a sense for the archaic nature of the original sin doctrine. If the forces that exact retribution in the 'Ancient Mariner' appear daemonic, this is not surprising: for Coleridge had long considered much of the legal narrative of orthodox Christianity to be brutal and primitive, unworthy of a rationalised moral religion. Indeed, are we not tracing something very similar to the Burkean concept of sublime divinity – a religious element of terror, punishment and force – noted in the previous chapter?

Finally, the inexpiability of the crime reflects the debate over human perfectibility, especially given Coleridge's ever-diminishing faith in such ethical and political advancement. Unitarianism was generally optimistic about humanity's prospects, holding it absurd and unscriptural that God would make moral demands that he knew would be impossible to fulfil. Unitarianism believes that human beings can be good, if the right social and political conditions were to come about. Thus, Priestley objects to the notion of innate depravity by arguing

> You cannot think that God would command, and expect obedience, when he had not given power to obey; and much less that he would

> urge men to provide for their own safety and happiness, when himself had put an effectual bar in the way of it.[27]

Yet in assenting to original sin as part of a description of human nature, Coleridge was halfway to acknowledging the fact that humans had an inherent inability to respond to moral demands – not just individual demands, but the overarching demand to follow the Good.[28] Facing a guilt one has no capacity to overcome is a moral horror we see clearly expressed in the 'Rime', and the moment where the Mariner bites his own arm in order to speak is perhaps emblematic of the terrible perversity of his helpless condition. Even Ulmer, who maintains the poem is primarily Unitarian in outlook, has to admit that it is shadowed with 'an unpurged Gothic guilt'.[29]

In short, if the 'Rime' is an expression of a moral order involving an innate guilt that Coleridge was yet to admit explicitly, then the terrors of the poem are due to the fact that such a moral order still appeared terrifying. For years, Coleridge had shared with mainstream Unitarianism a view that original sin was a doctrine of outrageous cruelty, especially when combined with corollary beliefs in hell and election. As Priestley puts it:

> An arbitrary and unreasonable partiality in favour of some of the human race, and the most cruel and unjust severity towards others, as condemning them to everlasting torments for crimes of which they could not be guilty, and expecting of them that which [God had] not enabled them to do.[30]

Yet, if the poem's obsession with guilt and expiation is anything to go by, he found this vision increasingly powerful, even though he found it difficult or impossible to rationalise. Thus, the poem speaks where the 1798 letter chooses not to pass comment, portraying the doctrine in monstrous hyperbole and thus reflecting its disturbing hold over Coleridge's shifting religious beliefs. This is the true ground for the gothic sublimity of the 'Rime'. It is surely the poem of a man who is reluctantly and terrifyingly drawn to the possibility that something he thought, and still thinks, irrational seems undeniable. What if we were indeed cursed with such a guilt? As such, the nightmarish quality of the poem is unsurprising, for it is a Unitarian nightmare – original sin – coming true.

By 1802, even if the final conversion to Anglicanism is some years away, Coleridge writes to his brother that 'the Socinian & Arian Hypotheses are utterly untenable' (*CL*, II.807), and asserts to John Prior Estlin that

Christianity under 'the Priestleyan Hypothesis' was void in so far as it denied original sin, redemption, grace and justification (*CL*, II.821). That guilt which, if my reading of the poem is correct, had haunted him as a possibility in 1798, became an explicit and avowed part of his own beliefs. As such, he was forced to come to terms with each of the irrational aspects that had menaced the coherence of the 'Rime': the nightmare portrait of original sin given by Unitarianism had to be assimilated. It is thus unsurprising that when Coleridge came to revise the text of 'The Rime of the Ancient Mariner', many of the changes made ensured that the points we have identified as irrational were contained and explicated rather more firmly in an Anglican framework.

The most important emendations were made for 1817's *Sibylline Leaves*, and subsequent editions of poetical works during his lifetime, including the 1834 version cited here. Important alterations were made to the spectre-ship scene, which might be seen as a concentrated emblem for all the forces that seem so resistant to rationalisation. The two spectral figures become capitalised allegories of death and life-in-death, the latter described as a 'Night-mare' (1834, l.193). This allegory not only diminishes the threat of a literal, daemonic order opposed to Christianity (and may even suggest the psychological projections of a dream world), it also means we now have some clue as to the punishment imposed on the Mariner. The scene becomes more intelligible: it seems that the Mariner could have been punished by death, or by a life of mortifying penance, and that the latter was chosen. In the same passage, from 1817 Coleridge replaced 'playing' (1798, l.192) with 'casting' (1834, l.196) dice, suggesting something more providential than arbitrary. Another important change was made as early as 1800, altering the closing scenes when the ship returns to the bay. Reanimation of the curse-bearing corpses, and the sections describing the red glare rising from the waves – both symbols of recurring guilt – are virtually excised, thus allowing the moonlight and the seraph band to dominate a less problematic homecoming.[31] This allows the narrative to conclude in a less agonised way, suggesting that the Mariner is undergoing a process of redemption, rather than being menaced by inexpiable guilt.

The most radical change of all was the addition of substantial paratext. The gloss, as Kathleen Wheeler has emphasised, delimits the narrative in a major way:

> the two most characteristic elements of the gloss ... are its geographical specifications and its technique of streamlining the narrative so that the sequence of events and their causal connections are made

> more clear. The verse is correspondingly vague on these three categories of time, space, and causality.[32]

Wheeler suggests that the gloss is ironic – a deliberately bad, reductive reading of the poem. Yet this assertion – also part of Leah Richards-Fisher's argument – is not incompatible with its evident rhetorical authority. As Jerome McGann's highly influential analysis of the 'Rime' proves, by creating an economy of text and commentary it sets in motion a certain hermeneutic to which the reader or critic finds him or herself bound from the off.[33] This hermeneutic is pre-eminently an Anglican one, which brings the body text under a more fixed Christian ideology. Confirmations of otherwise ambiguous supernatural occurrences are made throughout: the Virgin Mary intercedes for the Mariner, the presence and mission of the angel troop are made significantly clearer, and the Polar Spirit is identified and placed in a Christian penitential context.[34] Of course, these glosses also – in so far as the critic is bound to lend them a certain privilege – negate the possibility that the Mariner is an unreliable narrator.

The terrors of subjectivity

The glosses thus clarify a salvational trajectory, joining many of the penitential motifs into a more coherent progression in which the Mariner is punished for his killing of the albatross, blesses the water-snakes with the mediation of a guardian saint, expiates the curse of the dead crew, and receives 'the penance of life'.[35] In reference to our three major loci of obscurity and irrationality, the legal narrative of transgression and punishment is made more coherent; many of the daemonic elements are identified and incorporated into a Christian mythology; and, perhaps most importantly, the sin that the Mariner carries seems expiable. It is a less ambiguous poem, and definitely a more Anglican one. Yet, importantly, Coleridge did not totally void the poem of its horror, its obscurity and its 'Dutchness'. It maintained its disturbing sense of a sublimity that was stranger and more resistant to explication than the eighteenth-century taste for terror, which by now had passed into the cliché of gothic. For whilst Coleridge no longer saw originary guilt as horrifying and irrational in the sense he had back in 1797–8, that does not stop it being a doctrine that is fearsome and mysterious.

There has been a tradition of thinking within Christianity which has accepted, to an extent, all the criticisms of the kind made by Unitarianism about the foundations of its moral order. This tradition claims that only by accepting a brute and irrational fact at the root of existence, can existence itself be explicated. This is perhaps the greatest weakness of McGann's account, which has sometimes been claimed as a definitive advance beyond the Christianising versus counter-moral debate.[36] McGann defines the Christian ideology primarily as a hermeneutic which aims to create a totalised order of symbols, and thus he forestalls the possibility of irrationality or unreadability lying within a Christian thinking. Nevertheless, such a thinking does exist within Christianity and has a long, powerful history (beginning perhaps with 1 Corinthians 1:19–20, and Tertullian's maxim *Credo Quia Absurdum*, I believe it because it is impossible). For instance, Blaise Pascal contends that

> nothing shocks us more deeply than this doctrine [of original sin]. Nevertheless without this most incomprehensible of all mysteries we are incomprehensible to ourselves. Within this gnarled chasm lie the twists and turns of our condition.[37]

A similar admission is made by one of Coleridge's favourite theologians, Martin Luther, when he claims in 'The Smalcald Articles' (1537) that 'hereditary sin is so deep a corruption of nature that reason cannot understand it. It must be believed because of the revelation in the Scriptures.'[38] Original sin is admitted as a mystery of faith, inexplicable precisely because of its position as an existential ground on which all else depends.[39]

Coleridge joins this tradition. In 1802, he claims that he believes the drama of original sin and atonement 'not because I *understand* it; but because I *feel*, that it is not only suitable to, but needful for, my nature' (*CL*, II.807). Yet this is no short-lived, purely affective response. In his most thorough theological work, *Aids to Reflection* (1825), Coleridge continues to assert that what he accepts through faith is not rationally explicable. Indeed, some of his points on original sin are not far from Unitarian ones. Thus, he rejects the legalistic attempt to define and justify original sin as a hereditary punishment incurred by Adam as 'an outrage of common-sense' based on 'flimsy analogies drawn from the imperfections of human ordinances and human justice-courts'.[40] Nevertheless, the universality of evil is affirmed despite the fact that *all* wills are evil – that all wills have somehow chosen to be evil – is inexplicable. This is said to be a datum that lies at the base of all religions, not just Christianity. Thus, *Aids to Reflection* asserts that:

> A moral Evil is an Evil that has its origin in a Will. An Evil common to all must have a ground common to all ... that there is an Evil

> common to all is a Fact; and this Evil must therefore have a common ground. Now this evil ground cannot originate in the Divine Will: it must therefore be referred to the Will of Man. And this evil Ground we call Original Sin. It is a *Mystery*, that is, a Fact, which we see, but cannot explain; and the doctrine a truth which we apprehend, but can neither comprehend nor communicate. (p. 288)

Similarly, Coleridge – in a way familiar from Unitarian polemic – rejected a notion of original sin's expiation through *vicarious atonement*, i.e. a literal interpretation of Christ's crucifixion as a blood substitution. In *Aids to Reflection*, he dismissed such an interpretation as a 'species of sophistry' (p. 318). However, this does not mean that Coleridge thought there was no guilt and absolution involved in original sin and redemption:

> Do you rejoice when the Atonement made by the Priest has removed the civil stain from your name, restored you to your privileges ... Here is an atonement which takes away a deeper, worser stain, an eating Canker-Spot in the very heart of your personal Being! (p. 324)

As Coleridge's rhetorical question about 'civil stain' is trying to show, notions of ransom and debt are merely metaphors describing the *consequences* of redemption, taken from the most immediate experiences of those to whom those Christ was preaching. However, these figures are not applicable to the *nature* of redemption, which is 'a spiritual and transcendent Mystery' (p. 332) that Coleridge specifically pairs with the mystery of original sin: 'the mode, the possibility, we are not competent to know' (p. 324).

In short, the invocation of mystery allows Coleridge to accept apparently violent and troubling theological facts. Given this approach to sin and redemption, it would be wrong to simply see the irrationality in the 'Rime' as stemming solely from his fears about the doctrine of original sin at a time when his beliefs were shifting towards it. Rather, original sin remained a doctrine that he admitted as beyond knowledge and explication, which means that the relationship between irrationality and Christianity, even in the late text, is a strong one. Although Coleridge tried to approach the epistemological problems with a Kantian rigour (not applying phenomenal categories to divine matters and reining in speculative theology, for instance), the end result is as Pascal expressed it.[41] This incomprehensible fact comprehends us.

For Coleridge, we cannot understand ourselves without admitting mysteries – fearsome mysteries – into our world-view. The logic, of course, is one recurrently associated with the sublime: that of being brought to the limit of apprehension and comprehension. We do not understand our sense of intrinsic guilt, and we are terrified by the burden it brings, but we feel it nonetheless. The shock of such a mystery – expressed so well by Pascal – very much survives even in the late texts of the 'Rime'. We are now even further away from the conventional reading of the poem, whereby a Christian order is undermined by a non-Christian irrationality. Now we see that the irrational but brute fact of original sin that lies at the heart of the 'Rime' also lies close to the heart of Coleridge's Christianity. Even the late 'Rime' is a narrative of acts that are shadowed by an excess of ethical responsibility over and above the sum of those acts. This excess is the burden of original sin. The irrationality *is* a Christian avowal. And it is in this avowal where we can finally see the grounds for the exorbitant and disturbing nature of the poem's terror-sublime.

The 'Rime' shifts the grounds of the terror-sublime, destroying the empirical, Lockean subjectivity assumed and theorised by Burke and others. Above, I suggested more than once that the young Coleridge was haunted by the possibility of originary guilt. We now see that this is more than just a turn of phrase, for the logic of original sin is indeed a haunting of the subject. Here is a guilt and a responsibility which claims the subject – and which the subject must accept – which cannot be linked to any empirical act or motive of that subject. In contrast to the Unitarian subject, which was psychologically transparent to itself and considered a *tabula rasa*, this new and darker subject has guilt, possessing and possessed, at, or before, its origin. As *Aids to Reflection* remarks, 'let the evil be supposed such as to imply the impossibility of ... referring to any particular time at which it ... commenced' (p. 287).[42] Coleridge conceives of a split subject:

> the most frequent impediment to men's turning the mind inward upon themselves is that they are afraid of what they shall find there. There is an aching hollowness in the bosom, a dark cold speck at the heart, an obscure and boding sense of a somewhat, that must be kept *out of sight* of the conscience; some secret lodger, whom they can neither resolve to eject or retain. (p. 24)

Coleridge considers it imperative to stare this secret lodger in the face, this impurity or stain on the *tabula rasa*. The terror and sublimity of the 'Ancient Mariner' lie in its exploration of this transgression that is always already present at the heart of ethical subjectivity.

The contrast with the subject theorised by the *Philosophical Enquiry*, or even that assumed by 'The Destiny of Nations', is a radical and important one. Let us consider Burke first. Distance is a crucial element of the Burkean sublime which sets the perceiving subject off from the sublime object.[43] The definition of the sublime as a passion of self-preservation demands a spectatorial remove: indeed, it is precisely a purely observing subjectivity, not involved in the terror, that allows pain and violence to become sublimity. Tellingly, whereas the sense of touch – and thus contact – has an important role to play in Burke's theory of the beautiful, tactility plays little or no part in the sublime, unless it is as a function deduced from the visible (such as the roughness of a mountain slope). The same applies to taste. Both would suggest the sublime getting too close. Conversely, the terror-sublime of the 'Rime' abolishes all distance: it takes a horror and places it within; it demands we interrogate ourselves ethically and confronts us with guilt and an abyssal capacity for evil. Let us reiterate Coleridge's words: 'the most frequent impediment to men's turning the mind inward upon themselves is that they are afraid of what they shall find there'.

What of the ethical terror-sublime explored in the previous chapter? This differs from the Burkean sublime in closing the distance between spectator and terror: Joan of Arc feels the sufferings of others as her own, and the glory of that moral heroism is the positive content that 'The Destiny of Nations' extracts from the horrors of war and injustice. Yet in so far as that experience is theorised from within a Hartleian perspective, adapted to Unitarian radical ends, which posits the perfectibility of humanity, the 'Rime' destroys its possibility. The young Coleridge believed that the human subject could raise itself up: ethically, it could transcend its egoism in order to sympathise with others; socially, it could transcend injustice in order to form better societies; spiritually, it could embrace a sense of theopathy that would allow it to participate in a benevolent, providential divine order. This perfectibility, underwritten by a deterministic associationist philosophy that assumed that good stimuli would create good human beings, is ruined at the very foundation of the subject in the 'Rime' and Coleridge's later thought. There is a stain prior to any stimuli, any education, any political programme, corroding the human subject and condemning it to a certain law of evil.

There is an even deeper logic at work, however, which makes the terrors of the 'Rime' distinct from the Burkean sublime and Coleridge's own ethical terror-sublime. As mentioned in the previous chapter, both the *Philosophical Enquiry* and the *Observations on Man* utilise empirical models of subjectivity: their shared assumption, derived from Locke, is that the subject begins as a blank *tabula rasa*. The terrors of the sublime become particular kinds of stimuli affecting a subject that is, more or less, a passive perceptual screen. They are theorised, regulated and understood through a discourse of psychology that subsumes the discourse of the sublime. For Burke, the sublime is reduced to the plane of the physiological, determined as a passion of self-preservation and set dualistically alongside the gentler pleasures of the beautiful (which relax rather than exercise the nerves). In Coleridge's 'The Destiny of Nations', sublime terror has a function within an associationist understanding of ethical development, driving a perfectible humanity through sympathy towards a goal that ultimately embraces ethical, political and religious aspects (all of which are systematically theorised by Unitarian radicalism). In both cases, therefore, the sublime is an experience analysed alongside other experiences within a single psychological framework.

There is always a risk that such frameworks come under considerable pressure from the experience of the sublime, which is a uniquely intense and transformative affect. We can see this in the *Philosophical Enquiry*, for instance. Whilst distance from an object of terror may be essential to Burke's sublime in one sense, preserving the spectatorial subjectivity at a safe remove, there is also the interior dimension inherent to all empiricisms of the era. Is not Burke's sublime also an overwhelming inward experience, founded on absolutely private sensation?[44] After all, Burke borrows that classic eighteenth-century trope of a mind filled to – or beyond – its boundaries, to the point of paralysing astonishment: 'the mind is so entirely filled with its object, that it cannot entertain any other' (p. 53). We might want to relate this astonished self (etymologically from the Latin *attonare*, to be thunderstruck or dazed) with the trance that Joan of Arc undergoes in 'The Destiny of Nations'. In both cases, might not subjectivity itself be overthrown? Such rhetoric seems to suggest a self on the point of dissolution, outstripped by the very object it attempts to grasp: what kind of psychology is adequate to an experience which threatens to break the mind's bounds? Nevertheless, if empirical psychology finds a kind of limit here, it is only in response to greater and greater *degrees* of sensation (with sensation being the base unit of empiricism). By contrast, what happens in Coleridge's poem demands a different kind of psychology altogether.

In the 'Rime', I would argue, the sublime is no longer something that can be understood through a wider discourse of the subject at all: rather, the experience of subjectivity itself becomes sublime. The subject is something that can terrify itself and struggles to know itself: one's heart is 'dry as dust' (l.239), one hears the relentless tread of 'a frightful fiend' (l.456) at one's back, one is sometimes 'wrench'd / With a woeful agony' (ll.611–12). Subjectivity itself – or rather the capacity for evil of which it is capable – is an enigma. The hermit's question 'what manner man art thou?' (l.610) is not only addressed to a gothic anti-hero but to all, and the agony (*agon*, Greek, struggle or contest) of the soul that answers is, for Coleridge, the answer of a guilt resistant to rational explication, of a subjectivity that finds a terrifying burden at its root, shared by all. Whilst there is indeed a single act to which the Mariner's guilt can be linked, it is a rather arbitrary one. As the hermit implies, what is at stake is not just what the Mariner has done, but equally who he is and what he has become: the obscure motivelessness of the slaying seems to confirm that it is not so much he who claims the act, but rather the act which claims him. What is exposed, I would contend, is thus not a simple calculus of offence and debt, but rather the stain – the alien presence which one fears to confront – that marks the soul according to Coleridge's later theology.

This overrunning of subjectivity with the sublime is not dissimilar to what Peter De Bolla describes as a shift from the discourse *on* the sublime to the discourse *of* the sublime. De Bolla's contention, applied primarily to the rhetorical rather than the terror-sublime, is that eighteenth-century culture attempted to 'police the transport of the sublime experience'.[45] This meant that the excess characteristic of the sublime experience was checked by surrounding discourses such as rhetorical education or theology. The excess was, as it were, passed on to these other fields. However, it is claimed that after the 1760s, one finds the sublime actually transforming those discourses. In particular, the excess produced by the sublime creates a self-legislating 'I' which outstrips the very discourses which once regulated sublimity: one goes from a discourse *on* sublimity (contained within the general perspective of rhetorical, theological or indeed psychological discourse), to a discourse *of* sublimity (as a force which permeates and overruns many different discourses with a new experience of subjectivity).

As my earlier reading of the *Fears in Solitude* quarto should have shown, I think the notion of a self-legislating subjectivity runs into a great many problems very quickly. However, De Bolla's underused and very powerful distinction certainly seems applicable to the case of the terror-sublime. The regulating discourses of empiricism are suddenly overthrown: the sublime as a terrifying and difficult perceptual experience lying outside a transparent, normal subjectivity (even one under pressure) is displaced by an experience of a subject that now finds the perception *of itself* to be terrifying and difficult. A psychological discourse on the subject no longer comprehends the sublime: psychology has itself become incomprehensible. The terror-sublime has been moved inside oneself. This, I feel, is the root cause of the exorbitant, redoubled sublimity of the 'Rime'. It is more 'Dutch', disturbing, irrational and frightening than the classic eighteenth-century accounts of terror in *kind* and not just *degree*: because the perceiving subject had always just about maintained its externality to the experience, and now it *was* the experience. This is a subject that finds itself to be as spectral as any gothic machinery.[46]

This spectrality of the subject is something on which I want to focus in order to conclude. Coleridge gives us a picture of a subject who was claimed by guilt at or before the root of itself. He thus rediscovers and reframes the notion of original sin which Unitarianism had so forcefully rejected. Of course, to a secular world, the doctrine of original sin seems hopelessly archaic, but perhaps this is largely because we receive it in the mythic, hereditary form that Coleridge rejected. Coleridge turned it into a haunting of the subject and in this form – if not in content – it seems far more contemporary. Consider, for instance, Susan Eilenberg's interpretation of the poem through the uncanny experience of 'an alien spirit ... [coming] to inhabit the body of the Mariner's speech'.[47] Both possessed and dispossessed by a language that speaks *him* as much as he speaks it, the Mariner is divided from himself. Eilenberg's reading preempts Jacques Derrida's *Monolingualism of the Other* in showing that the 'I' is born into a language that is always already present, 'demonstrating the difficulty of saying "I am" in one's own voice'.[48] Thematically, Eilenberg largely belongs to the counter-moral tradition, dissolving moral or providential clusters 'favoured by those who insist upon the ... Christian implications of the poem' into arbitrary relations formed by accidental contiguities and metonymies.[49] Like McGann, she can only perceive religion as a totalising hermeneutic. Yet, in Coleridge's treatment of original sin as a haunting of the subject, we can see the same dividing of the 'I' from itself: a Christian experience of the very thing Eilenberg identifies. The language of the 'I' and the ethical burden of the 'I' both seem to come from a place other than the 'I'. Yet the 'I' must speak, and the 'I' must act.

The ethical turn of recent continental theory, and renewed attention to the unfashionable and contentious theme of evil, seems to render Coleridge's haunted and guilty subject more and more our contemporary. Kant was perhaps the first thinker to refigure original sin into a philosophical theory of radical evil in *Religion Within the Limits of Reason Alone*, where he suggests there is an inscrutable yet universal perversity in human beings to incline away from the moral law by mixing the maxims of duty with those of sensuous interest: 'this evil is *radical*, because it corrupts the ground of all maxims'.[50] The aporetic nature of this corrupted root is well attested to by one recent commentator who describes Kant as theorising 'a propensity to evil [that] is innate or inborn (angeboren), yet we are somehow responsible for it'.[51] However, Kant was certainly not the last thinker to fashion a darker selfhood, and raise from the Christian past the spectre of a primordial disposition to evil. Thinkers as varied as Sigmund Freud, Emmanuel Levinas and Jean-Luc Nancy have also put a kind of guilt at the root of, or prior to, the subject.[52] A self-divided subjectivity, terrified by its own deepest recesses, is hence one that is characteristically ours, as we pose the question of evil to ourselves afresh, after the collapse of the Enlightenment, after psychoanalysis, after the Holocaust. This is why this poem still appears forcefully compelling.

In conclusion, if the ambitions of the Unitarian subject seen in 'The Destiny of Nations' were built on an empirical, *tabula rasa* psychology and held out for the perfectibility of a potentially self-transparent subject, then the subject in the 'Rime' is always already divided. It is the anti-type of the Unitarian heroic subject valorised in 'The Destiny of Nations' and 'Religious Musings'. Most devastatingly for Unitarian hopes, it is always already claimed by guilt, thus ruining the dream of perfectibility for which Locke's philosophy opened space. However, as we have seen, this guilt is no merely external and legal matter, as in traditional theology: it is a speck on the heart, a secret lodger, a hollowness of the subject. It is a haunting, one that seems to speak to own sense (and rediscovery) of an evil shadowing humanity. The psychological discourses of the subject which comprehended the sublime as exterior perceptual content have now been overturned by an experience of the subject which is itself sublime, excessive, terrifying and at the limit of comprehension.

As I have argued, the 'Rime' does all this not *despite* but *because* of its own understanding of Christianity. Coleridge's poem appears here strikingly modern, perhaps precisely because it succeeded the collapse of an ethically optimistic, unitary model of subjectivity in the Enlightened tradition. As our psychoanalytic or phenomenologically decentred subjects follow the ruin of the Cartesian *cogito*, the anguished religious subject of the 'Rime' follows the ruin of a classically eighteenth-century perfectible self. The intertwining of religion and irrationalism no doubt troubles us in an age with a fragile secular-enlightened legacy, but the pre-Enlightenment nature of the doctrine of original sin is in a sense exactly what is at stake in the poem. This is whether or not we can have a subject exorcised of everything archaic that haunts it.

Part III
Representation, Kant, Theology

5

'Ye signs and wonders of the element! Utter forth God': Divine Presence and Divine Withdrawal in the Natural Sublime

'Hymn Before Sun-Rise', Coleridge's poem to Mont Blanc, is his most direct expression of the natural sublime – the sublimity of mountains and savage landscape that would become prototypical in Romantic literary and visual culture, as well as being the *locus classicus* of Kant's discussion in the *Critique of Judgment*. Hence, any discussion of sublimity in Coleridge's work must turn at some point to this poem, the writing and revision of which encompassed the period of Coleridge's first engagement with German philosophy.[1] Although the poem runs parallel to certain Kantian motifs and analyses of the natural sublime, it oversteps many of the limits of a Kantian treatment. In this chapter, I show how Coleridge's natural sublime differs from Kant's in asserting a visionary claim: a logic which reads off divine presence through signs of authorship which speak out in the landscape. As Raimonda Modiano and Seamus Perry have both noted, this version of the sublime wants to bring nature itself along in the sublime movement of transcendence, not negate it as in Kant.[2]

However, a close examination of the rhetoric and figures underlying this visionary claim leads one to find the violence of prosopopoeia (personifications) at the root of Coleridge's addresses to the landscape. Critical consensus on this poem, borrowing a deconstructive scepticism about the Romantic bond with nature and drawing out unfavourable comparisons with the materialism of Percy Bysshe Shelley's 'Mont Blanc', sees it as a set of visionary projections, appropriating the landscape for theological ends under the auspices of the sublime. However, returning to Kant's text, I identify two tropes – the veil of Isis and the Judaic interdiction on idols – which understand the relation between divinity and sublimity with a different kind of logic: a divine withdrawal *from* the world, not a divine presence *in* the world. Such a withdrawal is marked in the 'Hymn', despite running counter to the poem's leading rhetoric. Looking at the scene of praise that concludes 'Hymn Before Sun-Rise', and analysing the grammatical modality of prayer, I argue that an entirely different way of reading the text emerges.

The boundary of the phenomenal in 'Hymn Before Sun-Rise'

Initially, the poem prepares for its *visionary* claim by stretching the *visual* to breaking point. By this I mean that the categories of the empirical, space and time, are found to alter because the experience of Mont Blanc is so overwhelming. This pressure on space and time becomes a precondition for their ultimate disappearance and the shift to a visionary mode over and above visual perception. Thus, for example, the spatial form of the mountain outlined against the sky becomes forebodingly austere, merely two abstract and interlocking shapes. Detail, colour and even accurate appreciation of physical state (in the case of the opaque sky) all give way to a violent juxtaposition of the massive forms of heaven and mountain:

> Deep is the air and dark, substantial, black,
> An ebon mass: methinks thou piercest it,
> As with a wedge![3]

Meanwhile, the ceaseless motion of the rivers at the mountain's base contrasts with the eerie stillness of the peak itself, rising from a silent forest of pines, provoking a temporal distortion:

> Hast thou a charm to stay the morning-star
> In his steep course? So long he seems to pause
> On thy bald awful head, O sovran Blanc! (ll.1–3)

Sheer physical scale seems to affect the perception of time, in a way similar to that described in section 27 of the *Critique of Judgment*. There, Kant explains that the attempt to intuit a vast object as a whole, and thus instantaneously, is in conflict with the internal time series which accompanies the lengthy duration needed to take in all its parts. In Coleridge's poem, the perception of things moving, through which we get a sense of time, seems to lose precision; again, because of the vastness of the sublime object. The morning star – which we know *is* moving – seems to be frozen when we try to compare the scale of its motion with the scale of the mountain, simply because the former is too minute and the latter too massive. Mont Blanc seems to pause time itself.

As the senses lose their grasp on normal perceptions of time and space, Coleridge sketches a sudden transformation, anticipated by the striking image of Mont Blanc piercing the heavens as if rending the veil of phenomenality itself. When the narrator returns his gaze to the peak, the noumenal has suddenly imposed its forms on the world of sense. The sky, previously figured as a dark massy substance, is now 'thy crystal shrine, / Thy habitation from *eternity*!' (ll.11–12, my emphasis). The change from opacity to crystal suggests a revelatory moment, a newly transparent world: as he later writes, 'the effect of the Sky – how purely intellectual' (*N*4153). It is precisely when, as Kant puts it, 'the senses no longer see anything before them', that a vision of a different world may begin:[4]

> I gazed upon thee [Mont Blanc],
> Till thou, still present to the bodily sense,
> Didst vanish from my thought: entranced in prayer
> I worshipped the Invisible alone. (ll.13–16)

The poem's movement seems to follow a parallel logic to Kant in bringing the subject to the border between visible and invisible worlds. Although Coleridge would probably not have been aware of Kant's text when he first wrote the passage in 1802, the way he conceptualises what lies behind the visible (largely irrelevant to, for instance, Burke's sublime) does offer a number of points where their accounts converge. In the *Critique of Judgment*'s rendering of a sublime experience, at the very moment one's perceptual grasp on the sensible begins to founder, a supersensible idea is articulated, uplifting and liberating the subject. In the mathematical sublime, the imagination fails to find an appropriate measure to appreciate the scale of some vast object, but Reason intervenes with the idea of an absolute whole. In the dynamical sublime, the imagination is overwhelmed by the crushing power of nature over the physical fragility of the human being, but Reason provides the idea of humanity's vocation as a free being in the moral world. This failure of empirical perception, leading to the announcement of a relationship with the invisible, is thus a pattern common to both Kant's theory and Coleridge's poem.

Indeed, tracing the changes made between 1802 and later versions, we might well argue that Coleridge brings the poem closer to the Kantian analysis after he engaged with the *Critique of Judgment*. Both earlier and later versions of the 'Hymn' offer a transition between passivity and activity. Thus, the first *Morning Post* version runs as follows:

> But I awoke, and with a busier mind
> And active will self-conscious, offer now
> Not, as before, involuntary pray'r
> And passive adoration![5]

This passage becomes more elaborate in later texts, in which the relatively simple psychological opposition between perception and will is replaced by a rhetoric of transcendence:

> the dilating Soul, enrapt, transfused,
> Into the mighty vision passing – there
> As in her natural form, swelled vast to Heaven. (ll.21–3)

The passage of the soul into a higher, more authentic form suggests the influence of Kant. In the *Critique of Judgment*, Kant had strikingly suggested that the true source of sublimity lay not in the natural object (such as the mountain), but rather in the mind that was thus ennobled by the experience:

> We express ourselves on the whole incorrectly if we call some **object of nature** sublime ... we can say no more than that the object serves for the presentation of a sublimity that can be found in the mind. (p. 129)

The idea that true sublimity might lie with what the human being possesses over and above nature is echoed in the poem's attestation that nature blended 'with my life and life's own secret joy' (l.20). Whereas the 1802 version makes a straightforward shift from wonder to praise, the inserted passage on blending and dilation appears to take up, almost sublate, the glory of nature into the glory of the human subject. It is unclear what is more 'mighty': the vision of Mont Blanc, or the 'natural form' of the rapturous narrator.

However, there is an important and instructive difference between the Coleridgean and Kantian versions of natural sublimity. This difference lies in a lack of discontinuity between visible and invisible worlds. In 'Hymn Before Sun-Rise', the sensuous does indeed give way to the invisible, but there is no rupture between the two: rather the sensuous takes its place as something reconciled *with* the invisible. As Raimonda

Modiano has remarked, there is no sense of crisis in Coleridge's sublime, no vertigo in the passage over the chasm between phenomenal and noumenal perspectives.[6] What Coleridge has done is to bring the phenomenal and noumenal worlds together and let one flow into the other. The subject narrated in 'Hymn Before Sun-Rise' is passing over a boundary: dilating (from *di-latus*, broadened into two parts), enrapt (*en-rapere*, to be seized), and transfused (*trans-fundere*, to pour across from one vessel to another).

This transcendental passage is Coleridge's own particular inflection of what I will gloss from now on as the Romantic nature sublime. This is the sublime we find in William Wordsworth's *Prelude*, in Shelley's own Alpine poem 'Mont Blanc', and in Caspar David Friedrich's paintings: nature on the grandest scale, re-envisaged as a sacramental scene for the lone individual for whom deeper forces than those immediately perceptible (be they Platonic, pantheistic or theistic) are revealed. Modiano's chapter in *Coleridge and the Concept of Nature* still remains the most detailed account of Coleridge's nature sublime, and I would agree with her central contention that he 'wants to take nature along in the experience'.[7] More than with other Romantics, landscape receives a Christian charge based on tropes such as the splendour of Creation and nature as a second Book of God. Whilst all the Romantics tended to use the aesthetics of the sublime to posit a kind of epiphany above and beyond what the philosophers of the sublime theorised or permitted, Coleridge's nature sublime is more firmly entrenched in a theology of epiphany (something which in turn minimises the sense of human meaninglessness always risked). For Coleridge, nature is a site of revelation where man receives knowledge of his own condition as a created being, and the sum effect – noted by Modiano and confirmed by other critics – is to unify the sublime economy under the Godhead.

This differs greatly from the boundaries enforced around the Kantian subject. One can certainly argue that Kant allows the subject more and more scope for validly grounded experience as he moves through the Critiques. Günter Zöller, for example, suggests that 'the second and third Critiques supplement the phenomenal restriction of theoretical knowledge with the practical and reflective extension of knowledge beyond the limits of experience'.[8] Whilst this is true, the practical and reflective aspects that Zöller mentions are profoundly circumscribed. Whilst they extend knowledge as a whole, these extensions do not have the same validity as theoretical cognition. The *Critique of Judgment* is at pains to emphasise this point, and the transcendental spirit inherited from the First Critique thus ensures a carefully guarded boundary is maintained between phenomenal experience and ideas falling outside of time and space.

In the General Remark that closes his comments on the sublime, Kant warns against the false sublimity of visionary rapture, which is precisely the notion that an experience of sublimity involves an adequate representation of the supersensible: '**a delusion of being able to see something beyond all bounds of sensibility** ... to rave with reason' (p. 156). This visionary rapture is 'least of all compatible with the sublime ... brooding and absurd ... a disease' (p. 157). Kant makes clear that the sublime is and can only be a *negative* experience, i.e. the idea of Reason is signified only indirectly, as a moment of failure on the part of cognition operating in the phenomenal world. Kant restates this position many times: 'taken literally, and considered logically, ideas cannot be presented'; the sublime 'compels us to **think** nature itself in its totality ... without being able to produce this presentation **objectively**' (p. 151); and 'the **inscrutability of the idea of freedom** entirely precludes any positive presentation' (p. 156).

How does Coleridge achieve, then, this distinctly non-Kantian crossing of boundaries, a crossing that is upheld even in later versions of the poem that appear to draw directly on Kant? It is not as if Coleridge is inattentive to the nature of the crossing: it is actually described in considerable detail. The physical bulk of the mountain is said to 'vanish from my thought' (l.15) but nevertheless exists as 'still present to the bodily sense' (l.14). There is thus a perceptual under-presence, guaranteeing the absorbing of the physical into the spiritual, which Coleridge compares to a melody we are not even aware of hearing. I would argue that the poem's model here is the experience of signification, or language, for the rest of the poem does indeed unveil a nature that speaks and that seems to bear signs. It is an oddity that in perceiving a sign-system, what is nominally perceived – the signifier – is secondary. The sound contours of the voice, or the written mark, are easily occluded in the expression – occluded, indeed, much like the under-presence of melody that Coleridge invokes as his initial simile (notably, of course, the poem entitles itself a hymn – words over music).

If nature bears signs in this way, then it does seemingly bring together an ideal plane with a material one. For the semantic operates in a way that reconciles matter and idea, or as Coleridge puts it in a letter of 1801, a *coherence*:

> Both Words & Ideas derive their whole significancy from their coherence. The simple *Idea* Red dissevered from all, with which it has ever

> been cojoined, would be as unintelligible as the word *Red* [without the idea]. (*CL*, II.698)

As the poem proceeds, we find that the landscape does possess such a 'significancy', co-joining its physicality with something transcending that. Nature is revealed as a language of 'signs and wonders' (l.68), and as the poem iterates, the idea welded to its marks and sounds is the divine: 'Earth, with her thousand voices, praises God' (l.85). What is achieved in Coleridge's sublime is hence nothing short of a revelation of divine presence, expressing a long-standing faith that, as he put it in 1795, 'the Omnipotent has unfolded to us the Volume of the World, that there we may read the Transcript of himself'.[9] As Cian Duffy notes, the voiceless materiality of nature is transformed at a certain ecstatic point to voice, to revelation, and a visionary articulacy.[10] This semantic effect undergirds the sublime crossing forbidden by Kant: everywhere Coleridge looks in the landscape, he reads 'God'.

Consider, for instance, the relentless momentum of questioning built up in the second half of the poem:

> Who sank thy [Mont Blanc's] sunless pillars deep in the Earth?
> Who filled thy countenance with rosy light?
> Who made thee parent of perpetual streams? (ll.36–8)

After no less than nine ecstatic interrogatives, the answer comes in a surging refrain performed by streams and ice-flows, as if the manifest presence of God behind nature can no longer be contained within its phenomenal housing:

> God! let the torrents, like a shout of nations,
> Answer! and let the ice-plains echo, God!
> God! sing ye meadow-streams with gladsome voice! (ll.58–60)

There is almost a signatory effect here: concealed teleological gestures, which seek origin and design for the landscape's magnificence, seem to identify a series of signatures or maker's marks inscribed into the Alpine environment. In this sense, the poem seems to drift close to the theories of Jacob Behmen, whose book *Signatura Rerum*, or the signature of things, is a work with which Coleridge was fascinated. Although I do not wish to read the 'Hymn' as a strictly Behmenite poem, despite pertinent similarities like depicting the creation as 'a great Harmony of manifold Instruments', there is no doubt that his work greatly influenced

Coleridge's thinking about nature as a second Book of God.[11] Moreover, the comparison is worthwhile in not only finding a contemporary analogue for the divine semantics of the 'Hymn', but also because it reveals a major problem with such a notion.

Behmen claims that 'the whole outward visible World with all its Being is a Signature, or Figure of the inward spiritual World'.[12] The sign is thus invoked, as in Coleridge's text, to establish a relation between ideal and empirical planes, identifying 'the Language of Nature, whence every Thing speaks out its property'.[13] Nature echoes with the evidences of a divine performative:

> this World, with the Sun, Stars, and Elements, and with every creaturely Being, is nothing else but a Manifestation of the Eternity of the Eternal Will and Mind.[14]

However, one might query how such a signature is revealed. How is this text, which lies hidden within the objects of normal perception, to be read or deciphered? Behmen frames his system in theosophical terms: 'every one is not fit for, or capable of the Knowledge of the Eternal and Temporal Nature in its mysterious Operation'.[15] Yet, as Coleridge notes in marginalia to Behmen, such so-called knowledge is dangerously intuitive: 'frequently does he mistake ... the phantoms and witcheries ... of his own seething Fancy, for parts or symbols of a universal Process'.[16] The similarity between the visionary claim in the 'Hymn' and the theosophical claim found in Behmen should alert us to the problem that menaces Coleridge's nature sublime here. As Ben Brice has also noted, an eighteenth-century sceptical tradition which Coleridge knew well (and even deployed, as in the marginalia to Behmen) calls into question the Romantic understanding of the visionary: 'at moments of great psychological need or anxiety, it seems impossible to maintain a firm distinction between symbolic vision and delusional apprehension'.[17]

Prosopopoeia and veils: a deconstructive reading and a Kantian alternative

Perhaps ironically, the sceptical critique that Coleridge advances cautiously at Behmen is precisely the one that modern criticism has levelled at the Romantic nature sublime as it is articulated in poems like the 'Hymn'. Of the relatively small body of critical work on this text, there is consensus that Coleridge has imposed and projected signification upon the landscape, especially in comparison with Shelley's poem on the same subject. Cian Duffy takes this line, holding that the landscape is made to speak in order to conceal its actual silence. Louise Economides also reads the poem's religious sublimity as a flight from empirical reality (which is in turn identified as possessing a material sublimity avowed in Shelley's later text).[18] As Angela Esterhammer points out in her interpretation of the poem, there is 'the substitution of a human, poetic voice for the creative Logos that should resound from Mont Blanc'.[19] The operations of a visionary interiority seem impossible to disentangle from the supposed exteriority of the visionary text: whenever the Romantic poet claims to speak with nature, or make it speak, we suspect him of pathology.

There are still critical attempts to rehabilitate the Romantic bond with nature, notably in ecocriticism.[20] However, the important deconstructive criticism of the 1980s and 1990s has embedded a strong sceptical bulwark against the Romantic idea of nature, and the rhetorical manipulations that it involves. It is easy enough to apply a de Manian reading of this sort to 'Hymn Before Sun-Rise'. To initiate such an interpretation, we need only note that nature only speaks when called forth: as in so many Romantic poems of natural sublimity, it is the apostrophe that is absolutely central. De Man's work encourages a thorough interrogation of such tropes, suggesting that, as it is put in 'Shelley Disfigured', there is a forgotten rhetorical violence at work.[21] The apostrophe is a prime example of this since one can argue it conceals the trope of prosopopoeia: literally, the giving of a face. For de Man, any act of address also carries with it a certain image of the addressee, no more so than when the addressee in question is inanimate. The apostrophe is thus, although superficially a rhetoric opening equal dialogue, an act of force.

A deconstructive dismantling of the rhetoric and figures of the 'Hymn' radically undermines its visionary claim. In order to evoke the shift from the ordinary perception of nature-as-nature to the visionary reading of nature-as-text, nature must be made to speak. As such, the poem must personify natural objects in the same motion as addressing them, and the apostrophes reveal themselves as speech acts whose addressee is entirely a creation of their own enunciation. After all, Mont Blanc is only metaphorically speaking the 'sole sovran of the Vale!' (l.29), the five torrents pouring down its side do not really possess the emotion of fierce gladness (l.39), and so forth. It is only because the poem gives them a face, as the etymology of prosopopoeia demands, that the 'thousand voices' (l.85) of nature can speak a language. 'They too have a voice, yon piles of snow / And in their perilous fall shall thunder' (ll.62–3), the narrator announces, but of course this description, supposedly of voice, is itself the moment where voice is given. Before it, like Mont Blanc itself, the landscape is silent.

Cynthia Chase is one critic, following de Man, who has strongly emphasised the relation between apostrophe and prosopopoeia. For instance, in her discussion of Keats's 'Ode to a Nightingale', she notes that the use of apostrophe creates the impression of a dialogue, thus saving the poet-speaker from a lonely isolation: 'passing from a sign to a sound and a sense ... letting us conceive of the reading of a text as an intelligible, perceptual process like hearing'.[22] In short, if we feel that the poet is speaking to someone beside him or herself, even a bird, then the poem itself appears more like a living utterance. More interestingly still, Chase goes on to contend that the turn to the flowers at Keats's feet, often read as a humble turn to the earth (as opposed to the imaginative flights represented by the nightingale), is *also* founded on prosopopoeia. The sense of bonding with nature, whether nightingale or flower, is shown to be a rhetorical effect dissimulated by yoking nature into dialogue by giving it a face. We can see a similar process at work in 'Hymn Before Sun-Rise'. Unlike the Kantian sublime, where it is precisely the *in*humanity of a landscape's power that allows human freedom and morality to be posited in opposition to it, Coleridge's natural sublime wants to bring human and landscape together in a shared relation to God. Getting nature to answer the teleological questions that the narrator poses, as if it were a living interlocutor, transforms the experience of reading landscape into one that is humane, a 'perceptual process like hearing'.

Moreover, the more human and living a landscape seems, the more credible is the idea that it has been designed by an intelligent being. Coleridge's teleological gestures are thus reinforced by prosopopoeia: it is not just the fact that nature becomes articulate that is important, but also the qualities that the articulacy brings. The landscape is imbued with human affect throughout: the pleasant 'meadow-streams' have a voice that is 'gladsome' (l.60), whilst the torrents are praised for 'your fury, and your joy' (l.45). Even when the things in the poem are already living, Coleridge takes care to underscore their organicity: twice the narrator utters the tautologous '*living* flowers' (l.56, 64, my emphasis). It would seem these qualities have come *from* somewhere: whilst the answer may be nothing more than the poet's pen, the poem obviously suggests that they are reflections of a conscious mind at work in its design.

There is a certain necessity at work here. Nature can be seen as bluntly literal and meaning only itself. To raise nature to the level where it can bear meanings, its materiality must stand for something else: it must be *figured*. Yet, of course, this figuration must come from the poet-speaker. To what extent are rhetoric and figures *bringing out* supposedly teleological qualities (beauty, majesty, harmony etc.), and to what extent are they actually *creating* those qualities? Conventional readings of Coleridge's religious nature poetry, and the theories behind them, emphasise the central role played by consubstantiality, or the unity of all things in God, which validates connections made between different levels of being (human, natural and divine).[23] However, the prosopopoeia so fundamental to the textual workings of 'Hymn Before Sun-Rise' suggests the possibility of an alternative centre of unity lying in the poet: that it might be the poet who brings disparate things together in a single articulation, fashioning analogies between levels of being that only have rhetorical validity.

A deconstructive approach, then, can tear apart the very bond that the poem requires between human and nature, showing how meanings are imposed in the supposed act of reading them: as Cynthia Chase sums up the de Manian thesis, one confronts 'the arbitrary conferral of face on the diffusion of material traces'.[24] However, I think we can go beyond this well-established tradition of interpretation. There is something else going on in the poem, and to identify it, I want to make a return to Kant. For although framed in de Manian terms, our critique of prosopopoeia recapitulates a classic Kantian logic: that of *subreption*, or 'the subjective which offers itself to or even forces itself upon reason as objective'.[25] Coleridge overturns a major aspect of the Kantian sublime, which is that sublime objects (or, more accurately, objects that provoke the sublime) are *contra-purposive*: formless, being of magnitudes of size or force outstripping the usual range of human perception. Certainly, the 'Hymn' draws on the fact that the Alpine environs push our capacities of apprehension and comprehension to the limit. However, he demands unlike Kant that these hyperbolic wonders, at the edge of the empirical, imply something *outside* of the empirical world. Coleridge inserts what Kant terms a *physico-theological* argument into his aesthetics of the sublime. Given that Mont Blanc dwarfs all other elements of visible nature – 'sole sovran of the Vale' (l.29) – what else but some force beyond the empirical could have possibly placed it there? How could the 'sunless pillars' of this titanic mountain, themselves at the edge of our comprehension, have been rooted in the earth, except by the divine? However, for Kant, such a logic bears a fatal internal flaw.

For instance, consider the First Critique's handling of the kind of argument put forward by Coleridge's invocation of Mont Blanc's 'sunless pillars':

> Reason, ceaselessly elevated by the powerful though only empirical proofs that are always growing in its hands ... [throws] a glance on the wonders of nature and the majesty of the world's architecture,

> by which it elevates itself from magnitude to magnitude up to the highest of all, rising from the conditioned to the condition, up to the supreme and unconditioned author.[26]

Even though Kant assents that this train of thought represents a common philosophical position and a deep-rooted instinct of the human mind, it is invalid. Specifically, trying to find a cause that transcends nature is incoherent since causality is a category that as far as we know only applies to nature.[27] This refutation exemplifies the weakness of all speculative theology, which is that it involves 'extending one's cognition ... where no possible experience and hence no means suffices to secure objective reality for any of the concepts we have thought out'.[28] Discussing the conceptual leap made between human works and nature, Kant claims that it is unjustifiable for the mind to pass 'from a causality with which it is acquainted to obscure and unprovable grounds of explanation, with which it is not acquainted'.[29] An analogy existing only in the mind has been lent an ungrounded sense of externality and constitutive reality. This should be a familiar pattern, because it is the same kind of illusion deconstructed above in our discussion of apostrophe and prosopopoeia.

Similar logic applies to Coleridge's invocations of natural beauty. There are a number of teleological questions in the 'Hymn' that suggest aesthetic beauty as well as sheer power:

> Who made you glorious as the gates of Heaven
> Beneath the keen full moon? Who bade the sun
> Clothe you with rainbows? Who, with living flowers
> Of loveliest blue, spread garlands at your feet? (ll.54–7)

As Coleridge's questions all begin with the personal *who*, there is clearly a certain tautology here: the only way of access that Coleridge can conceive to these 'signs and wonders' (l.68) is a teleological one. Kant does not deny the temptation of such a conception. He is drawn, particularly in the *Critique of Judgment*, by the argument that beautiful things in nature are evidence of design, claiming that it is indeed hard to perceive them without thinking that 'they had actually been designed for our power of judgment' (p. 233).

Nevertheless, although Kant finds the argument linking beauty with design appealing – perhaps because the *Critique of Judgment* is a work in which he is persistent in trying to bridge parts of his system – he ultimately rejects it. Whilst beauty does show an unusually high level of conformity with our faculties, this only tells us something about ourselves: 'in such judging what is at issue is not what nature is or even what it is for us as a purpose, but how we take it in' (p. 224). In deploying an aesthetic feeling for God's existence, 'Hymn Before Sun-Rise' is illegitimate in Kantian terms. A feeling *as if* something has been designed for our own contemplation, to please and inspire the human subject, cannot be validly extended to suggest that it *has* been so designed. As Kant makes clear in section 58 of the *Critique of Judgment*, the purposiveness we sense is in fact purposiveness between our faculties, and not a purposiveness in nature itself. We've projected something we might feel *subjectively* into the *objective* world.

It is thus easy to see how close the sceptical positions in the First and Third Critiques run to certain aspects of deconstructive scepticism. There is a sense in which Kant provides a no less searching or ultimately fatal critique of the Romantic natural sublime (in the shape found in the 'Hymn Before Sun-Rise') than any modern critic. And as one can see in de Man's identification of a 'radical materiality of sublime vision' in section 29 of the *Critique of Judgement*, the resistance of a conceptless nature to bearing human sense, which is so important to the readings of Duffy and Economides, is already there, in some form, in Kant.[30] However, precisely because Kant anticipates so much of our reading thus far, it is interesting to see that he nevertheless repeatedly invokes God or gods. Does he point the way to an alternative way of conceiving the relationship between theology and the sublime? In particular, I'd like to analyse two tropes. Shifting the ground away from God's presence in the world to his transcendence, the veil of Isis and the Judaic interdiction on idols signify an alternate conceptualisation of theological presence (or otherwise), and lead to an entirely different understanding of how the name of God might function in 'Hymn Before Sun-Rise'.

Given that we know that the Kantian position possesses such deep reserves of scepticism – particularly to religious appropriation of the sublime – it is perhaps surprising to find the *Critique of Judgment* citing with approval the second commandment:

> Perhaps there is no more sublime passage in the Jewish Book of the Law than the commandment: Thou shalt not make unto thyself any graven image, nor any likeness either of that which is in heaven, or on the earth, or yet under the earth, etc. (p. 156)

However, this offers a totally different understanding of the relationship between religion and the sublime. Here, the divine is not rooted in the sensible (natural evidences such as mountains or living things) or the semantic (the name of God, readable in the landscape), but conversely in an excess over, or withdrawal from, the sensible and semantic. The work of analogy which underwrites the physico-theological approach is here displaced by an uncompromising attestation of *dis*-analogy. The sublimity of the commandment resides in its negativity, that is, in the imagination's inability to fix itself on to the graven, the visible and the representational:

> the imagination, although it certainly finds nothing beyond the sensible to which it can attach itself, nevertheless feels itself to be unbounded precisely because of this elimination of the limits of sensibility; and that separation is thus a presentation of the infinite. (p. 156)

What is at stake is not reference, but the absence of reference. As one can see from the Judaic tetragrammaton – YHWH – which inscribes the second commandment into a single signifier, the denotative aspect of any thinking of God has been displaced by different modalities: the interdictory (one shall not represent, one shall not write) and the negation (ultimately leading towards the negation of negative theology). One has not reference, but the separation of reference.

Just as interesting for our purposes, especially given the fact that Coleridge roots divine presence in the natural sublime, is Kant's gesture in the *Critique* to Isis as Mother Nature. Although merely a footnote, the superlative terms in which it is framed demand notice:

> Perhaps nothing more sublime has ever been said, or any thought more sublimely expressed, than in the inscription over the temple of **Isis** (Mother **Nature**): 'I am all that is, that was, and that will be, and my veil no mortal has removed.' (p. 194)

As the parallels with the Judaic interdiction make clear, the veil of Isis trope also explores negative representationality. The veil is a limit – a limit of the sensible, one might say – in so far as it is itself sensible but yet also marks what is hidden. Although itself part of the visible order, it exists in the visible order only for the function of rendering invisible: it is a visible trope of invisibility. As such, if nature includes a limit that is veiled, it would again run counter to Coleridge's teleological appropriation of the natural sublime. Instead of the perception of nature intimating the presence of God through its beauty and majesty (an analogy or adequation between nature-as-creation and God-as-creator), there would be a moment in the perception of the world that intimates something unworldly, something far in excess of the world. The analogies on which physico-theological thinking rests, and through which it understands something of the nature of God or gods, would be ruined by a negativity that insists on the hidden, the separated and the incomprehensible.

Both the Judaic and Egyptian interdictions, therefore, operate with a far different logic to that identified in the 'Hymn' so far. They signify a withdrawal of signification, and present a withdrawal of presentation, entirely opposed to the doctrine of a nature that speaks out. The signatures of the 'Hymn' name God by naming him as maker; the tetragrammaton 'names' God by not-naming him. The visionary text of the 'Hymn' reveals God by revealing him as maker; the veil of Isis 'reveals' the goddess by not revealing her. However, I want to argue that although 'Hymn Before Sun-Rise' does indeed found itself upon a visionary claim, the poem also includes something closer to the negative experience found in *The Critique of Judgment*. As the poem moves towards its close, the final stanzas shift away from a religious sublimity based on God's immanence, to one that exposes his transcendence. As with the two Kantian tropes, this will involve the overturning of reference in favour of a different modality. However, here, it is not that denotative discourse is overthrown by interdictory or negative discourse; rather, the name of God shifts from being a signature and a reference, to the vocative: a cry, an appellation and ultimately a prayer. Just like the tetragrammaton and the veil of Isis, however, the word of prayer attests not to something seen and grasped in nature, but to the Other of the sensible.

The Other of the sensible: withdrawal and prayer in 'Hymn Before Sun-Rise' and later poems

One might ask how a poem like 'Hymn Before Sun-Rise', which stages a landscape positively resounding with signs of divine presence, can possibly inscribe withdrawal. The beginning of an answer lies precisely with those signs, or rather the address made to them. A de Manian reading of the 'Hymn', such as the one worked out above, deconstructs the question-and-answer rhetorical structure that dominates the middle sections of Coleridge's poem, and reveals the concealed violence of prosopopoeia as the true root of apostrophe. But it is worth revisiting these very apostrophes from a different analytic angle: their etymological origin as a sudden turn to an addressee (*apo-strophe*, Greek, to turn from).[31] Given that this is a 'Hymn', it is perhaps striking that the expected address *to* God is continually deferred: the natural elements to which the speaker turns are, in a sense, turns away from the primary addressee; or at least a series of folds in this work of address. Temporally, we detect a subtle building of suspense, a delay in the very vocality that is so fundamental to the text: the apostrophes are themselves calls to apostrophise, such as 'let the ice-plains echo' (l.59), 'sing ye' (l.60) and 'shall thunder' (l.63).

Although impossible to identify absolutely, it is perhaps only in the penultimate stanza that the text's temporality shifts decisively into the present tense, when the mountain seems in firm simultaneity with the speaker's present moment:

> Ye living flowers that skirt the eternal frost!
> Ye wild goats sporting round the eagle's nest!
> Ye eagles, play-mates of the mountain-storm!
> Ye lightnings, the dread arrows of the clouds!
> Ye signs and wonders of the element!
> Utter forth God, and fill the hills with praise! (ll.64–9)

It is precisely at this point that the poem's sense of spatiality also radically shifts, outward from the Vale of Chamouni to the infinite spaces of the universe. Set in a sky strewn with stars and a rising sun, Mont Blanc is described as the 'dread ambassador from Earth to Heaven' (l.82) but 'Heaven' here surely bears a double semantic load, since the text's sense of scale has gone from the bounded to the truly boundless. In Kantian terms, the final stanza enacts the 'elimination of the limits of sensibility' (*Critique of Judgment*, p. 156). At the moment the voices elicited in the experience of natural sublimity finally gather together as a single Nature to enunciate the name of God, the fact that God lies outside nature must become manifest. What this deferral in temporality (and the concomitant shift in spatial sense) suggests is that rooting a religious sublimity in the natural sublime must, unless it is to become pantheistic, ultimately come to a point where it marks the alterity of God to a sensible, visible order. The richness and majesty of perceptual experience may be posited as theistic evidence, but there must also come a decisive turn away from perception, and a shattering of its horizons.

However, it is important to see this turn for what it is, which is a negative experience close to the two Kantian tropes examined above: it is a withdrawal scored into sensibility. Helpful here is Martin Heidegger's account of *Erscheinung* or appearance, in which the announcement of one thing's presence is made through another thing, as in 'indications, presentations, symptoms and symbols'.[32] Or, as Heidegger puts it, 'appearing is an announcing-itself through something that shows itself'.[33] However, this logic of presentation is inextricably linked with something close to the logic of the veil found in Kant. Heidegger notes that if something (x) announces itself through something else (y), then the *Erscheinung* of x is also a hiding of x, because of course x never shows itself in the same way that y shows itself. Thus, Heidegger can contend that 'appearing is a not-showing-itself'.[34] If we apply this structure of simultaneous announcement and concealment to the announcements in 'Hymn Before Sun-Rise', we see that God, even though announced, is also hidden. The very nature that announces God would also be his veil. God withdraws, even beyond the furthest horizons of the visible world evoked in the final stanza.

One obvious objection is simple: for all this Heideggerian subtlety, surely the poem simply posits God behind the veil? The turn I am arguing for would then be nothing more than a simple expansion of scope, underwritten by the Christian doctrine that has been involved from the very beginning of the poem. An argument like that made by Louise Economides, which argues that the only thing behind the veil of poetic figures in the Romantic sublime is radical and brute materiality, would see my reading at this point as recapitulating an all-too-common ideological position: 'to unify nature and language under the authority of a transcendental signified'.[35] This would only be true, however, were the name of God to be retained as a primarily referential or denotative part of language (i.e. a signified). By contrast, I would suggest that the alterity which makes itself felt in the temporal and spatial shifts also involves a sharp grammatical shift.

This is found in the movement towards a scene of prayer, announced most obviously in the line 'Ye signs and wonders of the element! / Utter forth God, and fill the hills with praise!' (ll.68–9). Mont Blanc is transformed into an altar, streaming heavenward like incense, and as the limits of the visible world in which the poem has rooted itself are massively expanded, the name of God undergoes a profound change in function. We noted above that when Kant discussed the veil of Isis and the Judaic commandment against idolatry, there was a grammatical disruption of referentiality by other modalities: negation and interdiction. Here, reference is displaced not by negation but by a radical vocative, a vocative that was always implicit in the poem, but becomes utterly dominant in the final stanzas. There is a distinct difference between 'God' as the answer to a teleological question, and 'God' as a shout of praise. If the horizon of worldhood has suddenly become dislocated in the final stanza, then the name of God becomes something cried out into infinity. In 'Confessions of an Inquiring Spirit' (1824), Coleridge describes the name of God, the I AM, as part of a religious category called *stasis*. Prayer, however, is part of *metastasis-anastasis* (change of state/rising up): the conflictual, dynamic, unfinished scene of human redemption that includes grace, love, hope and perseverance.[36] Whilst the teleological parts of the 'Hymn' attempt to enunciate the I AM, the maker's mark, its closing stanzas belong to *metastasis-anastasis*.

It is thus no surprise that a conspicuous sense of rising (*anastasis*) comes to dominate the end of the poem: the 'sky-pointing peaks' (l.70), the narrator's gaze, the sun and the voices all ascend 'from Earth to Heaven' (l.82). Notably, the movement of 'slow travelling' (l.77) ascent never ends, for prayer is a reaching out to a God that is fundamentally Other to his creation, due to his withdrawal. Calling out the name of God during prayer re-establishes the very distance between human subject and divine Other that the name of God as a sign or signature – an announcement in Heideggerian terms – is supposed to close. Thus whilst I would not deny the validity of our de Manian reading, nor that Coleridge's poem is primarily built on a physico-theological argument, a visionary claim and a transcendental signified, I would nevertheless draw attention to something else occurring at the end of the poem. This is the displacement of the visionary experience by an experience of the vocative, the sudden bursting of spatial boundedness and – most crucially of all – divine withdrawal.

As such, at its close, the poem overruns the boundaries of the Romantic nature sublime (or at least Coleridge's particular Christian appropriation thereof), and offers something much closer to the Kantian 'separation ... [as] a presentation of the infinite' (*Critique of Judgment*, p. 156). The experience of prayer is not one of reference, but of a vocative that displaces reference and may even call its possibility or relevance into question. Indeed, there is a strong relationship between prayer and non-referentiality. Augustine, for instance, is drawn to a question that implicitly places the performative (of confession, of love, of prayer) prior to reference: 'What, then, do I love when I love God?'[37] As Coleridge comments in a number of notebook entries, prayer is predicated on a disjunctive relationship which radically undermines a referential grasp of God. It is precisely God's excess over reference – 'Connection of Prayer with Faith ... the transcendency of religious Intuitions over Language' (*N*4183) – that means the name of God in prayer is a cry and not a designation. Elsewhere in the notebooks, he finds himself trapped in a language that he knows to be inadequate: 'I know indeed, that his ways are not our ways nor his Thoughts our Thoughts ... [yet] how can I love him, trust in him, call on him, but as a Man?' (*N*6155).

On the other hand, one might make an objection to this. Prayer's irreducibility to reference and signification has been challenged: after all, how does one pray to an addressee, without designating that addressee? In Derrida's words, the 'apostrophe of prayer' always implies the 'determination of encomium'.[38] What he means is that within the vocative of prayer there is always 'a predicative aim, however foreign it may be the "normal" ontological predication'.[39] 'The act of addressing oneself to the other as other' is always compromised in its grammatical purity by trying to designate, determine and delimit the Other.[40] Hent de Vries thus argues that 'prayer is from the outset and forever divided in and against itself'.[41] Yet whilst this admission of a predicative, denotative or referential necessity in prayer complicates my analysis, it is far from the problem it initially seems. For being-against-itself has always been very close to the essence of prayer. Derrida notes that 'there would be no prayer ... [without] writing, the code, repetition'.[42] Prayer must be considered as an experience of language, calling upon the name of God, which is perhaps the most improper and paradoxical word in language. Above, we noted that Coleridge put prayer into the category of *metastasis*, the primary signification of which is, interestingly, a transition between rhetorical figures. Arguably it is not the calling out for God *per se*, but the transition from reference to calling – the *metastasis* between the two – that is in question. Perhaps this wordless shift within a language of words is the truest and purest definition of prayer.[43]

The *metastasis* would be the moment when one's grasp on God begins to founder, a certain experience within and across the name of God, of doubt within faith, which opens the necessity for calling out. We see this marked in the very etymology of prayer: the Latin *precarium* signifying something granted at the pleasure of a superior and revocable at any moment. Prayer is precariousness. Prayer must occur within some context of referentiality, because it is itself the modality of speech appropriate to a crisis or limit of referentiality. It is when 'Hymn Before Sun-Rise' hits this negativity that its spatial scope suddenly explodes, in a Kantian fashion, to mark out the very edges of worldhood (the stars, the astronomical sphere, the infinite spaces of the universe), and the name of God undergoes its *metastasis* from signatory designator to vocative praise.

Coleridge's poetry is of course rich in many different representations of prayer: 'The Rime of the Ancient Mariner', 'Christabel', 'The Pains of

Sleep', 'To William Wordsworth' and many more. However, I will end this chapter with a brief look at two later texts that specifically continue the displacement of natural sublimity with an experience of prayer and divine withdrawal: 'To Nature' (probably written in 1820), and the 1833 lyric 'Love's Apparition and Evanishment'. The former poem begins its extended envoy in an apologetic tone:

> It may indeed be phantasy, when I
> Essay to draw from all created things
> Deep, heartfelt, inward joy that closely clings;
> And trace in leaves and flowers that round me lie
> Lessons of love and earnest piety.[44]

Of course, the poem signals itself by its title alone as fundamentally apostrophic, yet unlike 'Hymn Before Sun-Rise', this sonnet shows a sceptical and anxious awareness about the rhetorical problems surrounding apostrophe. The vocabulary of essaying, drawing and tracing is particularly interesting, conveying an awareness of linguistic power and the kind of exchanges and projections that may be carried on under the auspices of addressing a nature that speaks. Although Coleridge maintains a defiant 'so let it be' (l.6) and promises to 'build my altar in the fields' (l.9), the visionary claim so prominent in the 'Hymn' has been virtually dissolved, and the leading voice of a concert of creation has been reduced to the humble 'priest of this poor sacrifice' (l.14).

Looking closely at the sonnet's response to the problems of phantasy, described after the *volta*, we find that nature functions in a way different to that found in confidently visionary poetry such as 'Hymn Before Sun-Rise'. It acts not as a language of the noumenal, but rather as materials for worship. For instance, flowers are no longer evidences of design (as in 'Hymn Before Sun-Rise) but yield incense for the narrator's altar. The sky, which had been Mont Blanc's 'habitation from eternity' ('Hymn', l.12) and a kind of visionary window, is now the worshipper's 'fretted dome' ('To Nature', l.10). The landscape itself is far more quotidian than the sublime Alps, a place of individual leaves and flowers: instead of being a visionary text, it provides the rather more humble 'lessons of love and earnest piety' (l.5). The narrator is a much reduced figure from the glorified narrator of the 'Hymn' and his dilating soul: 'thou shalt not despise / Even me' (ll.13–14). 'To Nature', therefore, marks a retreat from the possibility of a visionary nature sublime. Instead, one has a decisive turn to the vocative. The world is a scene of offering, rather than of revelation, and in contrast to the insistent referentiality of the word God in the 'Hymn', here the interpersonal 'Thee' (l.12) has a clear grammatical priority. As such, we can see 'To Nature' as scaling back the grandeur of the Romantic nature sublime, and maintaining some sceptical distance from its own rhetoric.

'Love's Apparition and Evanishment' provides a rather different relationship between prayer and landscape. It is, in fact, not the poem as a whole in which I am interested, but the conceit of its first eight lines:

> Like a lone Arab, old and blind
> Some caravan had left behind
> Who sits beside a ruin'd well,
> Where the shy sand-asps bask and swell;
> And now he hangs his aged head aslant,
> And listens for a human sound – in vain!
> And now the aid, which Heaven alone can grant,
> Upturns his eyeless face from Heaven to gain; –[45]

Deserts are certainly environments with sublime overtones. Yet, in a far starker way than any mountainous landscape, the desert is evoked here as an ascesis of sensibility, where the ruined well can stand as a metaphor for the desolation of both nature (the absence of water) and human life (the abandoned structure). In turn, this desolation reflects the desertification of the anonymous human subject at the centre of the scene. The Arab is a degree zero of subjectivity. Blind and abandoned, deprived of all interrelationship and phenomenal experience ('listens for a human sound – in vain!' (l.6)), his consciousness is as barren as the waterless desert in which he sits.

Yet, having stripped away nearly everything from the human subject and set it in a stance of total exposure, Coleridge identifies a relationship that is somehow indestructibly there at the very root of being. Seeking the Other – God – even when his experience is reduced to desolation, the poem expresses a yearning that appears to be fundamental to, in the literal sense of at the foundation of, the subject. Instinctively, when all else is lost and human life exists only in its barest form, the Arab turns to God, asking for the relation 'which Heaven alone can grant'. Moreover, the prayer that is forced from the Arab by the ascesis of the sensible (this forcing would perhaps correspond to the moment of *metastasis* examined above) is strongly figured as a waiting. The upturning of the face, as a gesture of openness and exposure, is an act of what Jean-Louis Chrétien has described as *anthropophany*: a showing of the human to God, in contrast to the signs of theophany which the visionary seeks in order for God to show himself to humans.[46] The representation of the Arab comes about as close to a purely vocative prayer, in the passion and passivity of his waiting, as is possible.

The radical passivity of his prayer should also guard against the temptation to read the Arab in the tradition of visionary blindness. Whilst he is blind, this does not mean he is being portrayed as seeing pseudo-mystically into the supersensible in a way sanctioned by cultural history (e.g. Homer, John Milton) and not alien to Coleridge's poetry either (e.g. the watcher figure in 'Limbo'). Rather, as with the Kantian logic of the negative presentation, the veil of Isis or the interdiction of idols, what is at stake is separation: here figured as the radical dislocation of human subjectivity from its existence in sensibility. This is how the blindness of the Arab should be read. In the sublime, Kant's imagination is said to find nothing on which to fix itself; the Arab motif here expands this to the existential level, affecting the whole subject which faces sensibility as a desert, as a desolation. The Coleridgean twist on this Kantian theme is to lay bare, as something which underlies this desertified, deserted subjectivity, a necessity for prayer: radically passive, radically exposed, radically vocative. Where the prayer in 'To Nature' is articulated in a context that is guarded about the possibility of nature's spiritual significance, the prayer here is uttered in a context forcefully alienated from nature, taking to an extreme the position that prayer must be reverence of the invisible. In the deserted, inhuman sands of 'Love's Apparition and Evanishment', we are a long way from the rich natural teleology that underpinned the middle sections of Coleridge's paean to Mont Blanc.

It is interesting that we have, not for the first time, returned to the figure of a subjectivity exposed. Perhaps this is the logical product of a sublimity that, as I have argued throughout, may trace the limits of immanence without necessarily asserting the successful movement towards transcendence: that is, a subjectivity that must narrate a kind of ellipsis within itself. The emotionally potent 'I' that we previously identified as the centre of a Longinian poetics found itself transformed into an exposed self in the Sapphic mode, when the fabular staging of its emotional figures to itself was revealed as abyssal and groundless. Similarly, in 'The Rime of the Ancient Mariner', the unified, empiricist subjectivity that was used to frame experiences of terror was overturned by a subject which confronted a rift within itself: a dark stain, a hollow place in the self, and exposure to an ethical guilt which exists prior to any act. The drive to elevate the soul through a sacramental experience of nature is perhaps a more resilient aspect of Coleridge's aesthetics, and it offers the Romantic self's most powerful site for transcendence.

And yet even here we have found the possibility of a self exposed, in prayer.

In conclusion, we may identify 'Hymn Before Sun-Rise' as the high-water mark of Coleridge's theistic appropriation of the Romantic nature sublime. Whilst Coleridge never abandoned the possibilities of a rapturous Christian experience of nature – something of the kind is reiterated as part of *The Statesman's Manual*'s argument on symbolism, for example – he would never write such an explicit example again.[47] Not least, he began to show, as Raimonda Modiano suggests, 'an increasing preference for love objects, which displace natural objects as the means of fulfilling the self's aspiration of unity with the divine'.[48] Our reading of 'To Nature' and the opening motif of 'Love's Apparition and Evanishment' should have further confirmed this retreat. However, as I have shown, we should not treat 'Hymn Before Sun-Rise' simply and solely as an example of the visionary appropriation of nature under the auspices of the sublime. The poem also points beyond itself in a more nuanced way. In contrast to its highly problematic visionary claim, the final turn of the poem towards a scene of prayer, and the overrunning of the referential by the vocative, embraces a rather different logic. This is closer to Kant's treatment of divine names as negative presentations. Despite its attempts to root God firmly in the sensible world, the last stanzas of the poem attest decisively to something *other* than the sensible.

6
'What never is but only is to be': the Ontology of the Coleridgean Sublime

In the previous chapter, it was argued that prayer – as a grammatical modality that overran the referential with the vocative – attested to a divine withdrawal from the world, mirroring Kant's analysis of the Judaic interdiction on idols and the veil of Isis. Far from asserting reconciliation between the sensible and the transcendent (as Coleridge's visionary aesthetic demanded), the name marked its own inadequacy of reference in a complex, *negative* gesture towards the transcendent. Yet, although the name of God, the improper name on which prayer calls, is always intertwined with this strange and unique grammar, it does so through firmly theological presuppositions. We are impelled to ask, therefore, whether the motif of something beyond presentation can ever be thought in a way that does not demand to be grounded in theology? Jean-Luc Nancy, for instance, has suggested that the divine name has come to dominate our thinking of the non-presentable in a paralysing and limited way, 'as if "God" were in fragments, an Osiris dismembered throughout all our discourse'.[1] Philosophy, he goes on to argue, should reappropriate the possibility of this thought from its theological history. In this chapter, I want to look more closely at how Coleridge grounds his thinking on presentation, the beyond-of-presentation and sublimity, and assess the relationship between philosophy and theology in his late thought.

This will first involve looking at Coleridge's formalist definitions of the sublime, which are perhaps the most explicit and specific references in his corpus to the concept. Drawing on a long-standing association of the sublime with a sense of totality, sublimity is defined as a presentation of 'all-ness' where the so-called comparative power is suspended. However, probing the logic of this definition, we find it may well abolish the possibility of presentation, given that a thought of everything seemingly erases all distinctions and differences. The thought of *all* sensible being, as a totality, seems to end up with a thought of nothingness (similar to Hegel's famous definition of one kind of absolute as a night in which all the cows are black). However, by drawing the links between this sublime of all-ness and monism (the doctrine that the world is all one substance), we can look at Coleridge's metaphysical moves away from monism to find contexts for a different kind of sublime, a sublime that works from a radically different thought of presentation. He becomes increasingly interested not in how the world is presented, but why there is a world given in the first place. To what extent he can only think this givenness in theological terms – and *which* kind of theological terms – will be a question I consider at the end of this chapter, in dialogue with Jean-Luc Nancy's work on the sublime offering.

The suspension of the comparative power: all-ness and nothingness

Among the most concrete references to the sublime in Coleridge's work are two fragments of 1814, written at a time when he was taking an increasing interest in systematising philosophical positions on art. The texts entitled 'Definition of Aesthetic Terms' and 'On the Distinction Between the Picturesque and the Sublime' are – perhaps unusually given the preferences of the later Coleridge – formalist and empirical. They arrange carefully distinguished categories on the basis of the relations of part and whole as they exist in the perception of an object or scene. Although the lists differ slightly, a broad spectrum of types can be identified, moving from those characterised by clarity of perception and articulation, notably the beautiful, through a range of middle terms lessening the perceptual grip on the object, and culminating in the sublime. Thus, for example, the shapely involves a perception where both parts and whole are seen distinctly (the beautiful is characterised in one list by a clear rather than a distinct apprehension of parts, and with the addition of pleasure to the perception of the shapely in the other). The picturesque, in both fragments, involves a lessened sense of the whole whilst maintaining clear perception of parts, in contrast to categories like the statuesque or majestic, where a sense of the whole is dominant but perception of parts is absent or deficient.

Given that one end of this continuum involves clarity and distinctness in both part and whole, it is natural that an opposing category emerges to articulate the absence of both part *and* whole in the aesthetic perception. Sublimity occupies this place on the scale, defined in the 'Definition' thus: 'Let there be (i.e. ~~in our~~ as Objects of our Conscious

[? ~~At~~] Attention) neither Whole, or Parts, but in *All* suspending the Comparative Power, and there results the SUBLIME.'[2] The same emphases characterise the description in 'On the Distinction', which figures the sublime as 'neither Whole or parts – but Unity as boundless or endless *Allness*'.[3] Sublimity is thus a perception where the presentation of an object is radically suspended, and Coleridge's formalism reaches a terminal point as both part and whole cease to be perceived. What is left is an indeterminate sense of all-ness, a whole so perceptually absorbing that its very articulation as a whole disappears.

Coleridge's fomalisation of the sublime here mirrors some familiar Kantian themes. *The Critique of Judgment* had itself involved a theory of beauty which was formalist at heart, describing a free-play of the imagination over the perceived object and largely privileging purely formal aesthetic objects – such as patterns of arabesque – over representational ones. The formlessness of sublime objects identified later in the *Critique* mirrors Coleridge's definition of the sublime as the absence of both part and whole in the perception of the object, suggesting that the sublime is a vanishing point for the formalism in both Kantian aesthetics and the ideas Coleridge was exploring in 1814. Furthermore, in the 'Definition', we find an explicit Kantian economy initiated on the basis of the suspension of the comparative power. Coleridge asserts that 'objects of sense never can be of themselves *sublime*', claiming that objects are only sublime in so far as their perception – or perhaps more accurately, the disruption to their perception – excites sublime feelings and ideas.[4] This assertion, as discussed in the previous chapter, is one of Kant's major innovations. However, I feel that Coleridge's definitions betray a persistent negativity that not only parts him from Kant, but suggests a more radical thought – and threat – that all-ness will become a vacant and undifferentiated absolute: a totality turned into a negation.

Despite Kant's recurrent vocabulary of the negative, the notion of a failure of imagination to grasp its object is counterbalanced by an imagination liberated.[5] Kant allows a positive unleashing of the imagination at a point where forms seem to lose their formality. Coleridge's analysis of the sublime, however, seems to exclude this possibility. Suspension is the key trope in all Coleridge's discussions of form: it is not even that imagination rebounds off one of its limits with a certain energy, it is merely arrested by a stasis born of total absorption by and into its object. It is not so much a failed imagination but a paralysed one. Indeed, one might ask how the symbolic aspect mentioned in the 'Definition', where the formlessness of the perceived object stands in for some idea, can possibly work when the imagination is neither blocked nor liberated, but stilled. How can one have an essentially comparative relation, such as the one between object and idea, when the comparative power has been explicitly negated?

Within the perceptual schemas laid out in 1814, the suspension of the comparative power thus hints not at a liberated imagination, but at one abolished into the condition of non-perception. The all-ness Coleridge considers as sublime may become an abyssal sense of the whole, one into which the 'I' falls and confronts as negation itself. Like Hegel's famous night in which all the cows are black, this absolute is nothing rather than being. I would argue that this relationship between negation and all-ness needs to be recognised as a long-standing one. For example, a letter of 1797 to John Thellwall establishes a clear, if less theoretically complex, connection between the sublime and an undifferentiated sense of totality:

> My mind feels as if it ached to behold & know something *great* – something *one* & *indivisible* – and it is only in the faith of this that rocks or waterfalls, mountains or caverns give me the sense of sublimity or majesty! (*CL*, I.349)

Coleridge goes on to give this act of perception a theological aspect, quoting a rapt passage from his own 'This Lime-Tree Bower My Prison'. As one finds confirmed in a letter written two days later, Coleridge's sense of the whole is supposedly connected to transcendent longings. Whereas empiricists see the universe as 'a mass of *little things*', Coleridge states that he has 'a love of "the Great", & "the whole"', a love which has ensured that he 'never regarded [his] *senses* in any way as the criteria of [his] belief' (*CL*, I.354).

On the other hand, the possibility of a perception of the whole is haunted by something else. Coleridge also admits in his letter to Thelwall that 'it is but seldom that I raise & spiritualize my intellect to this height', and this is where a darker, more negative side to all-ness emerges. He states that

> at other times I adopt the Brahman Creed ... Death is the best of all! – I should much wish, like the Indian Vishna, to float about along an infinite ocean cradled in the flower of the Lotos, & wake once in a million years for a few minutes. (*CL*, I.350)

Drawing on metaphors of death, intoxication and sleep, Coleridge counterpoints the Western thought of transcendence with an Orientalist thought of self-abnegation, the dissolving of perception into an infinite yet strangely empty space. Whilst this supposedly Vishnaic existence encompasses a kind of absolute – this is a faith parallel to that in the '*one & indivisible*' mentioned earlier in the letter – it is one which draws the perceiver into the deathly embrace of a total, infinite negation.

We can also see a similar set of dynamics in the fragment 'Christmas Out of Doors', from an 1809 number of *The Friend*. Coleridge describes a winter storm breaking over the ice-bound waters of Lake Ratzeburg:

> During the whole night, such were the thunders and howlings of the breaking ice, that they have left a conviction on my mind, that there are sounds more sublime than any sight can be, more absolutely suspending the power of comparison, and more utterly absorbing the mind's self-consciousness in its total attention to the object working upon it. Part of the ice, which the vehemence of the wind had shattered, was driven shoreward and froze anew.

It is hard to square Coleridge's later insistence that objects are not themselves sublime with the description rendered here of the all-consuming and absolute sovereignty of the object.[6] The splintering and churning mass of ice, much like the infinite ocean in the 1797 letter, is a blank and chaotic field that absorbs perception into itself without remainder, rather than standing for anything outside of itself. Indeed, it is only the following day when locals set to work on the ice, driving holes through it in order to fish, that Coleridge gives the scene an overlay of transcendent meaning: 'it appeared as if the rich crimson light has shaped itself into these forms, figures, and attitudes, to make a glorious vision in mockery of earthly things'.[7] Before this human intervention, the icy lake is an all-ness that is abyssal for the imagination. Like the ice-fields of 'The Rime of the Ancient Mariner', there is a sense of overwhelming vacancy and paralysis for which the ice itself (cold, frozen, white) might stand as an appropriate metonym.

The same threat is thus raised both by Coleridge's theoretical analysis of the suspension of the comparative power and the more elaborate and concrete descriptions found in the letter to Thelwall and 'Christmas Out of Doors'. This threat is whether a thought of totality actually reverts to a thought of nothing. As he writes to his wife in March 1799, an undifferentiated whole risks becoming a substance voided of attributes and accidents: 'I have been so forsaken by all the *forms* and *colouring* of Existence, as if the *organs* of Life had been dried up, as if only simply BEING remained, blind and stagnant' (*CL*, I.470). It is with this reading of all-ness in mind that I want to turn to two poems: 'Coeli Enarrant' and 'Human Life: On the Denial of Immortality'.[8] These poems not only articulate and engage the threat of 'simply BEING ... blind and stagnant', but also reveal some of the spiritual and metaphysical issues at stake.

Two metaphysical lyrics: 'Coeli Enarrant' and 'Human Life'

The two lyrics I want to consider in this section shift the thought of all-ness firmly towards its most infinite dimensions: that is, a sense of all that exists, the whole of the universe itself. The all-embracing vision of 'Coeli Enarrant' is one that mirrors many of the elements found in the 1814 writings. It begins with a liminal perceptual state, where one finds a totality of form outstripping form itself. Coleridge describes a perception that is 'wakeful over all', reaching a point of bliss and which 'in its excess became a Dream'.[9] Just as the 1814 fragments posit the absence of both part and whole, here there is 'no gradation' (l.1). Time and space blur into one another and create a 'space like Time' (l.7): the formal frames that constitute individual objects – the Kantian conditions of possibility for the sensory manifold, if one will – are set trembling and a resultant sense of all-ness absorbs the 'I'. The perceived world at its formal limit becomes nothing more than a 'still spreading web' (l.8).

Whilst the poem does involve a vocabulary of transfiguration, any hint of transcendence is counterbalanced by the way the 'still-spreading web' exerts its paralysing perceptual sovereignty. One can even read the poem as describing a radical immanence: the absorbing of every sensible form into all other sensible forms, and the 'I' into that all-encompassing field. The perceiving subject is swallowed up in its own perception, so that sense, thought and sensation 'lived in my eye' (l.4). The final lines of the first stanza describe how 'on the still spreading web I still diffused / Lay still commensurate' (ll.8–9), the triple repetition of 'still' not only marking the infinitely expanding sense of all-ness, but also intimating the subject's passivity before this all-ness. The 'I' is 'commensurate', or of the same measure, with the totality in which it is diffused and absorbed. Such radical immanence is also apparent in a temporal register, where we find temporal arrest and absorption in the absolutely momentary:

> For memory & all undoubting Hope
> Sang the same note & in the selfsame Voice,
> with each sweet *now* of my Felicity (ll.10–12)

The horizons of the subject in past and future are rendered so they become identical reflections of the present, indistinguishable as 'mirrors each reflecting each' (l.17). The closest analogy that Coleridge can find for these experiences of time and space is infancy, the inarticulate, pre-symbolic, oceanic state where the 'Milk that coming comes & in its easy stream / Flows ever in' (ll.14–15). Such a simile is appropriate, because the subject has been wrenched back to an almost pre-conscious state of being at one with the universe.

The poem's initial verses, then, articulate a sense of all-ness and the passage of forms (gradation, time, space) into a single, all-absorbing, web-like totality. It is telling that the first stanza is dominated by the alliteration of 's', and the second by 'm', since the integration of all things into a single measure, such as the single note of the *now*, is the exact point at issue. However, the beatific sense of being at one with the world is but a midpoint, a hinge leading to two further stanzas that operate with a very different sense of the world's totality. As Edward Kessler puts it, 'the sublimity of these early lines, perhaps because they have mystical, trance-like overtones, is balanced ... by a darker vision'.[10] It is this darker vision that mirrors the Vishnaic death-sleep, the unmeaning terror of the Ratzeburg storm or the stagnancy of mere being. From an exultant embrace of all-ness, 'Coeli Enarrant' turns to the terrifying sense of an absolute characterised not by its 'excess' (l.2) but infinite vacancy and negation: 'what never is but only is to be' (l.18).

As this opening line of the third stanza makes clear, it is ontological issues that are in question. The juxtaposition of a serene absorption in being with a being that declares its own emptiness shifts Coleridge's tone from the blissful to the horrified: 'This is not Life – / O Hopeless Hope, and Death's Hypocrisy!' (ll.19–20). A sense of all-ness breaks the promise of transcendence hinted at in the twenty-first line, and instead Coleridge's vision of totality becomes one of all-encompassing nullity. The oceanic sense celebrated earlier once more reverts to the familiar figure of the abyss, as the most infinite formal boundaries of the universe – the celestial – suddenly turn blank and void:

> The stars that wont to start, as on a chase,
> And twinkling insult on Heaven's darkened Face,
> Like a conven'd Conspiracy of Spies
> Wink at each other with confiding eyes,
> Turn from the portent, all is blank on high,
> No constellations alphabet the Sky –
> The Heavens one large black letter only shews,

> And as a Child beneath its master's Blows
> Shrills out at once its Task and its Affright,
> The groaning world now learns to read aright,
> And with its Voice of Voices cries out, O! (ll.22–32)

The figure of the 'O!' here is particularly dense with meaning. It signifies the inarticulate cry of a world that can express only fear and pain, tortured by the sinister 'conspiracy' and prison of its own immanence (i.e. the fact that its being is mere being, and thus to Coleridge nihilistic). Yet, it is also suggestively linked with the 'one large black letter' that the world reads from its own celestial frame. Of course, such a single letter is, as with Shakespeare's quarto ending to *King Lear*, a zero too: the cipher of the purest negation. What the stars, those archetypal signifiers of transcendence, spell out is nothingness itself, a nothingness under which the world is crushed. The world's totality, the totality of perceived forms, thus adds up to nought. The immanence of the world to itself, troped by the very circularity of the letter 'O' as an image of the whole, is ultimately empty. What 'only is to be' never really is, but is non-being. Like the 'O' it is empty inside.

There are thus two radically different perceptions of all-ness at work in the poem. The initial whole without gradation that 'in its excess became a Dream' (l.2) is counterpoised against a world that as a whole means nothing, ontologically void: 'all is blank on high'. The lamenting 'Voice of Voices' with which the poem closes reverses the happy image of the first section, 'the Babe's murmuring Mouth' (l.16). The characteristic tautologies and involutions that trope sublime unity in the first section – 'each reflecting each' (l.17) and 'that coming comes' (l.14) – become disturbing paradoxes and negations in the second: 'Hopeless Hope' (l.20) and 'with perpetual Promise, breaks its Promises' (l.21). Raimonda Modiano notes, *pace* the sublime, that Coleridge always draws on 'the quality of perceptual indistinctness which allows certain objects to lose their individual form and blend with one another into a whole'.[11] She is correct, but perhaps overlooks this persistent threat of formal indistinction becoming ontological emptiness, as the perception of a totality leaves nothing more than undifferentiated, or stagnant, being. More so than in the texts examined so far, 'Coeli Enarrant' – with its imagery of conspiracy and violence – broaches the existential dimension of being part of such a nullity.

An even sharper combination of ontological with existential anxiety can be found in 'Human Life: On the Denial of Immortality'. Like 'Coeli Enarrant', it confronts the perception of all-ness that is haunted by nothingness. This may at first seem far from the text's obvious concern, which the title announces as the immortality of the soul. Yet, as one reads 'Human Life', one realises that it is just as much about the ontological state of the soul in this world as in heaven. Alongside the fear of non-being after death, 'Human Life' evokes a state of non-being in life itself. The poem's portrait of the consequences of materialism is nihilistic, the fear that we are

> As summer-gusts, of sudden birth and doom,
> Whose sound and motion not alone declare,
> But are their whole of being! If the breath
> Be life itself, and not its task and tent.[12]

What the poem fears – and argues against in the name of religion – is that human life can be assimilated to an immanent whole. If such a totality could be conceived, Coleridge avers, it would be a form of non-being. It would render existence a nothingness.

One can see this in two recurring figures: the image of a wasted surplus and the economy of zero-sum exchanges. The first tropes Coleridge's anxiety that human life cannot be given any ontological value separate from that of the totality of material nature. At best, it can be seen as a null excess, a purely contingent formation which, as with the summer winds, is only briefly autonomous and shall be swiftly reabsorbed into the whole from which it came:

> Surplus of nature's dread activity,
> Which as she gazed on some nigh-finished vase,
> Retreating slow, with meditative pause,
> She formed with restless hands unconsciously!
> Blank accident! nothing's anomaly! (ll.10–14)

The rhetoric of the craftsman is ironically inappropriate here, for human life is nothing more than an epiphenomenon, a hollow conduit for the forces of blind nature: 'O Man! thou vessel purposeless, unmeant' (l.9). There is no doubt that someone as metaphysically fluent as Coleridge would have used 'accident' with full awareness of its philosophical meaning, hinting that human life is merely an attribute or mode of a single substance, in a somewhat Spinozan fashion. The impression of meaningfulness, purposiveness, self-consciousness and freedom in human existence is just 'nothing's anomaly': an unusual and striking modification of a material substrate that is fundamentally meaningless, purposeless, unconscious and deterministic. This allows Coleridge to posit the nihilistic reversal this chapter has repeatedly identified as haunting the thought of all-ness: being into nothing, substance into the 'substanceless' (l.15).

The second figure is the meaningless exchange of qualities. In the context of a totality, the diversity of human existential meanings is shown to cancel itself out:

> Go, weigh thy dreams, and be thy hopes, thy fears,
> The counter-weights! – Thy laughter and thy tears
> Mean but themselves, each fittest to create,
> And to repay the other! (ll.16–19)

The radical immanence that we have seen threaten the thought of all-ness recurs here as a feeling that existence can be reduced to a form of mechanics. Things 'mean but themselves' – something that leads to a zero-sum in so far as the totality balances all its forces and it is impossible to refer meaning to anything outside the totality's own self-contained workings. The 'transcendent anti-diversitarianism' Seamus Perry rightly identifies as a strong element of Coleridge's thinking threatens to abolish meaning itself in its abolition of differences.[13] This leads one to repeat the nihilistic thought that the world does not form a sublime unity, but rather an empty cipher without meaning and value. Human life, if it can truly be absorbed into immanence, becomes for Coleridge a hollow play of counterbalancing fictions that can always be reduced to the blankness of pure, neutral being: 'Be sad! be glad! be neither! seek, or shun! / Thou hast no reason why!' (ll.27–8).

Given its dominant focus on the non-being of life within a materialist universe, therefore, we can see that 'Human Life' is not so much a poem about immortality as one about monism. As Perry points out, referring to the One Life doctrine which always threatened to revert to materialism, 'monist determinism is never far away'.[14] 'Human Life' portrays what Coleridge thought to be the consequences of such a monism: it envisages the totality of 'nature's dread activity' (l.10) where human life is but an empty efflorescence and the richness of human experience and value is but the hollow exchange of accidents, attributes and modes within a deathly whole of pure, neutral substance. Ontologically, Coleridge's conclusion is that such a substance, in the immanence of its all-embracing all-ness, is an abyssal '*total* gloom' (l.1, my emphasis), a non-being rather than a being. As the poem concludes, under such a hypothesis 'thy being's being is contradiction' (l.29).

Our reading of 'Human Life', in particular, highlights Coleridge's difficult relationship with monism as a relevant context for his formalist sublime. What I have argued is that a nominally transcendent perception of all-ness can lead to an undifferentiated negative abyss, swallowing all around it into a blank and moribund immanence. This, I would suggest, mirrors Coleridge's travails with pantheism, Spinozism and the One Life doctrine. There too a positive transcendence – a unity posited between the world and the divine – became threatening in so far as he feared a pantheistic absolute which absorbs everything into a single, deterministic system. This risks both the thesis of human freedom and autonomy that Coleridge took from Kant, and the personeity and transcendence of the Godhead that was fundamental to his later Christianity. In this sense, our readings in this chapter can be folded into a long tradition of Coleridge criticism on the existential and ontological dangers of totality: the classic reading being Thomas McFarland's still invaluable *Coleridge and the Pantheist Tradition*, and one of the most recent the impressive work of synthesis practised by Seamus Perry in his *Coleridge and the Uses of Division*. Whenever Coleridge invoked the faith in something one and indivisible, the presentation of formal all-ness was always haunted by the deathliness of the Vishnaic abyss. A thought of the all could quickly become a thought of infinite negation: the aesthetic counterpart to Coleridge's fear of monism.

Given the wider backdrop to the issues, I believe that it is important to be specific when tracing Coleridge's responses. For instance, merely invoking Christian doctrine as shorthand for Coleridge's evasion of pantheist or determinist implications is certainly not enough. One must follow this up with questions: What Christian doctrines? How do they function? How do the theological ideas relate to philosophical tropes? Even Perry's humanistic liberalism of ideas – suggesting that Coleridge permitted unity and diversity to sit together in a productive muddle – seems a little too easy. Coleridge, despite it all, tried to theorise a rigorous passage through his intellectual difficulties. In this vein, I believe that it is possible to identify a particular, coherent type of sublimity that succeeds his formalist sublime, reflecting his metaphysic's increasing distance from any monism. It is founded not on a sense of all-ness, but a sense of givenness. By this I mean that the aesthetic notes of 1814, and the other texts we have already discussed, reach the limit of formalism in strictly formalist terms. They work according to a logic of presentation. The sublime is the point when a form (in some cases, like the metaphysical lyrics, the world itself) can no longer be perceived with gradation, part, whole and distinction, but only as boundlessness and all-ness. However, Coleridge later shifts his emphasis away from the presentation of forms, to something that lies outside any logic of presentation. What increasingly strikes Coleridge is ontological and existential rather than perceptual and formal: not the boundlessness of a form that exists, but the fact – or riddle – that forms exist at all.

Being and givenness: 'The Consideration of Existence' in *The Friend*

We may get some hold on how Coleridge's preoccupations shift from formalism and presentation by returning to the questions of 'Human Life'. We noted there that he was at pains to resist the assimilation and absorption of human life into a totality: the homogenising embrace of all-ness was to be resisted in the name of difference. However, under what logic could such a difference be articulated? Certainly Coleridge's answer would always be theological (the non-materiality of the immortal soul), but it also involves a particular philosophical theme, as one can see if one turns to a poem on related concerns, 1811's 'The Suicide's Argument'. There is no doubt that this text, like 'Human Life', is Christian in its outlook, but it expresses its Christianity in terms that are philosophically very interesting. Human life ceases to become a question of physical or metaphysical identity (what is human life?), but an existential one. The answer to the essence of human life is to be a question itself:

> If the life was the question, a thing sent to try,
> And to live on be Yes; what can No be? to die.[15]

This, in turn, allows Coleridge to articulate themes of destining and the gift in order to answer the moral question of suicide. What is distinctive about human life is that it is given, and demands a response to (within) this givenness. Although couched in light and almost comic diction, it marks a fundamentally different way of seeing the being of the human, refusing to identify it as a substance, as it threatened to be in 'Human Life', and figuring it instead as a gift: 'Is't returned, as 'twas sent? Is't no worse for the wear?'[16]

This trope of the given becomes central to the remarkable culminating passage on being that one finds in the 1818 redaction of *The Friend*.[17] What is at stake here, whilst beginning from the consideration of forms, is deeper than form itself. This is the fact that forms are a given and that the contrary ('there is nothing') cannot be imagined:

> Hast thou ever said to thyself thoughtfully, It is! heedless in that moment, whether it were a man before thee, or a flower, or a grain of sand ... If thou hast indeed attained to this, thou wilt have felt

> the presence of a mystery, which must have fixed thy spirit in awe and wonder. The very words, There is nothing! or, There was a time, when there was nothing! are self-contradictory.[18]

As noted by Herbert Read, this stretch of prose bears an uncanny resemblance to certain elements of Heidegger's thought.[19] In particular, Heidegger's text 'What is Metaphysics?' pursues the paradoxical nature of the nothing noted by Coleridge into the experience of existential anxiety. Towards the end of the essay, he turns like Coleridge to an experience of wonder – tinged with more angst, no doubt, but nevertheless still rooted in the same intuitions as those noted by *The Friend*:

> Only because the nothing is manifest in the ground of Dasein can the total strangeness of beings overwhelm us. Only when the strangeness of beings oppresses us does it arouse and evoke wonder. Only on the ground of wonder – the revelation of the nothing – does the 'why?' loom before us.[20]

The irreducible givenness of being is an arche-question for both Coleridge and Heidegger: put simply, 'why are there beings at all, and why not rather nothing?'[21]

However, if being is a 'given', then this should be understood in its full semantic sense: not only as an irrefutable datum to existence, but as a kind of gift. Jean-Luc Marion has argued that Heidegger was too keen to occlude his own motif of the *es gibt* (the opening of being, the 'there is' as 'it gives') within a metaphysical horizon, and I believe that it is the *es gibt* that is fundamental to the experience that Coleridge analyses.[22] Certainly, the passage begins with what Heidegger would later formalise as the ontico-ontological difference: the consideration of the 'It is' (of being) as opposed to the ontic forms (or beings), such as flower, man or grain of sand. Yet, the discussion is not really about stripping away the ontic particularly of forms, leaving a vision of a category of pure being. Not least, that gesture would threaten to revert to the same undifferentiated absolute – the stagnancy of a universal substance without accidents – we saw again and again earlier in this chapter. Indeed, something of this danger is intimated when Coleridge warns against conceiving being on the level of the Kantian understanding, which would involve foolishly seeking 'absolute fulness in mere negation' (I.515).

Coleridge's emphasis is different. What fascinates him is the coming to pass of existence, the coming-to-be of being: the fact that set off against the possibility of nothingness, existents have arisen, and that a world has opened up. There is thus a kind of internal distance marked out in the thought of the world: between the presentation of particular forms and the originary opening up of presentation itself, between the fact of what a thing is, and the fact that it is (or things are) at all. The latter facts have a priority over the former, and it is this relationship that is the true source of the wonder: 'to no class of phaenomena or particulars can it [being] be referred, itself being none'.[23] Coleridge is not so much interested in being as a substance or metaphysical category, but as something that befalls us, that is gift and given. Like one's life in 'The Suicide's Argument', being is destined and offered. Just as Heidegger does, a rhetoric of arrival and advent emerges: 'the idea itself, which, like a mighty billow, at once overwhelms and bears aloft – what is it? Whence did it come?'[24] And again like Heidegger, Coleridge moves towards the motif of manifestation in order to attest to this coming. However, for *The Friend* (openly theological in a way that Heidegger disallowed) the manifestation, advent and gift of phenomenality become inevitably intertwined with revelation: 'And the manifesting power, the source and correlative of the idea thus manifested – is it not God? Either thou knowest it to be God, or thou hast called an idol by that awful name!'[25]

I will return to the crucial juncture where Coleridge shifts firmly to the theological register of revelation – framing and sublating the mystery of the TO BE with faith in the I AM that I AM – at the end of this chapter. However, before doing so, I want to return to the sublime. I believe that the wonder of being as conceptualised in *The Friend* can be formulated most accurately as a thought of the sublime. Most obviously, one can identify a series of familiar tropes structuring Coleridge's description. For instance, the figure of the billowing wave that simultaneously uplifts and overwhelms, cited above, partakes of the archetypally sublime combination of danger and transcendence. Equally, there is a prominent vocabulary of astoundment – 'fixed thy spirit in awe and wonder' – which has also been close to hand in discussions of the sublime. There are specific echoes too. Coleridge claims that the thought of being was one that 'in earlier ages seized the nobler minds ... with a sort of sacred horror', thus recalling a certain Burkean logic of religious terror. A Kantian emphasis on the moral nobility of humankind is apparent when he argues that 'this it was which first caused them to feel within themselves a something ineffably greater than their own individual nature ... projecting them to an ideal distance from themselves'. There is even a gesture towards his own favourite trope, that of all-ness: 'BEING limitless, comprehending its own limits in its dilation' (I.514).

At a more fundamental and structural level, the thought of givenness involves an excess over what is intuitable and comprehensible that possesses a classically sublime logic. As David Vallins has noted, Coleridge's later writings are often characterised by turning the sublime towards paradox and antinomy: 'effortful attempts to articulate those ideas which most resist expression'.[26] The facticity of being is irreducible and undeniable, but it is also impossible to fully understand or explain: 'Not to be, then, is impossible; to be, incomprehensible'.[27] Driven against itself, thought cannot grasp the one thing that it must always already presuppose: being. The inextricable counterpart to identifying the statement 'there *is* nothing' as impossible is to acknowledge 'there is ...' as a tautology. Thought sets off from being and must posit and accept the *is* at the heart of all its predications, always already given to it. As Coleridge puts it, the sense of being is not so much something we can possess (as an intuition, concept or thought), but something that possesses us:

> [One] bears witness of it [being] to his own mind, even as he describes life and light; and, with the silence of light, it describes itself and dwells in *us* only in as far as we dwell in *it*.[28]

Hence, there is an intuition that is necessary and yet impossible to articulate at the root of the world. The world fails to formalise itself, invoking a sense of paradox neatly described in *Aids to Reflection*: '*there is nothing, the absolute ground of which is not a Mystery*. The contrary were indeed a contradiction in terms: for how can that, which is to explain all things, be susceptible of an explanation?' (p. 139). This is sublime in so far as its logic traces out the very boundary of the thinkable.

I would argue, then, that when *The Friend* describes Coleridge's wonder at being, it is describing a form of sublimity. However, if so, it marks a fundamental shift away from the formalist analysis he earlier favoured. The difference is precisely because *The Friend* involves a sublime that thinks something logically prior to the formal: the question of why there are forms at all, rather than no forms, and why there is being rather than nothing. Hence, one moves from thinking the sublime formally (one cannot grasp the formal character of something that exists) to thinking it ontologically (one cannot grasp the *given* character of something that exists). Coleridge, in emphasising givenness rather than all-ness, opens up the possibility of a sublime that is *non-eidetic*, or outside of the logic of form and presentation. It is with this in mind that I want to compare the reading of *The Friend* I have just made with two contemporary examples of non-eidetic thinking: Jean-Luc Nancy's 'The Sublime Offering' and Jean-Luc Marion's *Being and Givenness*. Not only will these texts clarify how Coleridge's discussion of being in *The Friend* fits into the tradition and theory of the sublime, but they also return us to the question of revelation. To what extent is thinking a sublime of givenness a motif that we can detach from theology? This will allow us to return to the Christian turn in *The Friend* (and similar gestures made in other texts) and make a final judgement on the relationship to both theology *and* philosophy of Coleridge's thinking on something beyond presentation.

Givenness and givers: theology and the sublime

In the previous chapter, we argued that the negative presentation in Kant could best be interpreted as an overrunning of the referential function of language by other modalities: negation and interdiction. Jean-Luc Nancy has argued, however, for an even more radical logic at work in Kant:

> There can be no presentation of the unlimited. The expressions that Kant does not cease to attempt throughout the paragraphs dedicated to the sublime, those of 'negative presentation,' or 'indirect presentation,' as well as the 'so to speaks' and the 'in a certain sense' strewn throughout the text indicate merely his difficulty with the contradiction of a presentation *without* presentation. A presentation, even if it is negative or indirect, is always a presentation ... But the deep logic of Kant's text is not a logic of presentation and does not pursue the thread of these clumsy expressions.[29]

Nancy thus resists the temptation to assimilate the category of the sublime to the eidetic, the logic of forms and schematisms, even if in a negative or indirect way. That which Coleridge does explicitly in his 1814 formalist definitions – add the sublime to the same framework as the other aesthetic categories, the framework of perception and presentation – is what Nancy counsels us *not* to do. For Nancy, 'the sublime forms neither a second wing of aesthetics nor another kind of aesthetic ... it does not merely add itself to the beautiful ... [it] does not constitute in the general field of (re)presentation just one more instance or problematic: it transforms or redirects the entire motif of presentation'.[30]

Nancy's justification for this interpretation of Kant is grounded in a reading of *bild*, or form, that attends not to its internal edge (i.e. the presented thing that is enclosed by the contour of its shape), but its external edge: 'the unlimited begins on the external border of the limit'.[31] We can get a sense of Nancy's argument by imagining the white page or canvas that precedes the inscription of any form for an artist, or the silence between the notes that a composer must structure into musical composition. It is what Derrida or Kristeva might call a *chora*, the 'space' or spacing of space.[32] That naked indeterminacy out of which presentations emerge is what is felt in the sublime: 'a presentation takes place only if *all* the rest, *all* the unlimitedness from which it detaches itself, sets itself off along its border – and at once, in its own way, presents itself'.[33] As such, Nancy argues there is an experience of the sublime belonging to every form, at its edge, in so far as every form that is enclosed implies the dis-enclosed. The movement of presentation itself – the articulation of limits into and out of representational space – by definition cannot be presented: it 'takes place, happens, or occurs *in* presentation itself and in sum *through* it but [it] is not presentation'.[34]

There are a number of affinities between Nancy's reading of Kant and Coleridge's wonder at being in *The Friend*, which I hope will have already become apparent. Both are interested in the coming to existence of things, and how this coming is abyssal and unformalisable. Just as Coleridge's sublime is rooted simply in the fact that being *is*, Nancy's sublime exists because '*presentation takes place*'.[35] Just as being is felt as a kind of gift or revelation for Coleridge, presentation is inextricable from a certain offering or address for Nancy. Indeed, reading 'The Sublime Offering' alongside Nancy's *The Experience of Freedom* makes the analogies even clearer. In the latter text, he describes the facticity of the 'is' in the same terms of form, limit and arrival used in 'The Sublime Offering':

> The *there* of the 'there is' is not a receptacle or a place ... The *there* is itself the spacing (of space-time) of the coming, because there is *all* (and totality is not the fastening, the completion without remainder; it is the 'having there', the taking place, the unlimited 'coming there' of the delimited thing ...).[36]

Perhaps predictably, one does not have to look far in Nancy's text to find the very same wonder at being, and at the impossibility of nothing, articulated by Coleridge and Heidegger: 'there might not be *existence* ... if there were no existence, then there would not be nothing and yet there would not be something'.[37] The experience of being is a startling experience of givenness.

However, if Nancy turns to the motif of the offering to describe the coming to pass of existent forms, this raises a theological question: must an offering imply one who offers? Does a gift imply a giver? As mentioned at the beginning of this chapter, Nancy strives to liberate philosophy from theology when discussing such topics as being, transcendence and alterity. Thus, in the same way that his non-eidetic reading of Kant is keen to free the sublime from the so-called negative presentation (because it bears such a close relationship to negative theology and the divine name), 'The Sublime Offering' wants to dissociate the notion of offering from a theological gift or revealing. In this vein, he argues that the sublime should not be conceived of as a gift *per se*: 'what takes place is neither a coming-to-presence nor a gift ... the offering is the giving up of the gift ... what is offered is offered up – addressed, destined, abandoned'.[38] In emphasising the sheer immanence of the experience of the sublime offering, Nancy attempts to foreclose the suspicion of a transcendent or divine giver. Yet how severe is this risk? To what extent is givenness a concept necessarily woven with Christian overtones? This is where a turn to the work of Jean-Luc Marion is instructive. For Marion – like Coleridge, but unlike Nancy – has written theological works such as *God Without Being* that draw on the trope of the gift. Yet he has also tried, in the face of suspicious critique, to articulate a phenomenology of givenness *without* drawing on theological presuppositions.

Perhaps his most sustained attempt occurs in *Being Given: Toward a Phenomenology of Givenness*. There, he argues that givenness is the primordial category of experience. Phenomena are given to us (they arise before us) and are *a* given to us (they are non-negotiable and irreducible). However, generations of philosophers have overlooked givenness and appealed instead to more limited and de-limiting horizons of experience (e.g. all phenomena can be defined as objects, or all phenomena can be defined as beings).[39] (Marion's protest against this occlusion of givenness is similar to *The Friend*'s critique of the impoverished categories of the understanding.) Importantly, however, Marion also argues that givenness has always made itself known, since the givenness or gift of phenomenality sometimes overflows horizons such as objectness or being, thus proving and manifesting its primordiality. When such overflowing occurs, Marion terms this the *saturated phenomenon*.

Tellingly, two of Marion's key examples from the history of philosophy derive from Kant's *Critique of Judgment*. One is the aesthetic idea.[40] The other, closely linked, is the sublime. Marion reads the Kantian sublime as an intuition of the fundamental givenness of phenomenality, a moment when givenness reaches a stunning and manifest intensity and exceeds any lesser categories or horizons:

> Already with the sublime, it is an issue of a saturated phenomena ... in terms of quantity, the sublime has no form or order ... In terms of quality, it contradicts taste as a 'negative pleasure' ... In terms of relation, it very clearly escapes every analogy and every horizon since it is literally 'limitlessness' ... In terms of modality, finally, far from agreeing with our power of knowing, 'it may appear in such a way as to contradict the finality of our faculty of judgement'.[41]

In identifying the sublime as a precursor and type for the saturated phenomena, we find Marion's analysis runs close to Nancy, and indeed to Coleridge. The givenness of phenomenality (just like the givenness of form in 'The Sublime Offering', and the givenness of the IT IS in *The Friend*) is deeper than any conceptual or sensible representation, yet impresses itself nonetheless.

Nevertheless, Marion realises that to make his analysis phenomenologically rigorous, he must be able to justify the trope of the gift. As such, like Nancy, he is keen to prove that givenness is an experience which is immanent to the phenomena, i.e. it does not imply a transcendent giver and a subsequent economy between divine and human. As a result *Being Given* takes pains to note instances such as inheritance (where the giver is dead), secret charity (where the giver is unknown) or performance (where athletes and artists give pleasure to their audiences, but are unconscious of constituting themselves as givers). Such examples, he contends, prove that givenness can be defined solely as an experience of the given, and that 'even without the giver, the gift is accomplished'.[42] Moreover, like Nancy above, he emphasises the abandonment of the gift as a crucial element to it: 'it is a question of the pure and simple loss involved in giving with abandon'.[43] To be truly given, the gift *should* exist in the absence of its giver, who has left it behind.

If one accepts these arguments, givenness can be maintained as a philosophical, rather than theological, concept. Being as a given, as a gift, would not imply God as the giver. On the other hand, Marion provocatively assigns revelation as the limit-experience of givenness. Gathering together all figures of the saturated phenomena (temporal excess, visual excess, the flesh and the gaze), the incarnation and death of Christ is privileged as a second-degree saturated phenomenon: 'saturation passes beyond itself, exceeds the very concept of maximum, and finally gives its phenomenon without remainder or reserve'.[44] This raises certain problematic questions. Marion claims that he is merely sketching out a possibility intrinsic to the structure of givenness: suggesting how such an experience would be given, if it were to be given, but not commenting on the reality or otherwise of revelation. However, despite this, one can certainly see why suspicion still attaches to givenness and its apparent theological origins. It seems naturally to slide into a consideration of revelation as the phenomenon of givenness *par excellence*. Of course, this is precisely how *The Friend* positions things.

This is where I want to return to Coleridge. Given the difficulties surrounding the concept of givenness, not to mention the obvious Christian polemic of *The Friend,* one could suggest that the wonder of being is a theological sublime. One might argue, in fact, it is no less theological than the sublime based on the divine name in 'Hymn Before Sun-Rise'. However, on the other hand, I believe that the relationships here between theology and philosophy – and transcendence and immanence – are rather more complex. I certainly do not deny that Coleridge repeatedly appropriates antinomy and paradox in the name of Christianity. There is a consistent negative theological tendency at work in his late writings, where the very inarticulacy of a ground is taken as an opportunity to assert the very ultimacy of that ground. *Aids to Reflection,* for instance, often works in this way: 'in Wonder all Philosophy began: in Wonder it ends ... The First is the birth-throe of our knowledge: the Last is its euthanasy and apotheosis' (p. 236). One finds specific instances of this logic when Coleridge is discussing the necessary mysteriousness of any absolute ground (as in the quotation cited earlier), when considering the heteronomy of freedom (allowing him to insert a moral relation to a creator in the face of a deterministic nature), and when defining religious mysteries as intrinsically a-logical (as in the analysis of original sin we met in our reading of the 'Ancient Mariner'). Time and again, Coleridge welcomes the idea that spiritual things must be paradoxes, often invoking the Kantian Idea under the auspices of such a thesis.

In *The Friend,* we find this done when Coleridge invokes the gift-character of being. Unable to root the givenness of the world in any logic *of* the world, Coleridge claims – much as Descartes did with the idea of infinity – that it must have come from God.[45] As we think about the offering of being – as we enjoy existence *within* being – we are told that the experience of its givenness can be named, and that any other name but God is idolatrous. The unformalisability of the IT IS is thus taken as a chance to posit the ineffability of the divine I AM (such a manoeuvre is obviously reminiscent of the end of the first book of the *Biographia*

Literaria as well). After making this turn towards doctrinal Christianity, it is telling that Coleridge returns to much more traditional terms of reference. He brings the givenness of being within a metaphysical horizon (as Marion might put it) that allows him to articulate a classic ontological argument for the existence of God: 'It is absolutely one and that it is, and affirms itself to be, is its only predicate' (I.515). He also reinstates a much more formalist notion of being, thinking the totality of the world in terms of nothing other than our well-established schema of part and whole:

> we behold – first, a subjection to universal laws, by which each thing belongs to the whole, as interpenetrated by the powers of the whole; and, secondly, the intervention of particular laws by which the universal laws are suspended or tempered for the weal and sustenance of each particular class. (I.517)

At this point, givenness has been thoroughly appropriated by a theological analysis (indeed, an onto-theological analysis, in so far as the notion of God as absolute being has been extracted from Coleridge's original, more phenomenological perspective on being). This represents, doubtlessly, one very strong strand in Coleridge's late work.

Despite this, I want to emphasise two elements to the religious turn that make Coleridge's work rather more interesting, particularly to contemporary readers. Firstly, he starts firmly *from* immanence and the finite, and sublimity is rooted in them. The wonder of being is an intuition that can stem from almost any thing, here and now, down to a grain of sand. In thinking about a theological appropriation of the sublime, we should bear in mind that one would usually describe a religious sublime as the imposition of the infinite on to the finite. As Jean-Luc Nancy puts it, 'the presence of God ... overwhelms the sensible ... a presence that ruins all presentation and all representation ... the imposition of glory'.[46] Whilst this is something Coleridge works towards (as does Jean-Luc Marion, under the auspices of the second-degree of saturation and a phenomenology of revelation), *The Friend*'s initial description is not of the infinite failing to coincide with the finite. Rather, it is the finite failing to coincide *with itself*. Looking at what is closest to us, we find that existence cannot formalise itself and that the very simplest fact (arguably the fact of immanence *par excellence*, that something is) is both given, and yet as given remains indescribable. The root of Coleridge's analysis in finitude rather than infinitude should not be overlooked.

David Vallins, in a chapter called 'Language, Consciousness, and the Sublime', has been one of the few recent critics to fully note the importance of paradoxes and mysteries in the late Coleridge. Although the focus is on language rather than phenomenality, his point that the origin of description cannot itself be described (by definition) mirrors a recurrent motif in our own discussion.[47] Vallins primarily considers transcendent referents that are beyond 'the limitations of human intellects', a reading that perhaps shifts the locus of the sublime too far away from the experience of the here and now.[48] As a corrective, consider the following passage from earlier in *The Friend*, describing

> Objects, which their very sublimity renders indefinite, no less than their indefiniteness renders them sublime: namely ... the Ideas of Being, Form, Life, the Reason, the Law of Conscience, Freedom, Immortality, God.[49]

Being and form are precisely the two sublime givens on which this chapter has concentrated. Note that they are not only immanent, but they *are* the conditions of immanence itself. Of the next four, one can certainly see a transcendent and theological origin developed for the moral law and reason (as *logos*) across Coleridge's work, most deeply in the unfinished *Opus Maximum*. Nevertheless, they are essentially experiences which are familiar and close to us: to borrow a metaphor from *The Friend*, we dwell in them. Life itself, the intuition of freedom, the ability to reason and ethical demands are things inscribed at the point of finite, even quotidian, existence. As Coleridge puts it, 'the Life, we seek after, is a mystery; but *so both in itself and in its origin is the Life we have*' (p. 204, my emphasis).[50] Of the eight givens in *The Friend*, only 'the Life, we seek after' (immortality) and God itself, are terms that are unambiguously to be defined in terms of transcendence, Nancyean glory or a truly theological sublimity.

Coleridge's sublime, despite its Christian drift, is hence not about something other than the world, but about the world itself: a world that does not and cannot coincide logically with itself. As Coleridge writes in a notebook entry:

> The more I read & reflect on the arguments of the truly philosophical Theists & Atheists, the more I feel convinced that the ultimate difference is a moral rather than intellectual one / that the result is an X Y Z – an acknowledged Insufficiency of the Known to account for itself, and therefore a something Unknown – but to which the Theist dedicates his noblest feelings of Love, & Awe, & by a moral

> syllogism connects & unites it with his Conscience & Actions – while the Atheist leaves it a blank in the Heart, because it is a Blank in his Understanding. (*N*4030)

This fragment, I believe, exemplifies what is distinctive about Coleridge's late thinking on being. Where all-ness was always haunted by an all-absorbing, static sense of totality, here there is always an unsettledness, a non-coincidence, something cutting across the grain: an 'X Y Z' that remains unpresented and enigmatic. It is the imperative to respond to this X Y Z that I consider the second crucial and provocative thing about Coleridge's sublime here. He demands the active engagement of the subject, an existential decision: something in the practical rather than the intellectual domain, as the note puts it.

Obviously, this further parts this kind of sublimity from the formalist sublime, which always risked delivering the perceiving subject to a deathly passivity. More importantly, I think that it contextualises the theological movement whereby Coleridge's late texts move from the IT IS to the divine I AM. The existentialist overtones to his thought complicate the relationship between theological and philosophical theses. The unformalisability of the world to itself is not simply taken as an epistemological licence to posit something beyond knowing: there must be a decision to commit, to pass through, the very lacunae that a world that cannot account for itself presents. It is worth noting the claim that Coleridge makes in *Aids to Reflection*: 'Christianity is not a Theory, or a Speculation; but a *Life*. Not a *Philosophy* of Life, but a Life' (p. 202). Coleridge's Christian turn lies outside philosophy, but it comes out of a philosophical thought of the limits of philosophy: the point where the 'riddle of the world' – the edge of reason – demands an existential and moral decision, one way or another.[51] Together, these tropes of immanence and existentiality reveal a more textured and sophisticated relationship between theology and philosophy than one might imagine. We would be right to be suspicious of the path cut from givenness to revelation, from being to God, but we should not allow this to occlude Coleridge's keen cognisance of finitude, and a sublime which is originally articulated not between the infinite and the finite but between the finite and itself.

Conclusion

7

'A Specimen of the Sublime dashed to pieces': Sublimity in the *Biographia Literaria* and the Limbo Constellation

Throughout this study, I have contended that there is a need to acknowledge a finite Coleridge. In this chapter, I draw a deliberate contrast between the famous final pages of the first volume of the *Biographia Literaria* and the strange, compelling poetry found in the *Notebooks*, usually anthologised in fragments under titles such as 'On Donne's First Poem' or 'Limbo'. Treating the deduction of the imagination in terms of aesthetics, I argue that Coleridge makes a common Romantic gesture in trying to perfect the sublime by unifying it with the beautiful, thus creating an absolute aesthetic category. However, like similar gestures made by Schelling and Schiller, it is doomed to failure as a form of overreaching idealism. One can, however, identify a counter-aesthetic based on discontinuity and negativity in the margins of the *Biographia*. Moreover, one finds something approximating this counter-aesthetic more directly expressed in the Limbo poems. Fragmentary and self-interrupting, it is a text of finitude and non-absoluteness. The relationship between the two texts may be emblematic for the double-sidedness of Coleridge – and of the sublime – on which I have insisted throughout. I close the chapter by comparing my conception of a finite sublime with the dichotomy between positive and negative sublimity set up in Thomas Weiskel's *The Romantic Sublime: Studies in the Structure and Psychology of Transcendence* – still, perhaps, the definitive study on the topic.

The sublime and the beautiful in the *Biographia Literaria*

The deduction of the imagination from the *Biographia Literaria* is one of Coleridge's most influential stretches of writing – yet also one of the most frustratingly enigmatic. However, the work of many commentators and contextualisers has ensured that the passage can be rendered relatively lucid. I do not intend to depart from a broad scholarly consensus, reading the primary imagination via German idealism's analysis of the deepest grounds of consciousness, and the secondary imagination as the power of the aesthetic to reconcile subjective and objective poles, a breach alienating consciousness from itself in everyday existence. A recent article by Len Epp efficiently sums up the stakes of Coleridge's discussion, arguing that the imagination

> is creative insofar as it unifies, via the contemplation of art, the conscious and the unconscious, that are made distinct in the act of primary imagination, which itself generates the distinction between subject and object, and hence the world, nature ... [I]n art we can consciously reproduce the tension between the conscious and the unconscious which characterizes our everyday interaction with nature, and so make this very tension an object of contemplation.[1]

As mentioned above, I would identify the most relevant contexts as those of German philosophy and aesthetics, a position that has historically only had a few dissenters (such as Walter Bate, who argues that 'one may best approach Coleridge ... by viewing him in the line of British empirical intuitionalists').[2]

We may begin with Fichte and the early Schelling. Desirous of placing the tentative epistemology of Kant's philosophy on firmer ground, they identified a primordial principle in the shape of the absoluteness of the self. As Fichte argues:

> whatever we may think, we are that which thinks therein, and hence ... nothing could ever come to exist independently of us, for everything is necessarily related to our thinking.[3]

Despite some differences, especially Coleridge's tendency to draw in the reflexivity of empirical self-consciousness (myself perceiving myself), the *Biographia Literaria* generally follows the German lead.[4] Thesis VI places the SUM or I AM at the heart of existence. This elevation of self to a transcendent position helps explain the exaltation of the primary imagination as 'the living power and prime Agent of all human Perception' (I.304), and its otherwise enigmatic link to the act of divine creation. Coleridge's primary imagination is the auto-positing act of a self functioning as ultimate principle, as one finds confirmed in a similar pronouncement from Fichte's *Science of Knowledge*: 'imagination forms the basis for the possibility of our consciousness, our life, our existence for ourselves, that is, our existence as selves'.[5]

However, the formal and unconditioned position of the 'I' as a metaphysical absolute sharply contrasts to the predicament of the 'I' in the everyday or empirical world. The selves with which we are all familiar are thoroughly finite, facing the intransigence of external objects. As Fichte explores in tracing the movement of self-positing, consciousness is actually forever divided by the subject–object dichotomy, contradistinguished by what Fichte terms the not-I. As Coleridge suggests, the 'one power' of consciousness is riven by 'two inherent indestructible yet counteracting forces' (I.299). The unity and primordiality which Coleridge, following Fichte and Schelling, hoped to find in the absolute self is, in fact, a lost ground: the everyday 'I' is alienated from its own origin in the absolute 'I'. There is a kind of fall.[6] This is where the relationship between primary and secondary imaginations becomes interesting. If the primary imagination – the power that generates selfhood itself – produces a self alienated by an outside world, then the secondary imagination is drafted in to repair this very breach between subject and object. Put simply, philosophy posits an absolute unity of subjective and objective; everyday existence loses touch with that unity; and art recovers it.

One can see this by comparing the secondary imagination in the *Biographia* with Schelling's rather more explicit discussion in the *System of Transcendental Idealism* (one of the texts most thoroughly plagiarised by Coleridge). In the sixth part of the *System*, Schelling argues that the work of genius is characterised by a reconciliation between unintended activity and conscious intention: 'the objective and the conscious activities are here brought into unexpected harmony ... a dark unknown force ... supplies the element of completeness or objectivity to the piece-work of freedom'.[7] What is crucial is the artwork bringing together the exact two things sundered in empirical existence: subjectivity and objectivity. In the artwork, the finite self begins to overcome its alienation, coming to a knowledge of a harmony and identity between subject and object that is also a knowledge of its own origin in the absolute: 'the intelligence will therefore end with a complete recognition of the identity expressed in the product as an identity whose principle lies in the intelligence itself; it will end, that is, in a complete intuiting of itself'.[8]

Schelling's account of art runs parallel to Coleridge's account of secondary imagination. Just like Schelling's genius, Coleridge's secondary imagination is described as a reconciling force, healing a human subject otherwise divided between its own internal life and the world of sensate objects outside it. The secondary imagination harmoniously imbues objects in nature with human qualities, just as Schelling's artwork imbues unconscious materials with conscious intentions. Art recreates nature as a harmonious dwelling for human consciousness: 'it dissolves, diffuses, dissipates, in order to re-create ... it is essentially *vital*, even as all objects (*as* objects) are essentially fixed and dead' (I.304). Although objects *as objects* are dead, secondary imagination imbues them with life, and co-joins human life to them: thus mimicking the primal unity of the lost absolute. Therefore, we see the reflexive relationship between the two types of the imagination is a response to a certain post-Kantian dilemma: like Fichte and Schelling, Coleridge wants to posit an absolute unity which everyday life lacks, and whilst it can be theorised philosophically in the shape of the absolute self, it takes art to provide a concrete experience of what such unity might actually be like.

None of this is a particularly novel interpretation. In its lineaments, the idea that the aesthetic (secondary imagination) fashions a unity that consciousness and everyday perception (primary imagination) lack is extracted easily enough from a careful reading of the *Biographia*, and the publication of the exemplary Bollingen edition has made the German context more accessible. However, what I would like to do is to characterise the secondary imagination in the context of aesthetic categories. In particular, I want to argue that Coleridge is trying to unify the limitless scope of the sublime with the phenomenological satisfaction of the beautiful. In this, I am drawing on Andrzej Warminski's description of a Schillerian aesthetic which solves 'the problem of the sublime by recourse to the beautiful'. However, as Warminski also points out, the categories resist assimilation: there is an 'incommensurability and non-mediatability [between] the sublime task and the beautiful solution'.[9] One can find the attempt – and failure – to unify the sublime and the beautiful as a recurrent pattern in Romantic idealism, and I shall refer to Friedrich Schiller (the text studied by Warminski), Schelling (perhaps Coleridge's primary influence) and of course Coleridge himself.

What happens in Schiller's *Letters on the Aesthetic Education of Man* is that the aesthetic object is defined as possessing an elegant and playful form that does not seem to be the product of a deterministic nature. Instead, it intimates freedom. Whilst the emphasis on form comes from the Kantian analysis of the beautiful, the connection with freedom is more characteristic of the Kantian sublime. Schiller tries to argue that the aesthetic actually constitutes a sensible representation of freedom, freedom visibly in harmony with nature: something totally contrary to Kant's insistence that ideas such as freedom are impossible to represent. As Warminski suggests, Schiller is trying to bring the sublime into the beautiful. The same thing applies, I would suggest, to Schelling's aesthetics. There too, the artwork provides a place for freedom to constitute itself in the sensible, material world. There too, the aesthetic involves an adequate formal representation of the supersensible: 'it is as if, in [the man of genius] ... that unalterable identity, on which all existence is founded, had laid aside the veil wherewith it shrouds itself in others'.[10] Not surprisingly, then, we find that when Schelling turns to the categories of the beautiful and the sublime, his ultimate conclusion is to unify them: 'there is actually no true objective opposition between beauty and sublimity; the truly and absolutely beautiful is invariably also sublime, and the sublime (if it truly is so) is beautiful as well'.[11]

There is every suggestion that Coleridge attempts the same aesthetic gambit. We discover among the *Biographia*'s long list of pronouncements on the unifying force of the poetic imagination that poetry involves precisely 'the reconciliation ... of the general, with the concrete; the idea, with the image' (II.16–17). In so far as *ideas* are invoked, the Coleridgean poetic recalls the Kantian sublime. Yet, as with the natural sublime (see Chapter 5), discontinuity is abandoned in favour of reconciliation. Instead of *Widerstreit* (conflict), we find the poet 'bring[ing] the whole soul of man into activity, with the subordination of its faculties to each other, according to their relative worth and dignity ... diffus[ing] a tone, and spirit of unity, that blends ... each into each' (II.15–16). Coleridge's discussion of the total harmony of faculties recalls, if anything at all, Kant's 'Analytic of the Beautiful' in which the harmonious interplay of different faculties was the distinctive character and condition for the experience. Moreover, in believing that an idea can be conveyed by a symbol (I.156), Coleridge is reverting, as Warminski notes in regard to Schiller, to the formal adequacy of representation characteristic of beauty. As such, it is not surprising to find an important notebook entry evoking precisely the same kind of relative convergence posited by Schelling: the categories of the sublime and beautiful are part of a long list of dichotomous qualities that must be placed 'in due proportion & perfect harmony ... [by] the noblest Poem' (*N*3827).[12] No longer opposites, sublimity is fused with beauty to create a new Romantic category above both.

Discontinuity in the *Biographia Literaria*

However, there is a certain problem with trying to meld two very different categories: how can one unify finite form and infinite scope? Warminski argues that Schiller's argument is ultimately void:

> How does this *hypo*thesis of a possible experience become a *thesis*, the law ... that there ought to be such experience and hence that there

> must be beauty? ... it can take place only ... by the sheer positing of such experience ... this is indeed how the actual 'deduction' of the play-drive and its object, beauty, takes place in Schiller's text – based not on the transcendental grounds of Reason but on the ungrounded grounding power of pure positing.[13]

As Coleridge himself writes, 'all symbols [sensible representations of the supersensible] of necessity involve an apparent contradiction' (I.156): in this context, how does one transform logical paradox into transcendental necessity? Instead of finding itself articulated as a necessary condition of experience, as the Kantian method would demand, Schiller's aesthetic takes on a utopian drift, articulated through the hypothetical and imperative modalities of language. This is what art *should* be, but his idealism here is truly disconnected from logical possibility. What his deduction lacks, Warminski argues, is the constative mode that is the root of true philosophical discourse.[14]

The shape of this argument should be familiar to Coleridgeans, since the interruption of Schiller's deduction by a certain aporia recalls the more violent interruption in the *Biographia*'s deduction. Perhaps the classic reading of this interruption is Gayatri Chakravorty Spivak's 'The Letter as Cutting Edge', which analyses it as a rhetorical exit from a failing philosophical argument.[15] As we have noted, Coleridge seeks an absolute: posited by philosophy, lost in everyday perception and recovered by art. Yet being prior to both subjective and objective it escapes reflection, which requires precisely that very dichotomy between knowledge and being. As Jerome Christensen puts it, 'the condition of our knowledge ... can never directly be known'.[16] The argument of the *Biographia* shuttles between subjective and objective poles, seeking vainly to reflect on the inarticulable ground of both. What happens in the end is notorious: Coleridge inserts a fictitious letter from a friend, complaining about the obscurity of the (non-existent) deduction of the imagination. On this pretence, the deduction is never made, and its (supposed) conclusions merely schematised, leaving us with the gnomic statements that conclude the first volume. As Spivak notes, the letter from a friend cuts cleanly across the logical knots and 'allows the Law to spring forth full-fledged'.[17]

The inability of either Schiller or Coleridge to make the deduction of their central aesthetic category (the Schillerian beautiful, the imagination), and their necessary turn to the force of a rhetorical sleight-of-hand, can be derived from the incommensurability of the sublime and beautiful. The unity of freedom and nature sought in the 'Letters on the Aesthetic Education of Man', and the closely related unity of subjective and objective desired by the *Biographia Literaria*, essentially require a formal closure characteristic of the beautiful. Yet, the irreducible gap between freedom and nature, or subject and object (attested in the Kantian sublime through conflict and difference) cannot be closed. What Warminski and Spivak highlight, in their readings, is how Schiller and Coleridge push rhetorically through this contradiction. However, I would argue that there is more to be read than merely a refutation of the overwrought ambitions of Romantic theory. Here I want to turn to Philippe Lacoue-Labarthe and Jean-Luc Nancy and their reading of Schelling, whom we have already identified as a key influence on the aesthetics of the *Biographia*.

For Schelling, as we have seen in our earlier discussion, art takes on the task of presenting the absolute: 'a "precritical" return towards the goal of a pure auto-presentation'. However, when he turns to a concrete example – the purest being Homeric epic – he also institutes a history: 'a historical product situated on one side of the historical difference (of ancient and modern)'.[18] This, in turn, initiates a tension between the formal universality of the philosophical idea of art, and its historical situatedness. The very heterogeneity and immanence of individual examples runs counter to the uniformity and transcendence of the initial conception. Artworks are not 'indifferent vis-à-vis one another in their relation to the Absolute'.[19] In fact, the history of art turns out to mark a series of differences and lacks: the varying distance between individual historical forms and the conception of the absolute artwork. Each artwork retains a necessary singularity, an echo of its particular critical and historical setting. As Lacoue-Labarthe and Nancy explain, tracing the analysis into Schlegel, one finds this difference most pronounced in modernity, an epoch defined precisely by its difficult historicity and its distance from the ideal: 'an epoch that founds itself, so to speak, on a loss of origin; always on the loss of a great poetry (the Greek, the romantic)'.[20]

I want to note two things about this analysis, which will orientate my own reading. Firstly, like Warminski on Schiller and Spivak on Coleridge, *The Literary Absolute* undoes the idealistic gambit of Romantic aesthetics: the transcendent idea of art and the history of its individual forms cannot be unified, just as nature and freedom, or subjectivity and objectivity, cannot be unified. If one looks at Schelling's own history of art, we find that he is forced to concede that the infinite aspirations ushered in by the modern age have not yet been reconciled with the kind of formal achievements completed by the ancients: in short, sublimity has not yet been unified with beauty. Modern art is still an art of striving, *'possible only as a transition or as characterized by nonabsoluteness'*.[21] However, unlike Warminski and Spivak, the authors of *The Literary Absolute* emphasise the production of something else at the site of the discontinuity. If beauty could be unified with sublimity, in essence, there would be no history of art, because all art would be the same. However, because it cannot be so unified, art emerges with a critical sense of its own historicity and its own particular non-coincidence with an ahistorical ideal of art. Out of the paradoxes of Romantic idealism, then, something else founded on lack is shown to spring: what they call 'another idealism' and 'an altogether different art'.[22]

It is this element of productivity, or 'something else' that I want to add to the classic, broadly deconstructive readings of Coleridge's *Biographia*. If one looks at the letter itself, the crucial 'cut' in Spivak's interpretation, then it functions through the very gestures of negativity characteristic of the Kantian sublime but repressed in the sublime–beautiful aesthetics of the absolute:

> *placed, and left alone, in one of our largest Gothic cathedrals ... in palpable darkness not without a chilly sensation of terror; then suddenly emerging into broad yet visionary lights.* (I.301)

The tropes are of an encounter with lack and discontinuity: terror comes to the forefront, there is a weight placed on incomprehensibility, and the whole is sketched as a crisis in perception. In contrast to the luminous ideals of reconciliation, the evocation of the gothic foregrounds a series of motifs that opens the possibility of a different kind of aesthetic: one that might be founded on fragmentation, obscurity and disorientating reversals. I want to argue firstly that this aesthetic is very much legible in the margins of the *Biographia*, haunting the idealistic aesthetic project carried out there. Just as in German Romanticism a certain new aesthetic (critical, historical, striving) is produced for art at the moment the aesthetics of the absolute fail, here we find a certain sublime negativity occupying the site of Coleridge's own crisis. Secondly, I want to suggest that such a counter-aesthetic is very much available for Coleridge's use elsewhere: indeed, we shall find this poetic of lack – of finitude – fully explored and developed in the appropriately marginal and private space of his *Notebooks*. Together, these two analyses will bear witness to the double-edgedness of Coleridge, the sublime and – naturally – the Coleridgean sublime.

To give a sense of how a different aesthetic is inscribed as the spectral counterpart of Romantic idealism, even in Coleridge's most public and supposedly authoritative pronouncements of such, I want to look at one particular episode in the *Biographia*. This is the case of suspected demonic possession recounted at the end of Chapter 6. The reader is told of an illiterate German girl who began 'incessantly talking Latin, Greek, and Hebrew' (I.112), a phenomenon which remained an inexplicable mystery until it emerged she was retrieving fragments from early childhood experience. Having been raised by a pastor who used to recite biblical and rabbinical texts aloud, these very words were reproduced in a random order from the depths of her memory. This tale is initially introduced to suggest the consequences of associationist psychology: all consciousness, Coleridge avers, would be as delirious and fragmented as the girl's incoherent speech, were David Hartley's passive theory of mind to be taken seriously. However, the tale seems to have resonances that outstrip its stated purpose.

Jerome Christensen suggests one key problem: despite being recounted in order to refute a passive theory of mind, it turns out to be a phenomenon which is explained precisely by associationist theories: 'why has Coleridge bothered to tell a story, which, if it performs any function, reinforces the position of his adversary, albeit in a pathological extreme?'[23] Christensen believes that the narrative is one of disguised identification: Coleridge himself, given the extensive plagiarisms in the *Biographia*, has been possessed by the texts of Kant, Schelling and others. More generally, the narrative unconsciously assents to broader implications of ventriloquism and possession in Coleridge's theory. Despite the *Biographia*'s emphasis on the will, Christensen believes that it nevertheless attests that 'no one can fully possess anything – certainly not language, least of all himself'.[24] After all, is not finite consciousness just a repetition of the I AM, always already secondary and in a manner possessed?

I would also like to read this episode as one that haunts the system of the *Biographia* with unforeseen consequences; as Eilenberg puts it, 'moments when the book ... seems to frighten itself ... insisting upon its difference from the delirious mimics whose stories it tells'.[25] In simple terms, although the girl is evoked as an example for the delirium-fancy axis, the prophetic and religious overtones of her utterances seem to bring her closer to the cluster surrounding imagination and mania. She is, after all, citing from holy texts in holy languages. Compare, for instance, Coleridge's description of prophecy made in marginalia to Johann Eichhorn:

> sudden changes produced without any conscious act of their own will, both on their bodies and their minds – and the sum of all, that

> with more or less excitement, ~~equ~~ greater or lesser disturbance of their nervous system they passed into a state of *inner vision*, a *state* ... in all points identical with that of Extasy or Clair-voyance.[26]

Moreover, the girl's illiteracy appears to anticipate Chapter 9's 'illiterate and ... simple' (I.148) mystics such as Jacob Behmen and George Fox. Coleridge is very favourable to these writers, describing them as 'truly inspired ... the originals themselves' (I.149).

Although medical science analyses the facts of the case, and brings the possession under the logic of delirium that Coleridge wants to enforce, the overtones of mysterious truths uttered by illiterate prophets are not erased. Compelled by these overtones, perhaps, Coleridge creates another set of significations for the event. The case is read as strong evidence that all experiences may be eternally preserved in a deep state of memory. The German girl's ravings suggest

> that all thoughts are in themselves imperishable; and, that if the intelligent faculty should be rendered more comprehensive, it would require only a different and apportioned organization, *the body celestial* instead of *the body terrestrial*, to bring before every human soul the collective experience of its whole past existence. And this, this, perchance, is the dread book of judgement, in whose mysterious hieroglyphics every idle word is recorded! Yea ... it may be more possible that heaven and earth should pass away, than that a single act, a single thought, should be loosened or lost from that living chain of causes, to all whose links, conscious or unconscious, the free-will, our only absolute *self*, is co-extensive and co-present. But not now dare I longer discourse of this, waiting for a loftier mood. (I.114)

The shift to the 'body celestial' refigures and reorganises the girl's utterances into something close to a form of revelation. In empirical and scientific terms, the sentences are meaningless, troping a kind of prophetic discourse but in reality just the products of a disordered nervous system retrieving words heard in childhood. However, *as* products of imperishable memory, they have a spiritual signification as fragments intimating the existence of an immortal archive of consciousness.

Indeed, this second signification is said to mark nothing less than 'our absolute *self*', which we already know as the ground of being and knowing: that which the *Biographia* has sought all along! The girl gives us shards of an otherwise inaccessible absolute: not through *what* is being said, but *how* it is being said. In a dazzling reversal, the German girl's gnomic speech has passed from signifying the pathological, disordered extremities of fancy and the 'phantasmal chaos of association' (I.116), to usurping the imagination's task of presenting the absolute. Its discursive similarities to religious prophecy and mystic illiteracy have asserted themselves through this second signification. However, in invoking the idea of an eternal archive, Coleridge relates to the absolute self in a way that is very different to the adequacy of presentation attributed to the artwork, the '*Forma formans per formam formatam translucens*' (II.215).

The division between the celestial and terrestrial bodies reasserts the boundary between finite and infinite that the artwork purports to dissolve. Whereas the organisation of the celestial body is a seamless archive of the absolute, a structure from which no act or thought can be parted, the girl's empirical body expresses this archive through a fragmentary, pathological discourse: 'sentences, coherent and intelligible each for itself, but with little or no connection with each other' (I.112–13). In Coleridge's theory of the artwork, we are granted luminous expressions that reconcile 'the idea, with the image' (II.17). Here, the expression is discordant and disassociated, and implies signs that exist hidden behind the fragments, at a deeper inaccessible level: 'the dread book of judgement, in whose mysterious heiroglyphics every idle word is recorded'. This unread 'dread book', to be opened in an apocalyptic future, renders the absolute secret and thus shows the books of the human imagination to be comparatively blind and delimited, just as the fearsome heiroglyphs can be read as doubles that refute the ambitions of the Coleridgean symbol. Revelation in this episode is imbued with negativity: the fragmentary nature of the girl's speech signifies the very hiddenness of the absolute.

As such, Coleridge's attempt to exorcise the fragmentary from his philosophy of imagination has ended up asserting a fragmentary concept of revelation which stands alongside, but in conflict with, his theory of the artwork. Whereas the latter aims for a pure presentation of the absolute through reconciled symbols, the narrative portrays the absolute as something hidden and only intimated through disordered and enigmatic utterances. This nodal point in Coleridge's system, where he attempts to invoke pathology in order to decisively divide imagination from fancy, ends up not only failing to maintain this distinction, but offering an entirely different mode of revelation and presentation. Whilst the *Biographia* thus articulates the grandest ambitions of the Romantic ideology, the glory of the secondary imagination is shadowed by the possibility of its failure, and an alternative experience of discontinuity and finitude: a counter-aesthetic, as it were. The attempt to unify the sublime and the beautiful is interrupted by a more radical sublime remainder.

As mentioned above, Nancy and Lacoue-Labarthe emphasise, in a way that Spivak and Warminski do not, that such a remainder can be productive. In fact, the moment in German idealism where art falls short of its philosophical ideal is also that which 'decidedly opens the entire history that leads to the present'.[27] Not an impasse, then, but an opening: Romanticism does not simply drive itself vainly into the ground. In Coleridge, I would argue that the discontinuity which articulates itself in the margins of the *Biographia* (and in doing so dis-articulates the aesthetic idealism fundamental to that text) finds another more profound and spacious opening in the *Notebooks*. A new poetic, a different poetics, is inscribed there. In particular, I would like to – somewhat rhetorically – juxtapose the authoritative critical voice of Coleridge with the private poetic writing of the 1811 fragments of the Limbo constellation.[28] Although written four years before he began the *Biographia Literaria*, they initiate an interesting parallel history: poetry that remained unpublished, in some cases for decades, written in the shadow of his growing public stature as critic, intellectual and privileged reader of Wordsworth.

At the edge of the poem: Limbo

From the perspective of the sublime, the watcher figure that stands at the centre of the fragment often anthologised under the title 'Limbo' must draw our attention: 'An old Man with a steady Look sublime / That stops his earthly Task to watch the Skies'.[29] As the turn away from the earth suggests, transcendent vision is at stake, a theme confirmed by the hyper-optical tropes used to describe the seer: 'an Organ full of silent Sight' and 'his eyeless Face all Eye'. As such, he stands counterpoised to blind materialism, those who

> creep back from Light, then listen for its Sound –
> See but to dread, and dread they know not why
> The natural Alien of their negative Eye.

Moreover, it is possible to link this cluster of imagery to parallels in Coleridge's prose: for example, his rendering of Kantian Reason as 'an organ bearing the same relation to spiritual objects, the Universal, the Eternal, and the Necessary, as the eye bears to material and contingent phaenomena'.[30] For Edward Kessler, this figure is the hope on which the poem centres: 'not knowing what they seek, the Limbo souls are deprived of both darkness and light ... striving only for what they *were*. But the blind old man, likewise denied both light and darkness, sees what he can *be*.'[31]

However, if the sublime here marks the spiritualisation of sight, there are certain problems. What is to part the 'negative Eye' from the 'eyeless Face' of the watcher? How to distinguish two types of blindness from each other, one less than sight, one more than sight? Coleridge wrenches vision through paradox when he turns to the old man's blindness. But in doing this, the passage is threatened by a disturbing stasis or petrifaction: a lack of seeing. It is hard to square the rejoicing face with the paralysis depicted as 'Lip touching Lip, ~~with~~ all moveless, Bust and Limb'. The *bust* in the latter line gestures back at another, equally troubling, depiction of the watcher's blindness: 'a statue hath such Eyes'. The watcher's eyes seem to be threateningly empty. Although it is the watcher and not the watched that is described as the statue, there are certainly overtones of idolatry here. Not least, given that the watcher is depicted gazing at the moon 'with moon-like Countenance', we cannot avoid suspecting that there is some form of narcissism apparent. The frozen, immobile gaze and the circularity of the moon imagery both suggest a kind of enthralment that is characteristic of the idol.

If the undecidable knot of blindness and sight suggests something problematic about the watcher figure – also marked by the sudden flurry of similes that subtly undercut the description with a certain hesitation and suspension – this is also borne out by the fact that the 'steady Look sublime' is in no way the climax of the poem.[32] The watcher passage is enveloped between depictions of limbo and closed off with a renunciation – 'No such sweet Sights doth Limbo Den immure'. It is identified as a wish fantasised from within a state it would represent the escape from: as Morton Paley points out, the watcher 'significantly is *not* in "Limbo Den"'.[33] This leaves us, where else, but in limbo. If the watcher would see beyond the limit of the earth, this fragment finds itself at the limit: torn from the certainties of the earth but unable to cross to the heaven intimated in the constellation's early stages. Instead of the visionary sublime of the watcher, one truly has an experience of the pure limit. Coleridge's alter-ego here is Charon, the boatman crossing endlessly between realms, rather than the watcher.

As such, Coleridge is caught in the half-place that is limbo. And his poetry is too. Instead of the spiritual light bathing the watcher's face, there is only 'ghost-Light'. Although space and time recede to virtually nothing, the supervention of spiritual being is not forthcoming, leaving just a series of absences and withdrawals:

> Time & ~~hungry~~ weary Space
> Fetter'd from flight, with night-mair sense of Fleeing
> Strive for their last crepuscular Half-being –
> Lank Space, and <scytheless> Time with ~~scytheless~~ branny Hands
> Barren and soundless as the measuring Sands
> Mark'd but by Flit of Shades – unmeaning they
> As Moonlight on the Dial of the Day.

The deletion of 'hunger' in favour of 'weary' is both telling and appropriate, as if suggesting the tenor of the passage – and by extension, poetic language – shuttles between desire for fuller being and its own exhaustion. There is undoubtedly something beautiful about moonlight falling across a sundial, but equally the figures thus illuminated are meaningless and deceptive. They are false signifiers. The language in this poem describes limbo, but this limbo is itself a perfect description of language's 'last crepuscular Half-being'. Language is wandering in the desert of its own limits, 'barren and soundless'.

Indeed, I would argue that the final stanzas of the 'Limbo' segment themselves enact an exhaustion characteristic of the endlessly self-dividing state of limbo. Coleridge finds himself turning back on himself, the form of the poem breaking down as he attempts to write in the wake of the image of the watcher, which could or should have been the transcending moment of spiritual vision. The description of the crossing with which the poem began returns as Coleridge repeats but truncates the line 'Unchang'd it cross'd & shall &c', thus drawing the poem back in a wide circle to its earliest sections. He also drafts two versions of a single quatrain. As enveloped ABBA rhymes, they both suggest a sudden slowing when compared with the momentum of previous rhymed couplets. Moreover, the fact that an entire quatrain has been repeated deepens the sense of inertia and fragmentation, especially when we see the sestet between them itself breaks down in an unrhymed line, and a '& shall &c'. Coleridge appears to be unable to write, or to write on.

Of course, one can argue that these are just drafts, and it is true that they were later tidied up for publication. Yet, regardless of this, the increasingly fragmented set of stanzas suggests that with visionary hope renounced, one type of aesthetic had been irreversibly overturned, and the poem suffered a 'night-mair sense of Fleeing'. As the draft closes, Coleridge himself attests to the brokenness of his language, arguably using comedy to play down the darkness of the regions he had been traversing: 'A Specimen of the Sublime dashed to pieces by cutting too close with her fiery Four in Hand round the corner of Non-sense'. This is a fascinating motif. It is clear that Coleridge persistently associated the sublime with the whole: as in the formalist definitions discussed in Chapter 6, for example. Yet, equally, the sublime had a long-standing association with fracture and violence. Longinus on textual fragments, Burke on the irregular and obscure, and Kant on formlessness all evoke a sublimity of the broken or non-whole, reinforcing a visual tradition that took storms, volcanoes and ruins as some of its central motifs. Equally, note it is 'Non-sense' and not nonsense: this corner of non-sense is arguably the very fulcrum of the sublime, as one can see in Burke's valorisation of poetic language that is obscure, confused and on the limit of sense. To dash the sublime to pieces, to non-sense, then, may not negate the sublime, but actually redouble it. Certainly, the fragment that follows on from the sheared text of limbo tellingly pursues the logic of a shattered language, and the title under which it is sometimes given – 'Ne Plus Ultra', or no more beyond – suggests the continued exploration of an aesthetic that is liminal, fragmentary and sublime.[34] It exemplifies the fact that shattering the sublime may reorientate rather than repudiate a sublime aesthetic.

The violence of 'Ne Plus Ultra' fits into an apocalyptic tradition, owing much to St John of Patmos and the imaginings of the Hebrew prophets. Many of the images have biblical analogues. The 'one Sceptre' is an eschatological image of the Messiah from Numbers 24:17. 'The Shadow, Death!' appears frequently in both Job and the Psalms. Scorpion imagery is found in Revelation 9, and 'The Dragon foul and fell!' is obviously the terrifying seven-headed dragon of Revelation 12. Coleridge combines these biblical intertexts into the expression of a principle of destruction inherent in existence. The darkness of the world (counterpointed to Christ as the light of the world) rushes towards its eschatological end as the earth itself is annihilated:

> Fate's only Essence! Primal Scorpion Rod!
>   The one permitted Opposite of God!
>   Condensed Blackness, and Abysmal Storm.

Hence, instead of a visionary infinite we are presented with the apocalypse of the finite; instead of a poetics of light, there is a poetics of darkness. The fragmentation and violence of this apocalyptic mode is also apparent in the section's form. 'Ne Plus Ultra' settles appropriately into the Pindaric, the most irregular of all modes.[35] Its lines differ considerably in length and, in combination with a steadily more complex rhyme scheme (AABBCDCDEFFEFGHGIHIHH), create a chiming, broken effect. It is, to borrow Kessler's term, a shattered icon.[36]

However, more striking than either metre or rhyme is the intensely concentrated nature of the imagery. As if mimicking the final concentrating of finitude's finitude into the moment of its own destruction – 'Condensed Blackness ... Compacted to one Sceptre' – the poem is dominated by concentrated, self-contained appellations. Verbs and any kind of complex syntax are notable by their scarcity in this section; regular end-stopping and even caesura are carried out with the potent weight of exclamation marks. Coleridge also displays a penchant for filling trimeters with single images. As such, the verse is noticeably atomic. Gnomic and discontinuous, the language itself is in a process of fragmentation even more marked than in other forms influenced by the Pindaric. This kind of fragmentation should be distinguished from that we identified in the 'Limbo' section: whereas there repetition signified an exhaustion of form into inertia, here the restless rhyme scheme and hammer blows of the exclamation marks signify energy, or the destruction of form into raw atoms or elements, notably the name.

Nevertheless, it would be a mistake to see this condensation of language into naming as signifying purity or efficacy, a diabolic counterpart to the tradition of divine names, for instance. The names in 'Ne Plus Ultra' are themselves apocalypses; they are – as Coleridge anticipates in the final line of the 'Limbo' section – positive negations. 'Antipathist of Light' and 'the Shadow' are defined negatively, 'Abysmal Storm' is an absolute dis-ordering of order, whilst 'The Intercepter' and 'Sole Interdict of all-bedewing Prayer' are interruptions. Such names refer to nothing else but the unmaking or arrest of being, the undoing of the referential foundation on which language itself rests. Coleridge lays waste to language, drawing on irregular forms and negations to depict the apocalypse of the finite. However, there is something which Coleridge refuses to name, and indeed considers unnameable:

> Revealed to none of all th' Angelic State,
>   Save to the Lampads seven
>   That watch the Throne of Heaven!

When language and being are in the process of disintegration, Coleridge affirms something whose withdrawal appears precisely in that breach: the unsaid, the unnamed. There is thus a secret name behind the apocalyptic names: the name of the eschatological 'x' is preserved by making it encrypted, unknown 'save to the Lampads seven'. Aesthetically, this is the very opposite of the visionary hope represented by the watcher. Moreover, if one would want to connect the watcher and his 'steady Look sublime' to the idealism of the *Biographia*'s primary aesthetic, then the apocalyptic 'Ne Plus Ultra' is far closer to the counter-aesthetic identified in its margins. Like the delirious discourse of the raving girl, Coleridge's Pindaric is violently discordant, and like the enigmatic hieroglyphs brokenly intimated in her speech, it involves something dread, hidden and unsayable.

To some extent, this gesture of apophasis (or not-saying) is controlled. Within the context of 'Ne Plus Ultra' alone, it initiates a negative theological economy of sorts. One has only a single *blockage* as Jonathan Culler, following Neil Hertz, would have it: a blockage that is easily appropriated through a rhetorical reversal which affirms the existence of the 'x' all the more strongly by saying that it is beyond description.[37] A critic like Morton Paley seems to have accepted the validity of such an economy, in so far as he asserts that the constellation ends with a vision parallel to that of the *Biographia Literaria*: 'though dark ... one of reconciliation'.[38] By contrast, I believe there is a more radical sense of apophasis at work. 'Ne Plus Ultra' is the coda to a much wider, and more multiple text, and its rhetoric of apophasis overspills the bounds of a single gesture. Apophasis, in the sense of a not-saying or a not-being-able-to-say, haunts the entire constellation. What is *named* by apophasis in this broader sense is not a hyper-essential 'x' outside of names and languages, but the experience of the failure of the name, of language, itself.

This more uncontrollable, exorbitant sense of apophasis is nothing other than a sublime dashed to pieces, and reinscribed with its transcendent pretensions thoroughly chastened. It is a fragmentary sublime, rather than one of wholeness; it is an aesthetic of the limit, rather than beyond-the-limit. Across the disarticulated parts of the constellation, language enacts its own finitude. 'Ne Plus Ultra' practises an apocalypse of language, concluding with its enigmatic refrain, with the secret: 'save to the Lampads seven'. The main stretch of text, often entitled simply 'Limbo', hollows out language at its own edge, occupying the pure limit. One can look earlier in the constellation too. In the playful prose text that prefaces the poetic fragments, and in the comic verse on John Donne, Coleridge wittily juxtaposes the spiritual ambitions of poetry with its stubborn materiality. Donne's poem *The Flea* is figured as crossing from earth to heaven: 'What 'tho that great ancestral Flea be gone / Immortal with immortalizing Donne'. Yet the privileged metaphysical wit of Donne runs close to a much more arbitrary material manipulation of language.[39] The initial prose *jeu d'esprit*, in particular, is full of random, sliding significations (thoughts that run, fleas that crawl), decompositions of words, the semiotics of speech (the saliva dribbling from Copioso's mouth, the stutter of Tungstic) and the force of the letter: 'At most his Lice & his Sense ... differ only as the note of a Cat & a Hawk – the one *mews*, & the other *pews* – the L~~ouse~~ice crawl~~s~~ & the Thoughts drawl'.

Even at its beginning then, the constellation is tracing the limits of language. There is no reason to exclude this comic side from the text as a (fractured) whole, as many editorial works of excerpting and selecting do.[40] It too is one of the shards of a sublime dashed to pieces. One of the crucial things – perhaps the crucial thing – about the constellation is its multi-voicedness and its fragmentary textuality. It is the discontinuous surface of the notebook drafts that most fundamentally attests to the finitude of its language, and the finitude of the counter-aesthetic. The constellation is divided and re-divided, precisely because it is poetry that knows itself to be founded on lack: it is a ceaseless interruption of itself. It is a ruin of sorts. This ruination is the more fundamental and radical sense of apophasis at work in the text: not just a single rhetorical trope, but an intractable experience of language. The Limbo constellation expresses what was always haunting the margins of the *Biographia*: the *other* sublime, the shattered sublime, produced at the moment the transcendent sublime fails.

The fact that such a counter-aesthetic appears so powerfully in the *Notebooks* is perhaps not coincidental. At the time, Coleridge's poetic writing was in the main a very private affair. Given that he had renounced his claim to be a poet – repeatedly mythologising his own poetic death in poems like 'To William Wordsworth' – the poetry he was writing (which he presumably considered on one level *not* to be poetry) is an interesting contrast to the public aspirations he had for literature, as embodied in Wordsworth. From 'Dejection: An Ode' onwards, Coleridge had accepted a certain self-representation which should be approached cautiously by critics, but nevertheless does mirror a drastic reduction in output and an almost total refusal to publish until 1817. This is thus a poetry that is, in essence, *post*-poetic for Coleridge. Even before the Romantic era was over, then, Coleridge was already in a sense displaced from it, thinking poetry in a way otherwise from that conceptualised in his own ambitious aesthetics. A poetry, in every sense, on the edge of poetry.

Conclusion: from transcendence to finitude

The difference between the *Biographia Literaria* and the Limbo constellation could be said to be emblematic of Coleridge's relationship with the sublime. The deduction of the imagination belongs to the Coleridge whom Vallins describes as the 'foremost advocate of the aesthetic of transcendence'.[41] I have characterised the secondary imagination as an attempt to unify the beautiful and the sublime, providing formal adequacy and harmony, but also invoking supersensible ideas and infinite horizons. However, almost inevitably, one can read the undoing of this desire for transcendence in the very process of its articulation: hence, the fictitious letter from a friend cutting in, as Spivak puts it, to produce the law of the imagination, and hence also the existence of a counter-aesthetic (e.g. the tale of the German girl, the representation of the gothic cathedral) in the margins. Whilst the potential crisis is to some extent averted through rhetorical sleight-of-hand, it cannot be erased. I have read the Limbo constellation as a new finite form of sublimity that, whilst involving its own gestures towards transcendence (e.g. the watcher figure, the negative theology of 'Ne Plus Ultra'), ultimately enacts a ruined poetics. As Nancy and Lacoue-Labarthe put it, 'Romanticism ... could never have protected, defended, or preserved itself from its "unworking" – its incalculable and uncontrollable incompletion'.[42] This is language that does not coincide with itself: multiple, hollowed, broken, interrupted. Yet, this is arguably the very language that post-Romanticism must speak in.

This threefold movement – a transcendent ambition, an arc of crisis, and a renewed sense of the finite – is the same one we have met throughout this study. In considering the Longinian sublime, the possession of a passion that authenticated a privileged space of interiority, outside of the normal rules of discourse, was shown to become increasingly problematic despite its centrality to both Coleridge's lyric and political identities. By contrast, 'Frost at Midnight' engaged with an experience of affect that dispossessed and dislocated the lyric 'I', rather than being possessed by it. In 'The Destiny of Nations', the transcendent ambition for a perfectible subject founded on an ethical terror-sublime ran into crisis as the sublime reverted to more archaic forms: the terror of divine vengeance and the stain of evil on humanity. The guilty subject of 'The Rime of the Ancient Mariner' succeeds the collapse of such hopes, haunted by its own terrifying depths. Finally, in Chapters 5 and 6, we saw various theological sublimities committed to transcendence, counterbalanced by other, more finite, experiences: the withdrawal of the divine in prayer, and the givenness of being. None of these finite experiences need be described as abandoning the discourse of the sublime. Quite the opposite, in fact: they remain sublime, based – speaking schematically – on a non-coincidence, non-formalisability and ungraspability within what is here and now. We encounter the haunting of emotion by itself, of the subject by itself, of being by itself, and of language by itself. As I have argued in my reading of the Limbo constellation, the dashing to pieces of a transcendent sublimity opens up the possibility for redoubling and rearticulating the sublime in a different, finite register.

There is thus a two-sidedness in both Coleridge and the Romantic sublime which demands attention. The end of the transcendent sublime is the opening of a finite sublime. One might justly ask if this is the very same relationship as that between the positive and negative sublimes identified by Thomas Weiskel in *The Romantic Sublime*. Given the importance of the latter study, it is a query that deserves consideration. Certainly, Weiskel seems more alive to an ambivalence within the sublime than many more recent Romantic critics, and at various points there is a structural similarity between his argument and mine: for instance, when he claims that 'the egotistical [or positive] sublime ends precisely at the point of ambivalence in which we found the beginnings of the negative sublime'.[43] As mentioned in the introduction, of course, Coleridge is given relatively short shrift in Weiskel's book, considered in the same transcendent, idealist frame as that assumed by most subsequent critics. He is invoked primarily as the architect of the Romantic imagination, and whilst Weiskel acknowledges 'the "absence" in the work of the Imagination', he does not consider Coleridge traverses this absence in any particularly interesting way.[44] Other than the positive sublime, the paths Weiskel tracks Coleridge along – the beautiful and the de-sublimated – are not those in which we have been interested.[45] However, even putting this to one side, there are nevertheless crucial differences between what I have identified as a finite sublime and Weiskel's negative sublime.

What is at stake is intimated by the very difference in terminology: Weiskel's negative sublime is more purely a category of negativity than what I have called finite sublimity. In contrast to the positive sublime (an excess of meaning to which the self binds itself in a movement of expansion and glorification, in Weiskel's analysis), the negative sublime tends towards privation, violence and annihilating force. In the book's crowning interpretation of Wordsworth, the negative sublime reveals itself as the 'annunciation of death'.[46] Within the psychoanalytic structures that Weiskel weaves around tropes such as the stronger precursor, the Godhead or the archaic Word, the individual always faces 'the anxiety of self-effacement'.[47] We have met such destructive force in our interpretations – the archaic images of punishment that menace 'The Destiny of Nations' (Chapter 3), the abolition of self in a sublime of all-ness (Chapter 6), and the fear of the 'corner of Non-sense' in the Limbo constellation (Chapter 7). Yet, this has generally not been the final moment in our readings: I am not so much interested in privation which destroys the self (a logic of death), but the lack at the heart of existence (a logic of living on). What Coleridge's sense of the finite has always involved is the articulation of experiences (subjectivities, poetics ...) that are *founded* – and continue to exist – on lack. The finite sublime is, put simply, more positive than Weiskel's negative sublime.

One finds this reflected in a persistent sense that Weiskel arranges his two sublimes so that the negative sublime is merely the dark shadow of Romanticism. This type of reading proved fairly influential in the 1970s, and is related to a certain interpretation of gothic as the repressed Other of Romanticism.[48] This tendency is at its most obvious when Weiskel invokes an explicit sense of repression in his final chapter, arguing that *The Prelude* deliberately occludes the spectre of the Gondo Gorge episode in order to maintain a positive, egotistical sublime. The 'terror of the defile' is buried out of sight, and the poem divided. Weiskel insists that 'no moment of consciousness unites the two passages ... they remain dialectically confronted, side by side ... the positive and negative poles of the Romantic sublime'.[49] I don't believe that the relationship between transcendence and finitude in Coleridge is anywhere near as starkly dichotomous.

Whether it is in refiguring his lyric voice, exploring new forms of ethical subjectivity, or attempting to articulate a sense of human finitude within Christian faith and theology, Coleridge's poetry and thought increasingly bears witness to lack, aporia and limit. Yet he does so whilst still maintaining a conscious and critical rapport with the transcendent, or at least the limits of the immanent. The finite sublime is not the repressed Other of Coleridge's Romanticism, so much as a new articulation of it, or within it. Indeed, just as I have argued with the Limbo constellation, it could be seen as a form of post-Romantic poetic emerging at the limits of Romanticism: limits that Coleridge keenly felt. Of course, he never lost that ambitious, transcendent side so marked by existing criticism (including that of Weiskel). He remains, in one sense, the pre-eminent Romantic ideologist in the British tradition. Yet, there is also a fascinatingly *finite* Coleridge available if only we read him carefully and sympathetically. The passage he traces from transcendence to finitude, across the fault-line of the sublime, stands him at the origin of an aesthetic and intellectual legacy that still holds us even if its necessary failure is equally evident. Both sides of Coleridge are hence vital and contemporary.

Notes

Introduction

1. See, for example, Albert O. Wlecke, *Wordsworth and the Sublime* (Berkeley: University of California Press, 1973); Vincent de Luca, *Words of Eternity: Blake and the Poetics of the Sublime* (Princeton: Princeton University Press, 1990); Angela Leighton, *Shelley and the Sublime: An Interpretation of the Major Poems* (Cambridge: Cambridge University Press, 1984); and Stuart Ende, *Keats and the Sublime* (New Haven: Yale University Press, 1976).
2. *On the Sublime*, ed. David Vallins, Coleridge's Writings 5 (Basingstoke: Palgrave Macmillan, 2003).
3. Paul Magnuson, *Coleridge's Nightmare Poetry* (Charlottesville: University Press of Virginia, 1974).
4. Seamus Perry, *Coleridge and the Uses of Division* (Oxford: Clarendon Press, 1999), p. 135.
5. *On the Sublime*, ed. Vallins, p. 1.
6. Raimonda Modiano, *Coleridge and the Concept of Nature* (Basingstoke: Macmillan, 1985), p. 101.
7. Ibid., p. 122.
8. Ibid., p. 137.
9. Steven Knapp, *Personification and the Sublime* (Cambridge, MA: Harvard University Press, 1985), pp. 16–23 and 77–80.
10. Thomas Weiskel, *The Romantic Sublime: Studies in the Structure and Psychology of Transcendence* (Baltimore: Johns Hopkins University Press, 1976), see pp. 53–9 and 158–62.
11. Perry, *Uses of Division*, p. 78, my emphasis.
12. David Vallins, *Coleridge and the Psychology of Romanticism: Feeling and Thought* (Basingstoke: Macmillan, 2000), p. 165.
13. Weiskel, *Romantic Sublime*, p. 57.
14. Jerome McGann, *The Romantic Ideology: A Critical Investigation* (Chicago: University of Chicago Press, 1983), p. 107.
15. Ibid., p. 105.
16. Indeed, sometimes the most relevant context for a poem is a limited and circumscribed one. Whilst I always endeavour to recover whatever I can of Coleridge's contemporary force, this does not efface the necessity of acknowledging very specific historical backdrops, as in my reading of 'The Destiny of Nations' alongside David Hartley and Unitarian radicalism.
17. See Simon Critchley, *The Ethics of Deconstruction: Derrida and Levinas* (Oxford: Blackwell, 1992) and Dominique Janicaud et al., *Phenomenology and the 'Theological Turn': The French Debate*, trans. Bernard G. Prusach (New York: Fordham University Press, 2000) for seminal texts on the ethical and theological turns respectively.

18. Jean-Luc Nancy, 'Preface to the French Edition', Jean-François Courtine et al., *Of the Sublime: Presence in Question*, trans. Jeffrey S. Librett (New York: SUNY Press, 1993), p. 1.
19. Lyotard's most important works on the sublime are *The Inhuman: Reflections on Time*, trans. Geoffrey Bennington and Rachel Bowlby (Cambridge: Polity Press, 1991) and *Lessons on the Analytic of the Sublime*, trans. Elizabeth Rottenberg (Stanford: Stanford University Press, 1994). Courtine et al., *Of the Sublime*, gives a good indication of the range of French writers to cover the sublime. Jacques Derrida offers an analysis of the sublime in *The Truth in Painting*, trans. Geoffrey Bennington and Ian MacLeod (Chicago: University of Chicago Press, 1987), and J. M. Bernstein has gone so far as to represent Derrida's work as a philosophy of the sublime; see *The Fate of Art: Aesthetic Alienation from Kant to Derrida and Adorno* (Cambridge: Polity Press, 1992), pp. 136–75.
20. Tilottama Rajan, *Dark Interpreter: The Discourse of Romanticism* (Ithaca: Cornell University Press, 1980), pp. 249, 263.
21. Susan Eilenberg, *Strange Power of Speech: Wordsworth, Coleridge, and Literary Possession* (Oxford: Oxford University Press, 1992), p. 5.
22. Jerome Christensen, *Coleridge's Blessed Machine of Language* (Ithaca: Cornell University Press, 1981).
23. Jacques Derrida, 'In Memoriam: Of the Soul', in *The Work of Mourning*, ed. Pascale-Anne Brault and Michael Naas (Chicago: University of Chicago Press, 2001), p. 73.
24. Defined in more precise and technical terms, the departure of my analysis from the ironic norms of high deconstruction of a 1980s type would have to refer back to currents in German Romanticism, notably the work of Friedrich Schlegel. Put schematically, where irony in both Romantic and deconstructive forms takes finitude to be a site of infinite potentiality – a world-creating capacity in the absence of transcendental centres – the sublimity which I analyse in this study divides the finite with an internal limit. This is not an experience of power, but an experience characteristically dualistic and thus characteristically sublime.
25. Paul de Man, 'Phenomenality and Materiality in Kant', in *The Textual Sublime: Deconstruction and its Differences*, ed. Hugh J. Silverman and Gary E. Aylesworth (New York: SUNY Press, 1990), pp. 87–108. See also de Man's *Aesthetic Ideology*, ed. Andrzej Warminski (Minneapolis: University of Minnesota Press, 1996).
26. De Man, 'Phenomenality', p. 104.
27. Ibid., p. 105.
28. Derrida, 'Memoriam', p. 73.
29. If one was to identify a beyond-of-irony in de Man's reading of the sublime, it would probably lie in his comments on materiality. See Andrzej Warminski, '"As the Poets Do It": On the Material Sublime', in *Material Events: Paul de Man and the Afterlife of Theory*, ed. Tom Cohen et al. (Minneapolis: University of Minnesota Press, 2001), pp. 3–31.
30. Richard Kearney, 'Deconstruction and the Other: Dialogue with Derrida', in *Dialogue with Contemporary Continental Thinkers: The Phenomenological Heritage* (Manchester: Manchester University Press, 1984), p. 123.
31. Vallins, *Psychology*, p. 8.

32. See, for instance, the essay collections *Who Comes After the Subject?*, ed. Eduardo Cadava et al. (London: Routledge, 1991) and *Deconstructive Subjectivities*, ed. Simon Critchley and Peter Dews (Albany: SUNY Press, 1996).
33. A position explored in (critical) detail by Justin Clemens in *The Romanticism of Contemporary Theory: Institution, Aesthetics, Nihilism* (Aldershot: Ashgate, 2003).
34. Nancy, 'Preface', p. 1.
35. Paul Hamilton, *Coleridge and German Philosophy: The Poet in the Land of Logic* (London: Continuum, 2007), pp. 7–11. Other Romanticist criticism taking a broadly similar approach would include the readings of Wordsworth's materialism in Simon Jarvis, *Wordsworth's Philosophical Song* (Cambridge: Cambridge University Press, 2006) and David S. Ferris's analysis of aesthetics and politics in *Silent Urns: Romanticism, Hellenism, Modernity* (Stanford: Stanford University Press, 2000).
36. Samuel Taylor Coleridge, *Aids to Reflection*, ed. John Beer, Bollingen Collected Works 9 (Princeton: Princeton University Press, 1993), p. 204.
37. Jean-François Lyotard, 'The Sublime and the Avant-Garde', in *The Inhuman*, p. 93.
38. Peter de Bolla, *The Discourse of the Sublime: Readings in History, Aesthetics and the Subject* (Oxford: Blackwell, 1989).

Chapter 1

1. Longinus, 'On Sublimity', trans. D. A. Russell in *Classical Literary Criticism*, ed. D. A. Russell and Michael Winterbottom (Oxford: Oxford University Press, 1989), p. 143. Further references incorporated into text.
2. Theodore Wood, *The Word 'Sublime' and Its Context 1650–1760* (The Hague: Mouton, 1972), and Andrew Ashfield and Peter de Bolla (eds), *The Sublime: A Reader in British Eighteenth-Century Theory* (Cambridge: Cambridge University Press, 1996).
3. The best studies of the Romantic sublime already do this: see, for example, Frances Ferguson's reflections on the relations between the rhetorical and natural sublime in *Solitude and the Sublime: Romanticism and the Aesthetics of Individualism* (New York: Routledge, 1992), pp. 42–53.
4. See John L. Mahoney, 'The Classical Tradition in Eighteenth Century English Rhetorical Education', *History of Education Journal* 9 (1958): 93–7, and, for an enquiry into the specific classical texts studied in an undergraduate course such as that pursued by Coleridge, Russel M. Wyland, 'An Archival Study of Rhetoric Texts and Teaching at the University of Oxford, 1785–1820', *Rhetorica* 21 (2003): 175–95.
5. The 'cloud-climb'd rock, sublime and vast' in 'Epistle IV: To the Author of Poems published anonymously at Bristol', l.19, *Poems on Various Subjects* (London: G. G. and J. Robinson, 1796), pp. 125–8.
6. Samuel Taylor Coleridge, 'Effusion V', l.4, *Poems on Various Subjects*, p. 49.
7. Jacques Derrida, *Writing and Difference*, trans. Alan Bass (London: Routledge, 2001), p. 17.
8. Another aspect of this genealogy of the genius is Longinus's analysis of the sublime tradition: 'When we are working on something which needs

loftiness of expression and greatness of thought, it is good to imagine how Homer would have said the same thing, or how Plato or Demosthenes or ... Thucydides would have invested it with sublimity' (pp. 158–9).

9. Michel Deguy, 'The Discourse of Exaltation: Contribution to a Rereading of Pseudo-Longinus', in Courtine et al., *Of the Sublime*, p. 22.
10. Ibid., p. 7.
11. Ibid., p. 23.
12. Orrin N. C. Wang has identified a similar chiasmus affecting Kant's conception of genius in the *Critique of Judgment*, claiming that 'genius's grounding in nature merely begs the question of genius's ability to give the rule to art ... what enables artistic beauty? – genius. What is genius? – that which enables artistic beauty.' See 'Kant's Strange Light: Romanticism, Periodicity, and the Catachresis of Genius', *Diacritics* 30 (2000), p. 26.
13. Paul de Man, *Allegories of Reading: Figural Language in Rousseau, Nietzsche, Rilke and Proust* (New Haven: Yale University Press, 1979), p. 37.
14. Ibid., pp. 59–67 and 178–87.
15. Ibid., p. 36.
16. Rei Terada, *Feeling in Theory: Emotion after the 'Death of the Subject'* (Cambridge, MA: Harvard University Press, 2001).
17. Sir Richard Blackmore, 'from *Essays upon several subjects*' (1716), in Ashfield and de Bolla (eds), *The Sublime*, pp. 41–2.
18. James Burgh, *The Art of Speaking* (London: T. Longman/J. Buckland/W. Fenner, 1761), p. 29.
19. Ibid., pp. 32–46.
20. Ibid., p. 30.
21. Ibid., p. 31.
22. John Lawson, *Lectures Concerning Oratory* (Dublin: George Faulkner, 1758), p. 165. Further references incorporated into text.
23. Suzanne Guerlac, 'Longinus and the Subject of the Sublime', *NLH* 16 (1985): 275–89.
24. A point made by David Fairer, in 'Coleridge's Sonnets from Various Authors (1796): A Lost Conversation Poem?', *Studies in Romanticism* 41 (2002): 585–604.
25. Samuel Taylor Coleridge, '[Introduction] to *A Sheet of Sonnets*', in *The Complete Poetical Works of Samuel Taylor Coleridge*, ed. Ernest Hartley Coleridge, 2 vols (Oxford: Clarendon Press, 1912), II.1139. Further references incorporated into text.
26. Samuel Taylor Coleridge, 'Preface', *Poems on Various Subjects*, p. vi. Further references incorporated into text.
27. Samuel Taylor Coleridge, 'Effusion XXIV: In the Manner of Spenser', ll.11, 15. Further references incorporated into text, referring to *Poems on Various Subjects*, pp. 73–6.
28. Terada, *Feeling in Theory*, p. 22
29. Samuel Taylor Coleridge, 'Effusion XXXI: Imitated from the Welch', ll.1–4, *Poems on Various Subjects*, p. 88. The source is Edward Jones, *Musical and Poetical Relicks of the Welsh Bards* (London, 1784), p. 32. Jones's translation is rendered: 'If doubtful of my truth you stand / Place on my breast your lovely hand / Yet gently touch; nor aid the smart / That heaves my fond expiring heart?'

30. An analogous question relates to the poems of Charles Lamb within the 1796 *Poems*, which are marked as such even though Coleridge claims, as his poetics implies, that they are already distinguished by a separate stylistic 'signature' (p. xi).
31. More commonly known as 'Lines on an Autumnal Evening'.
32. Samuel Taylor Coleridge, 'Effusion XXXVI: Written in Early Youth', ll.14–15. Further references incorporated into text, referring to *Poems on Various Subjects*, pp. 101–8.
33. Paul de Man, 'The Rhetoric of Temporality', *Blindness and Insight: Essays in the Rhetoric of Contemporary Criticism*, 2nd edn (London: Methuen, 1983), p. 197.
34. Moreover, as Coleridge was forced to admit in later editions, this passage was plagiarised, thus proving in another sense the Protean nature of the poem's author.
35. Terada, *Feeling in Theory*, p. 102.
36. Ibid., p. 103.
37. Daniel Robinson, '"Work without Hope": Anxiety and Embarrassment in Coleridge's Sonnets', *Studies in Romanticism* 39 (2000): 81–110. The three sonnets can be found in *CP*, pp. 144–5.

Chapter 2

A version of the material in this chapter has been published in the *European Romantic Review* 20.1: 57–76.

1. Samuel Taylor Coleridge, 'Ode to the Departing Year', ll.10, 12, *CP*, pp. 126–31.
2. Paul H. Fry, *The Poet's Calling in the English Ode* (New Haven: Yale University Press, 1980), pp. 1–8.
3. Ibid., p. 8.
4. Ibid., p. 138.
5. Samuel Taylor Coleridge, 'France: An Ode', ll.11–14. Further references incorporated into text, referring to *Fears in Solitude, Written in 1798, During the Alarm of an Invasion. To Which are Added, France: An Ode; and Frost at Midnight* (London: J. Johnson, 1798), pp. 13–18.
6. *CP*, p. 522.
7. See Ann Matheson, 'The Influence of Cowper's *The Task* on Coleridge's Conversation Poems', in *New Approaches to Coleridge: Biographical and Critical Essays*, ed. Donald Sultana (London: Vision Press, 1981), pp. 137–50.
8. Samuel Taylor Coleridge, 'Fears in Solitude', ll.29–32. Further references incorporated into text, referring to *Fears in Solitude*, pp. 1–12.
9. *CP*, p. 522.
10. Cited by Longinus, pp. 167, 173. The Dionysius quotation is reported by Herodotus, and the Demosthenes text is 'On the Crown'.
11. Tim Fulford, *Coleridge's Figurative Language* (Basingstoke: Macmillan, 1991), p. 8.
12. l.57 of the 1817 version. See *CP*, p. 240.
13. Michael Simpson, 'The Morning (Post) After: Apocalypses and Bathos in Coleridge's "Fears in Solitude"', in *Romanticism and Millenarianism*, ed. Tim Fulford (Basingstoke: Palgrave Macmillan, 2002), p. 75.

14. Mark Jones, 'Alarmism, Public-Sphere Performatives, and the Lyric Turn: Or, What is "Fears in Solitude" Afraid of?', *Boundary 2* 30 (2003): 67–105.
15. Ibid., p. 96.
16. Ibid.
17. My analysis of oaths has been influenced by Jacques Derrida, *Limited Inc*, ed. Gerald Graff (Evanston: Northwestern University Press, 1988) and Simon Morgan Worthan, 'Neither Fire Nor Flame', an unpublished paper given at the 'Reading the Post Card Colloquium', Oxford University, April 2005.
18. Jon Mee, *Romanticism, Enthusiasm, and Regulation: Poetics and the Policing of Culture in the Romantic Period* (Oxford: Oxford University Press, 2003), p. 144.
19. Angela Esterhammer, *The Romantic Performative: Language and Action in British and German Romanticism* (Stanford: Stanford University Press, 2000), p. 148.
20. Kelvin Everest, *Coleridge's Secret Ministry: The Context of the Conversation Poems* (Hassocks: Harvester Press, 1979), p. 84.
21. See Paul Magnuson, 'The Politics of "Frost at Midnight"', *Wordsworth Circle* 22 (1991): 3–11, and Judith Thompson, 'An Autumnal Blast, a Killing Frost: Coleridge's Poetic Conversation with John Thelwall', *Studies in Romanticism* 36 (1997): 427–56.
22. Samuel Taylor Coleridge, 'Frost at Midnight', ll.59–69. Further references incorporated into text, referring to *Fears in Solitude*, pp. 19–23.
23. Eilenberg, *Strange Power of Speech*, p. 23.
24. Rajan, *Dark Interpreter*, p. 231.
25. Eilenberg, *Strange Power of Speech*, p. 23.
26. *Fears in Solitude*, p. 20.
27. Thomas M. Greene, 'Coleridge and the Energy of Asking', *ELH* 62 (1995), pp. 918–20.
28. Nicholas Royle, 'A Letter on Poetry', in *Telepathy and Literature: Essays on the Reading Mind* (Oxford: Blackwell, 1991), p. 122.
29. Matthew Vanwinkle, 'Fluttering on the Grate: Revision in "Frost at Midnight"', *Studies in Romanticism* 43 (2004), p. 587.
30. Ben Brice, *Coleridge and Scepticism* (Oxford: Oxford University Press, 2007), p. 141.
31. 'Self-watching' could apply both to the sense that the self is observing its own projections (or 'transfusions') in order to constitute feeling, and also to the self's observation of that very process. In fact, there is the possibility of a vertiginous regress here. For a similar analysis in more abstract terms, see Grovesnor Powell, 'Coleridge's "Imagination" and the Infinite Regress of Consciousness', *ELH* 39 (1972): 266–78.
32. Samuel Taylor Coleridge, 'Frost at Midnight', ll.20–4, *CP*, pp. 231–3.
33. Terada, *Feeling in Theory*, p. 69.
34. Ibid., p. 13.
35. Richard Berkeley, *Coleridge and the Crisis of Reason* (Basingstoke: Palgrave Macmillan, 2007), pp. 15–23.
36. Markus Poetsch, *'Visionary Dreariness': Readings in Romanticism's Quotidian Sublime* (London: Routledge, 2006), p. 46.
37. Anne Williams, *Art of Darkness: A Poetics of Gothic* (Chicago: University of Chicago Press, 1995), pp. 202–4.
38. Terada, *Feeling in Theory*, p. 31.
39. Ibid., p. 84.

40. Neil Hertz, *The End of the Line: Essays on Psychoanalysis and the Sublime* (New York: Columbia University Press, 1985) and Weiskel, *Romantic Sublime.*
41. Timothy Clark, *The Poetics of Singularity: The Counter-Culturalist Turn in Heidegger, Derrida, Blanchot and the later Gadamer* (Edinburgh: Edinburgh University Press, 2005), p. 73.
42. Guerlac argues for 'a more radical force at work in the Longinian sublime, one which threatens ... the unified self-identity of the subject' ('Longinus', p. 275).
43. Yopie Prins, *Victorian Sappho* (Princeton: Princeton University Press, 1999), p. 39.
44. Jonathan Culler, 'The Hertzian Sublime', *MLN* 120 (2005), p. 975.
45. Sappho, 'Fragment 31', cited by Longinus, p. 154.

Chapter 3

1. John Axcelson, 'Timing the Apocalypse: The Career of *Religious Musings*', *European Romantic Review* 16 (2005), p. 440, and Peter Kitson, '"To Milton's Trump": Coleridge and the Unitarian Sublime', in *Romanticism and Millenarianism*, ed. Fulford, pp. 37–52.
2. The poem has a complex textual history. It begins with material originally contributed to Book II of Robert Southey's epic poem *Joan of Arc*, before shifting into the newer and more naturalistic episode with the refugees. This breaks off, and the rest of the poem is a series of unfinished drafts in a visionary style. It was not actually published until 1817, although the refugee narrative was published separately in the *Morning Post* of 25 December 1797, entitled 'The Visions of the Maid of Orleans. A Fragment, by S. T. Coleridge'.
3. Samuel Taylor Coleridge, 'The Destiny of Nations', ll.197–202. Further references incorporated into text, referring to *CP*, pp. 95–107.
4. These parts of the poem were adapted directly from the real-life war journalism. See *The Watchman*, ed. Lewis Patton, Bollingen Collected Works 2 (Princeton: Princeton University Press, 1970), pp. 239–41.
5. See *CP*, p. 450.
6. Edmund Burke, *A Philosophical Enquiry into the Origin of our Ideas of the Sublime and Beautiful*, ed. Adam Phillips (Oxford: Oxford University Press, 1990), p. 36. Further references incorporated into text.
7. Ibid., pp. 119–22, 128–9, 131–3, 75–6.
8. Ferguson, *Solitude and the Sublime*, p. 57.
9. Ibid., p. 47.
10. David Hartley, *Observations on Man, His Frame, His Duty, and His Expectations*, 2 vols (London: S. Richardson, 1749), I.11–12.
11. Ibid., I.56–9.
12. It is worth noting that Burke does invoke association in the final section of the *Enquiry* on language, which reflects the fact that association was an integral part of British empiricism – although not in the systematic and overwhelmingly central way found in Hartley's system.
13. Richard C. Allen, *David Hartley on Human Nature* (Albany: SUNY Press, 1999), p. 355.
14. Hartley, *Observations*, II.283.

15. 'Sonnet: To the Author of the Robbers', *CP*, p. 61.
16. Nicola Trott, 'The Coleridge Circle and the "Answer to Godwin"', *Review of English Studies* 41 (1990), p. 214.
17. 'Religious Musings', ll.126–30, *CP*, pp. 107–17.
18. Of course, Coleridge's language is resolutely masculine: hence, 'the sublime of man', the notion of fraternity, and so forth. Perhaps this can be explained precisely by Joan's excess of *feeling*, as opposed to the *knowledge* in 'Religious Musings' – although this does not change the fact that feeling, sympathy and compassion are a necessary and continued foundation for moral sense. This would suggest a binary between the contemporary Unitarian hero, gendered masculine with full moral enlightenment, and Joan of Arc as a heroine, possessing a radical intensity of sympathy which is the undeveloped germ of the former. This would certainly fit in with Joan of Arc's proleptic position as a French revolutionary in 'The Destiny of Nations', where she aids her nation without full knowledge: 'Much hast thou seen, nor all canst understand – / But this be thy best omen – Save thy Country!' (ll.455–6).
19. Robert Sternbach, 'Coleridge, Joan of Arc, and the Idea of Progress', *ELH* 46 (1979), p. 259.
20. William A. Ulmer, 'The Alienation of the Elect in Coleridge's Unitarian Prophecies', *Review of English Studies* 57 (2006), p. 543.
21. Sternbach, 'Idea of Progress', p. 257.
22. Ulmer, 'Alienation', p. 542.
23. 'Religious Musings', ll.119–21.
24. Thomas de Quincey, *Confessions of an English Opium-Eater and Other Writings*, ed. Grevel Lindop (Oxford: Oxford University Press, 1996), p. 91.
25. Sigmund Freud, 'Mourning and Melancholia', *On Metapsychology: The Theory of Psychoanalysis*, ed. Angela Richards, Penguin Freud Library 11 (London: Penguin, 1984), p. 252.
26. Joseph Priestley, *The Doctrine of Philosophical Necessity Illustrated* (London: J. Johnson, 1777), p. 7.
27. Ibid., pp. 1–8 and 25–56.
28. Ibid., p. 65.
29. Joseph Priestley, *Lectures on History and General Policy* (Dublin: Byrne, 1788), p. 294.
30. William Godwin, *An Enquiry Concerning Political Justice*, ed. Mark Philp, Writings of William Godwin 3 (London: Pickering, 1993), p. 368.
31. Ibid., p. 279. For his critique of the psychological make-up of monarchs, see pp. 208–21.
32. Ibid., p. 468.
33. Peter Kitson, 'Coleridge, the French Revolution, and "The Ancient Mariner": Collective Guilt and Individual Salvation', *Yearbook of English Studies* 19 (1989), p. 201.
34. Julia Kristeva, *Powers of Horror: An Essay on Abjection*, trans. Leon S. Roudiez (New York: Columbia University Press, 1982), p. 114.
35. Joseph Priestley, *Three Tracts* (London, 1791), p. 98.
36. Joseph Priestley, *A Comparison of the Institutions of Moses with those of the Hindoos* (Northumberland: A. Kennedy, 1799), p. 205.
37. Priestley, *Three Tracts*, p. 10.

38. Samuel Taylor Coleridge, *Lectures 1795: On Politics and Religion*, ed. Lewis Patton and Peter Mann, Bollingen Collected Works 1 (Princeton: Princeton University Press, 1971), pp. 202–8.
39. Priestley, *Institutions*, p. 205.
40. Coleridge, *Lectures 1795*, pp. 112–18.
41. William Ulmer, 'Virtue of Necessity: Coleridge's Unitarian Moral Theory', *Modern Philology* 102 (2005), p. 393.

Chapter 4

1. A version of the material in this chapter is forthcoming in *Studies in Romanticism*.
2. *Coleridge: The Critical Heritage*, ed. J. R. de J. Jackson (London: Routledge, 1970), p. 53.
3. See David Chandler, 'Southey's "German Sublimity" and Coleridge's "Dutch Attempt"', *Romanticism on the Net* 32–3 (2003–4) (http://www.erudit.org/revue/ron/2003/v/n32-33/009257ar.html) (accessed 17 October 2009).
4. *Heritage*, ed. Jackson, p. 439, my emphases. One might argue that the polarised judgements are simply a matter of the changing historical context, in that Lockhart had the benefit of two decades of hindsight and a less hysterical political climate. However, this would be mistaken, for the *Monthly Review* – also in 1819 – reviewed the poem in an anti-German and anti-gothic vein very reminiscent of the negative reviews from the 1790s. See *Heritage*, p. 403.
5. I am initially working from the 1798 text, and many of the things I will identify as ambiguous or unintelligible are elucidated by Coleridge's later revisions. I shall move on to consider these revisions below.
6. For example, David S. Miall, 'Guilt and Death: The Predicament of The Ancient Mariner', *Studies in English Literature, 1500–1900* 24 (1984): 633–53 and Leah Richards-Fisher, 'Where There's a Rime, Is There a Reason? Defining the Personae in Coleridge's *The Rime of the Ancient Mariner*', *Coleridge Bulletin* 20 (2002): 63–8.
7. Raimonda Modiano, 'Words and "Languageless" Meanings: Limits of Expression in *The Rime of the Ancient Mariner*', *Modern Language Quarterly* 38 (1977): 40–61.
8. The classic *one life* reading is Robert Penn Warren, 'A Poem of Pure Imagination: An Experiment in Reading', *Selected Essays* (London: Eyre and Spottiswoode, 1964), pp. 198–305.
9. See ibid., and G. Wilson Knight, *The Starlit Dome: Studies in the Poetry of Vision* (Oxford: Oxford University Press, 1941), pp. 84–90. A Christian tradition of interpretation still continues. Graham Davidson foregrounds the themes of charity and mediation in *Coleridge's Career* (Basingstoke: Macmillan, 1990), pp. 45–73. Peter Kitson's article 'Collective Guilt' considers the 'Rime' as the representation of the inner, moral revolution – 'a personal millennium' (p. 206) – that might precede a political one. Thomas Dilworth argues for the poem's moral integrity through a spatial pattern of verbal echoes that centres on the blessing of the water-snakes in 'Symbolic Spatial Form in *The Rime of the Ancient Mariner* and the Problem of God', *Review of English Studies* 58 (2007): 500–30.

10. Edward E. Bostetter, 'The Nightmare World of *The Ancient Mariner*', *Studies in Romanticism* 1 (1961–2), p. 243.
11. Modiano, 'Words', p. 41.
12. Miall, 'Guilt', p. 635.
13. Anne Williams, 'An I for an Eye: "Spectral Persecution" in *The Rime of the Ancient Mariner*', *PMLA* 108 (1993), p. 1125.
14. Williams, 'Persecution', p. 1124.
15. Richards-Fisher, 'Where There's a Rime', p. 63.
16. Coleridge, *Lectures 1795*, p. 105.
17. On Coleridge's passage from Unitarianism to Anglicanism, see Thomas McFarland, *Coleridge and the Pantheist Tradition* (Oxford: Clarendon Press, 1969), pp. 169–81 and 223–55.
18. Ulmer, 'Virtue', p. 398.
19. Ibid., p. 399.
20. William Ulmer, 'Necessary Evils: Unitarian Theodicy in The Rime of the Ancyent Marinere', *Studies in Romanticism* 43 (2004), p. 350.
21. Ibid., pp. 353–4.
22. Ulmer, 'Virtue', p. 399.
23. The motiveless nature of the crime is an irrationality that Christianising interpretations of the poem have sometimes accepted. For example, Robert Penn Warren claims that 'the lack of motivation, the perversity ... re-enacts the Fall' ('Poem of Pure Imagination', p. 227). However, this is in strong contrast to the order imposed on the rest of the poem.
24. Priestley, *Three Tracts*, p. 10.
25. Ibid., p. 167.
26. Coleridge, *Lectures 1795*, p. 205.
27. Priestley, *Three Tracts*, p. 6.
28. Indeed, a slightly different way of reading the terrors of inexpiability is to suggest that Coleridge was beginning to believe that humanity did require redemption from outside, and yet his Unitarianism, which treated Jesus Christ merely as an exemplary human, failed to provide a redeemer.
29. Ulmer, 'Necessary Evils', p. 353.
30. Priestley, *Three Tracts*, p. 167.
31. Compare ll.477–506 of the 1798 version with ll.472–9 in 1834.
32. Kathleen Wheeler, *The Creative Mind in Coleridge's Poetry* (Cambridge, MA: Harvard University Press, 1981), p. 52.
33. Jerome J. McGann, 'The Meaning of The Ancient Mariner', *Critical Inquiry* 8 (1981–2): 35–67.
34. See *CP*, pp. 176 and 178–9.
35. *CP*, p. 185.
36. For example, Richards-Fisher, 'Where There's a Rime', p. 63.
37. Blaise Pascal, *Pensées and Other Writings*, trans. Honor Levi (Oxford: Oxford University Press, 1995), p. 43.
38. *A Reformation Reader: Primary Texts with Introductions*, ed. Denis R. Janz (Minneapolis: Fortress Press, 1999), p. 128.
39. Ben Brice foregrounds a parallel Calvinist influence on Coleridge, where the terms of God's justice seem outrageous and inscrutable to the fallen human intellect. See Brice, *Coleridge and Scepticism*, pp. 25–7.
40. *Aids*, p. 280, 274. Further references incorporated into text.

41. For Coleridge's treatment of election, see *Aids*, pp. 170–4.
42. This particular section, suggesting a relation to evil outside of the categories of time and space, seems indebted to the first part of Kant's *Religion within the Limits of Reason Alone*. Elinor Shaffer has explored the links between the two texts in 'Metaphysics of Culture: Kant and Coleridge's *Aids to Reflection*', *Journal of the History of Ideas* 31 (1970): 199–218.
43. Burke, *Enquiry*, p. 36.
44. I am indebted to my reader at Palgrave Macmillan for this insightful point.
45. De Bolla, *Discourse*, p. 37.
46. Indeed, this shift to a terrifying sense of subjectivity (rather than having terror perceived by a subject) is not unrelated to certain shifts in gothic that would become apparent in the late Romantic and Victorian age. See Fred Botting, *Gothic* (London: Routledge, 1996), pp. 10–13.
47. Eilenberg, *Strange Power of Speech*, p. 34.
48. Ibid., p. 59. See Jacques Derrida, *The Monolingualism of the Other; or, The Prosthesis of Origin*, trans. Patrick Mensah (Stanford: Stanford University Press, 1998).
49. Eilenberg, *Strange Power of Speech*, p. 51.
50. Immanuel Kant, *Religion Within the Limits of Reason Alone*, trans. Theodore M. Greene and Hoyt H. Hudson (New York: Harper, 1960), p. 32.
51. Richard J. Bernstein, *Radical Evil: A Philosophical Investigation* (Cambridge: Polity Press, 2002), p. 31.
52. Freud, of course, did so in *Totem and Taboo*, and guilt continues to play an important function in the psychoanalytic theories of Jacques Lacan and Melanie Klein. Readings that entwine Levinas's responsibility for the Other with guilt include Alon Kantor's 'Levinas's Law', *American Imago* 56 (1999): 357–85, and Philippe Van Haute's 'Law, Guilt and Subjectivity: Reflections on Freud, Nancy, and Derrida', in *Deconstructive Subjectivities*, ed. Critchley and Dews, pp. 185–200. Jean-Luc Nancy considers that evil and freedom are co-originary, freedom implying a decision made without prior laws or foundations, a decision that must as such pass through the possibility of violence – see *The Experience of Freedom*, trans. Bridget McDonald (Stanford: Stanford University Press, 1993), pp. 121–41.

Chapter 5

1. Initially written in 1802 and published in the *Morning Post*, the poem underwent several later revisions. The reading text for this chapter – and most modern editions – is from 1817's *Sibylline Leaves*. Exactly when Coleridge became properly familiar with Kant is unclear. Although Kant's name arises as early as 1796 (see *CL*, I.209), the famous letter to Thomas Poole (from March 1801) in which Coleridge claims to have overthrown associationism and 'extricated the notions of Time, and Space' (*CL*, II.706) is generally taken as the earliest unambiguous sign of adopting a distinctly Kantian perspective. The period of 1801–2 is also suggested by *Biographia Literaria*, where Coleridge claims 'fifteen years familiarity' with Kant's works. See *Biographia Literaria*, ed. James Engell and W. Jackson Bate, Bollingen Collected Works 7, 2 vols (Princeton: Princeton University Press, 1983), I.153.

2. Modiano, *Concept of Nature*, p. 137; Perry, *Uses of Division*, p. 78.
3. Samuel Taylor Coleridge, 'Hymn Before Sun-Rise, in the Vale of Chamouni', ll.8–10. Further references incorporated into text, referring to *CP*, pp. 323–5.
4. Immanuel Kant, *Critique of the Power of Judgment*, ed. and trans. Paul Guyer (Cambridge: Cambridge University Press, 2000), p. 156. Further references incorporated into text.
5. ll.20–3 of *Morning Post* version, *CP*, p. 563.
6. Modiano, *Concept of Nature*, pp. 134–7.
7. Ibid., p. 122.
8. Günter Zöller, 'From Critique to Metacritique: Fichte's Transformation of Kant's Transcendental Idealism', in *The Reception of Kant's Critical Philosophy: Fichte, Schelling, and Hegel*, ed. Sally Sedgwick (Cambridge: Cambridge University Press, 2000), p. 131.
9. Coleridge, *Lectures 1795*, p. 94.
10. Cian Duffy, 'Mont Blanc's Revolutionary "Voice": Shelley and the Discourse on the Sublime', in *Silence, Sublimity and Suppression in the Romantic Period*, ed. Fiona L. Price and Scott Masson (Lewiston: Edwin Mellon Press, 2002), p. 23.
11. Jacob Behmen, 'Signatura Rerum; the Signature of all Things', *Works*, 4 vols (London: G. Robinson, 1764–81), IV.132.
12. Ibid., p. 59.
13. Ibid., p. 11.
14. Ibid., p. 23.
15. Ibid., p. 4.
16. Samuel Taylor Coleridge, *Marginalia*, ed. George Whalley, Bollingen Collected Works 12, 6 vols (Princeton: Princeton University Press, 1980–2001), I.558.
17. Brice, *Coleridge and Scepticism*, p. 164.
18. Louise Economides, '"Mont Blanc" and the Sublimity of Materiality', *Cultural Critique* 61 (2005): 87–114.
19. Esterhammer, *Romantic Performative*, p. 173.
20. For instance, Helena Feder's 'Ecocriticism, New Historicism, and Romantic Apostrophe', in *The Greening of Literary Scholarship: Literature, Theory, and the Environment*, ed. Steven Rosendale (Iowa City: University of Iowa Press, 2002), pp. 42–58.
21. Paul de Man, *The Rhetoric of Romanticism* (New York: Columbia University Press, 1984), pp. 116–21.
22. Cynthia Chase, *Decomposing Forms: Rhetorical Readings in the Romantic Tradition* (Baltimore: Johns Hopkins University Press, 1986), p. 69.
23. Such as J. Robert Barth, *The Symbolic Imagination: Coleridge and the Romantic Tradition* (Princeton: Princeton University Press, 1977), pp. 13, 42–50; and James S. Cutsinger, *The Form of Transformed Vision: Coleridge and the Knowledge of God* (Macon: Mercer University Press, 1987), pp. 35–6.
24. Chase, *Decomposing Forms*, p. 106.
25. Immanuel Kant, *Critique of Pure Reason*, trans. and ed. Paul Guyer and Allen W. Wood (Cambridge: Cambridge University Press, 1998), p. 670.
26. Ibid., p. 580.
27. Ibid., p. 572.
28. Ibid., pp. 587–8.
29. Ibid., p. 581.
30. De Man, 'Phenomenality', p. 101. See also Warminski, 'Material Sublime'.

31. See Douglas J. Kneale, 'Romantic Aversions: Apostrophe Reconsidered', *ELH* 58 (1991): 141–65.
32. Martin Heidegger, *Being and Time*, trans. John Macquarrie and Edward Robinson (Oxford: Blackwell, 1962), p. 52.
33. Ibid., p. 53.
34. Ibid., p. 52.
35. Economides, '"Mont Blanc"', p. 89.
36. Samuel Taylor Coleridge, *Shorter Works and Fragments*, ed. H. J. and J. R. de J. Jackson, Bollingen Collected Works 11, 2 vols (Princeton: Princeton University Press, 1995), II.1118–19.
37. Augustine, *Confessions*, trans. R. S. Pine-Coffin (London: Penguin, 1961), p. 213.
38. Jacques Derrida, 'How to Avoid Speaking: Denials', trans. Ken Frieden, in *Languages of the Unsayable: The Play of Negativity in Literature and Literary Theory*, ed. Sanford Budick and Wolfgang Iser (New York: Columbia University Press, 1989), p. 42.
39. Ibid., p. 67.
40. Ibid., p. 41.
41. Hent de Vries, *Philosophy and the Turn to Religion* (Baltimore: Johns Hopkins University Press, 1999), p. 137.
42. Derrida, 'How to Avoid Speaking', p. 62.
43. For a much more detailed discussion, see Christopher Stokes, 'Coleridge's Philosophy of Prayer: Responsibility, Parergon, Catachresis', *Journal of Religion* 89.4 (2009): 541–63.
44. Samuel Taylor Coleridge, 'To Nature', ll.1–5. Further references incorporated into text, referring to *CP*, pp. 370–1.
45. 'Love's Apparition and Evanishment', ll.1–8. *CP*, pp. 414–15.
46. Jean-Louis Chrétien, 'The Wounded Word: The Phenomenology of Prayer', in Janicaud et al., *Phenomenology and the 'Theological Turn'*, p. 150.
47. Samuel Taylor Coleridge, *Lay Sermons*, ed. R. J. White, Bollingen Collected Works 6 (Princeton: Princeton University Press, 1972), pp. 70–3.
48. Modiano, *Concept of Nature*, p. 85.

Chapter 6

1. Jean-Luc Nancy, *The Inoperative Community*, ed. Peter Connor, trans. Peter Connor et al. (Minneapolis: University of Minnesota Press, 1991), p. 112.
2. Coleridge, *Shorter Works*, I.351.
3. Ibid., I.353.
4. Ibid., I.352.
5. See, for example, Paul Guyer's analysis of failed and liberated imagination in *Kant and the Experience of Freedom: Essays on Aesthetics and Morality* (Cambridge: Cambridge University Press, 1996), pp. 215–16.
6. Seamus Perry describes a 'sublime self-abnegation' in the face of the object, although he perhaps considers such an experience rather more positively than my interpretations. See Perry, *Uses of Division*, p. 159.
7. *The Friend*, ed. Barbara E. Rooke, Bollingen Collected Works 4, 2 vols (Princeton: Princeton University Press, 1969), I.367.

8. Strictly speaking, the title 'Coeli Enarrant' ('the heavens declare ...') refers only to the final stanza of a longer piece of untitled notebook verse, included in Keach's edition with the title '[Lines from a notebook – July 1807]'. I refer to the whole text as 'Coeli Enarrant' purely for reasons of convenience.
9. '[Lines from a notebook – July 1807]', ll.1, 2. Further references incorporated into the text, referring to *CP*, pp. 337–8.
10. Edward Kessler, *Coleridge's Metaphors of Being* (Princeton: Princeton University Press, 1979), p. 156.
11. Modiano, *Concept of Nature*, p. 115.
12. 'Human Life: On the Denial of Immortality', ll.3–6. Further references incorporated into the text, referring to *CP*, p. 362.
13. Perry, *Uses of Division*, p. 64.
14. Ibid., p. 80.
15. 'The Suicide's Argument', ll.3–4, *CP*, p. 359.
16. Ibid., l.5.
17. Strictly speaking, *The Friend* is not completed by this passage, but by the 'Third Landing Place' and a biographical sketch of Sir Alexander Ball. However, the main philosophical and theological thrust of the text reaches its conclusion here.
18. Coleridge, *The Friend*, I.514.
19. Herbert Read, *Coleridge as Critic* (London: Faber, 1949).
20. Martin Heidegger, 'What is Metaphysics', *Basic Writings*, ed. David Farrell Krell (San Francisco: HarperCollins, 1977), p. 109.
21. Ibid., p. 110.
22. Jean-Luc Marion, *Being Given: Toward a Phenomenology of Givenness*, trans. Jeffrey L. Kosky (Stanford: Stanford University Press, 2002), pp. 33–9.
23. Coleridge, *The Friend*, I.515.
24. Ibid., I.514.
25. Ibid., I.516.
26. Vallins, *Psychology*, p. 152.
27. Coleridge, *The Friend*, I.516.
28. Ibid., I.515.
29. Jean-Luc Nancy, 'The Sublime Offering', in *A Finite Thinking*, ed. Simon Sparks (Stanford: Stanford University Press, 2003), p. 224. All further references incorporated into the text.
30. Ibid., p. 221.
31. Ibid., p. 223.
32. The difficulty is not trying to imagine this pre-formal indeterminacy in formal terms, as a kind of space, place, totality or field. Nancy is insistent that the indeterminacy is not itself represented in any way in the sublime (this would be impossible), but rather *felt* on the edge of forms.
33. Nancy, 'Offering', p. 227.
34. Ibid., p. 225.
35. Ibid., p. 228.
36. Nancy, *Experience*, p. 158.
37. Ibid., p. 53.
38. Nancy, 'Offering', p. 237.
39. Marion's initial example is the painting, the phenomenality of which cannot be reduced to objectivity or even being, because it outstrips any single

determination of its presence (commercial, critical, aesthetic) and, more fundamentally, because it is different each time it is viewed (thus there is always a reserve or remainder of experience outside of the grasp). Other phenomena that Marion identifies as in excess of being and objectness are time, one's life, one's word, death, peace and meaning. See *Being Given*, pp. 39–53.

40. Ibid., p. 198.
41. Ibid., p. 220.
42. Ibid., p. 102.
43. Ibid., p. 86. See also p. 36.
44. Ibid., p. 241.
45. Not coincidentally, Cartesian infinity is one of Marion's other examples of a saturated phenomenon from the history of philosophy.
46. Nancy, *Inoperative*, p. 130.
47. Vallins, *Psychology*, pp. 144–6.
48. Ibid., pp. 157, 161.
49. Coleridge, *The Friend*, I.106.
50. See also p. 324 for the same sentiment.
51. Coleridge, *The Friend*, p. 109.

Chapter 7

1. Len Epp, 'Coleridge and the Non-empirical Imagination', *Coleridge Bulletin* 16 (2000), p. 46.
2. Walter Jackson Bate, 'Coleridge on the Function of Art', in *Perspectives of Criticism* (Cambridge, MA: Harvard University Press, 1950), p. 130.
3. J. G. Fichte, *The Science of Knowledge*, ed and trans. Peter Heath and John Lachs (Cambridge: Cambridge University Press, 1982), p. 71.
4. See David S. Ferris, 'Coleridge's Ventriloquy: The Abduction from the *Biographia*', *Studies in Romanticism* 24 (1985), pp. 46–56. David Baulch also highlights the assimilation of the radical German 'I' to a Cartesian tradition in 'The "Perpetual Exercise of an Interminable Quest": The *Biographia Literaria* and the Kantian Revolution', *Studies in Romanticism* 43 (2004): 557–81.
5. Fichte, *Science*, p. 202.
6. See Robert F. Brown, 'The Transcendental Fall in Kant and Schelling', *Idealistic Studies* 14 (1984): 49–66.
7. F. W. J. Schelling, *System of Transcendental Idealism*, trans. Peter Heath (Charlottesville: University Press of Virginia, 1978), pp. 221–2.
8. Ibid., p. 221.
9. Andrzej Warminski, 'Returns of the Sublime: Positing and Performative in Kant, Fichte, and Schiller, *MLN* 116 (2001), p. 975.
10. Schelling, *System*, p. 222.
11. Ibid., p. 226. This quotation comes from a passage added in the author's copy.
12. The editors of the Bollingen edition of the *Biographia* cite this notebook entry as a crucial precursor for the famous reconciliation-of-opposites passage in the text: see II.16, fn.2.

13. Warminski, 'Returns', p. 973.
14. This argument is similar to that made by Tim Milnes about Coleridge's deduction of the imagination in 'Eclipsing Art: Method and Metaphysics in Coleridge's *Biographia Literaria*', *Journal of the History of Ideas* 60 (1999), p. 136.
15. Gayatri Chakravorty Spivak, 'The Letter as Cutting Edge', *Yale French Studies* 55–6 (1977): 208–26.
16. Jerome Christensen, '"Like a Guilty Thing Surprised": Coleridge, Deconstruction, and the Apostasy of Criticism', in *Coleridge's Biographia Literaria: Text and Meaning*, ed. Frederick Burwick (Columbus: Ohio State University Press, 1989), p. 180.
17. Spivak, 'Letter', p. 220.
18. Philippe Lacoue-Labarthe and Jean-Luc Nancy, *The Literary Absolute: The Theory of Literature in German Romanticism*, trans. Philip Barnard and Cheryl Lester (Albany: SUNY Press, 1988), p. 107.
19. Ibid., p. 108.
20. Ibid., p. 110.
21. F. W. J. Schelling, *The Philosophy of Art*, ed and trans. Douglas W. Stott (Minneapolis: University of Minnesota Press, 1989), p. 82.
22. Lacoue-Labarthe and Nancy, *Literary Absolute*, pp. 111, 117.
23. Christensen, *Blessed Machine*, p. 111.
24. Ibid., p. 113.
25. Eilenberg, *Strange Power of Speech*, p. 167.
26. Coleridge, *Marginalia*, II.402.
27. Lacoue-Labarthe and Nancy, *Literary Absolute*, p. 111.
28. I borrow the term Limbo constellation from Morton D. Paley's *Coleridge's Later Poetry* (Oxford: Clarendon Press, 1996), p. 43.
29. As the poem is generally anthologised in separate parts, and I wish to treat it in its original notebook form, the reader is referred to volume 3 of the *Notebooks*, N4073–4, for all citations.
30. Coleridge, *The Friend*, I.155–6.
31. Kessler, *Metaphors of Being*, p. 103.
32. On simile as a disjunctive or suspending figure, see Susan J. Wolfson, '"Comparing Power": Coleridge and Simile', in *Coleridge's Theory of Imagination Today*, ed. Christine Gallant (New York: AMS Press, 1989), pp. 167–95.
33. Paley, *Later Poetry*, p. 52.
34. Although probably given by Henry Nelson Coleridge, Coleridge himself may have been aware of this title. See *CP*, p. 585.
35. Kessler, *Metaphors of Being*, p. 113.
36. Ibid., p. 9.
37. Culler, 'Hertzian Sublime', p. 980.
38. Paley, *Later Poetry*, p. 61.
39. On metaphysical wit in this section of the constellation, see John A. Hodgson, 'Coleridge, Puns, and "Donne's First Poem": The Limbo of Rhetoric and the Conceptions of Wit', *John Donne Journal* 4 (1985): 181–200.
40. One may, of course, invoke the possibility of a comic sublime: see Raimonda Modiano, 'Humanism and the Comic Sublime: From Kant to Friedrich Theodor Vischer', *Studies in Romanticism* 26 (1987): 231–44.
41. Coleridge, *On the Sublime*, ed. Vallins, p. 1.
42. Lacoue-Labarthe and Nancy, *Literary Absolute*, p. 59.

43. Weiskel, *Romantic Sublime*, p. 162.
44. Ibid., p. 161.
45. For desublimation, see ibid., p. 57; for beauty – in a brief reading of 'Frost at Midnight' – see p. 59.
46. Ibid., p. 190.
47. Ibid., p. 203.
48. See, for example, *The Gothic Imagination: Essays in Dark Romanticism*, ed. G. R. Thompson (Pullman: Washington State University Press, 1974).
49. Weiskel, *Romantic Sublime*, p. 204.

Bibliography

Primary sources

Ashfield, Andrew and de Bolla, Peter (eds), *The Sublime: A Reader in British Eighteenth-Century Theory* (Cambridge: Cambridge University Press, 1996)

Augustine, *Confessions*, trans. R. S. Pine-Coffin (London: Penguin, 1961)

Behmen, Jacob, 'Signatura Rerum; the Signature of all Things', *Works*, 4 vols (London: G. Robinson, 1764–81), IV.2–140

Burgh, James, *The Art of Speaking* (London: T. Longman/J. Buckland/W. Fenner, 1761)

Burke, Edmund, *A Philosophical Enquiry into the Origin of our Ideas of the Sublime and Beautiful*, ed. Adam Phillips (Oxford: Oxford University Press, 1990)

Coleridge, Samuel Taylor, *Poems on Various Subjects* (London: G. G. and J. Robinson, 1796)

—— *Fears in Solitude, Written in 1798, During the Alarm of an Invasion. To Which are Added, France: An Ode; and Frost at Midnight* (London: J. Johnson, 1798)

—— *The Complete Poetical Works of Samuel Taylor Coleridge*, ed. Ernest Hartley Coleridge, 2 vols (Oxford: Clarendon Press, 1912)

—— *Collected Letters of Samuel Taylor Coleridge*, ed. E. L. Griggs, 6 vols (Oxford: Clarendon Press, 1956–71)

—— *The Notebooks of Samuel Taylor Coleridge*, ed. Kathleen Coburn, 5 vols (London: Routledge, 1957–2002)

—— *The Friend*, ed. Barbara E. Rooke, Bollingen Collected Works 4, 2 vols (Princeton: Princeton University Press, 1969)

—— *The Watchman*, ed. Lewis Patton, Bollingen Collected Works 2 (Princeton: Princeton University Press, 1970)

—— *Lectures 1795: On Politics and Religion*, ed. Lewis Patton and Peter Mann, Bollingen Collected Works 1 (Princeton: Princeton University Press, 1971)

—— *Lay Sermons*, ed. R. J. White, Bollingen Collected Works 6 (Princeton: Princeton University Press, 1972)

—— *Marginalia*, ed. George Whalley, Bollingen Collected Works 12, 6 vols (Princeton: Princeton University Press, 1980–2001)

—— *Biographia Literaria*, ed. James Engell and W. Jackson Bate, Bollingen Collected Works 7, 2 vols (Princeton: Princeton University Press, 1983)

—— *Lectures 1808–1819: On Literature*, ed. R. A. Foakes, Bollingen Collected Works 5, 2 vols (Princeton: Princeton University Press, 1987)

—— *Aids to Reflection*, ed. John Beer, Bollingen Collected Works 9 (Princeton: Princeton University Press, 1993)

—— *Shorter Works and Fragments*, ed. H. J. and J. R. de J. Jackson, Bollingen Collected Works 11, 2 vols (Princeton: Princeton University Press, 1995)

—— *The Complete Poems*, ed. William Keach (Harmondsworth: Penguin, 1997)

—— *Poetical Works II: Poems (Variorum Text)*, ed. J. C. C. Mays, Bollingen Collected Works 16.2, 2 parts (Princeton: Princeton University Press, 2001)

—— *On the Sublime*, ed. David Vallins, Coleridge's Writings 5 (Basingstoke: Palgrave Macmillan, 2003)
De Quincey, Thomas, *Confessions of an English Opium-Eater and Other Writings*, ed. Grevel Lindop (Oxford: Oxford University Press, 1996)
Fichte, J. G., *The Science of Knowledge*, ed. and trans. Peter Heath and John Lachs (1794; Cambridge: Cambridge University Press, 1982)
Godwin, William, *An Enquiry Concerning Political Justice*, ed. Mark Philp, Writings of William Godwin 3 (London: Pickering, 1993)
Hartley, David, *Observations on Man, His Frame, His Duty, and His Expectations*, 2 vols (London: S. Richardson, 1749)
Janz, Denis R. (ed.), *A Reformation Reader: Primary Texts with Introductions* (Minneapolis: Fortress Press, 1999)
Jones, Edward, *Musical and Poetical Relicks of the Welsh Bards* (London, 1784)
Kant, Immanuel, *Religion Within the Limits of Reason Alone*, trans. Theodore M. Greene and Hoyt H. Hudson (New York: Harper, 1960)
—— *Critique of Pure Reason*, ed. and trans. Paul Guyer and Allen W. Wood (Cambridge: Cambridge University Press, 1998)
—— *Critique of the Power of Judgment*, ed. and trans. Paul Guyer (Cambridge: Cambridge University Press, 2000)
Lawson, John, *Lectures Concerning Oratory* (Dublin: George Faulkner, 1758)
Longinus, 'On Sublimity', trans. D. A. Russell, in *Classical Literary Criticism*, ed. D. A. Russell and Michael Winterbottom (Oxford: Oxford University Press, 1989), 143–87
Pascal, Blaise, *Pensées and Other Writings*, trans. Honor Levi (Oxford: Oxford University Press, 1995)
Priestley, Joseph, *The Doctrine of Philosophical Necessity Illustrated* (London: J. Johnson, 1777)
—— *Lectures on History and General Policy* (Dublin: P. Byrne, 1788)
—— *Three Tracts* (London, 1791)
—— *A Comparison of the Institutions of Moses with those of the Hindoos* (Northumberland: A. Kennedy, 1799)
Schelling, F. W. J., *System of Transcendental Idealism*, trans. Peter Heath (Charlottesville: University Press of Virginia, 1978)
—— *The Philosophy of Art*, ed. and trans. Douglas W. Stott (Minneapolis: University of Minnesota Press, 1989)
Schiller, Friedrich, *Aesthetical and Philosophical Essays* (Honolulu: University Press of the Pacific, 2001)
Southey, Robert, *Joan of Arc: An Epic Poem* (Boston: J. Nancrede, 1798)

Secondary sources

Aarsleff, Hans, *From Locke to Saussure: Essays on the Study of Language and Intellectual History* (London: Athlone, 1982)
Albrecht, W. P., *The Sublime Pleasures of Tragedy: A Study of Critical Theory from Dennis to Keats* (Lawrence: University Press of Kansas, 1975)
Allen, Richard C., *David Hartley on Human Nature* (Albany: SUNY Press, 1999)
Allison, Henry E., *Kant's Theory of Taste: A Rereading of the Critique of Aesthetic Judgment* (Cambridge: Cambridge University Press, 2001)

Appleyard, J. A., *Coleridge's Philosophy of Literature: The Development of a Concept of Poetry 1791–1819* (Cambridge, MA: Harvard University Press, 1965)

Ashton, Rosemary, *The German Idea: Four English Writers and the Reception of German Thought, 1800–1860* (Cambridge: Cambridge University Press, 1980)

Austin, Linda M. 'Children of Childhood: Nostalgia and the Romantic Legacy', *Studies in Romanticism* 42 (2003): 75–98

Axcelson, John, 'Timing the Apocalypse: The Career of *Religious Musings*', *European Romantic Review* 16 (2005): 439–54

Balfour, Ian, *The Rhetoric of Romantic Prophecy* (Stanford: Stanford University Press, 2002)

Barbeau, Jeffrey W., 'The Development of Coleridge's Notion of Human Freedom: The Translation and Re-formation of German Idealism in England', *Journal of Religion* 80 (2000): 576–94

Barfield, Owen, *What Coleridge Thought* (Oxford: Oxford University Press, 1972)

Barry, Peter, 'Coleridge the Revisionary: Surrogacy and Structure in the Conversation Poems', *Review of English Studies* 51 (2000): 600–16

Barth, J. Robert, *Coleridge and Christian Doctrine* (Cambridge, MA: Harvard University Press, 1969)

—— *The Symbolic Imagination: Coleridge and the Romantic Tradition* (Princeton: Princeton University Press, 1977)

Bate, Walter Jackson, 'Coleridge on the Function of Art', in *Perspectives of Criticism* (Cambridge, MA: Harvard University Press, 1950), 125–59

Baulch, David M., 'The "Perpetual Exercise of an Interminable Quest": The *Biographia Literaria* and the Kantian Revolution', *Studies in Romanticism* 43 (2004): 557–81

Berkeley, Richard, *Coleridge and the Crisis of Reason* (Basingstoke: Palgrave Macmillan, 2007)

Bernstein, J. M., *The Fate of Art: Aesthetic Alienation from Kant to Derrida and Adorno* (Cambridge: Polity Press, 1992)

Bernstein, Richard J., *Radical Evil: A Philosophical Investigation* (Cambridge: Polity Press, 2002)

Bialostosky, Don H., 'Coleridge's Interpretation of Wordsworth's Preface to *Lyrical Ballads*', *PMLA* 93 (1978): 912–24

Bostetter, Edward E., 'The Nightmare World of *The Ancient Mariner*', *Studies in Romanticism* 1 (1961–2): 241–54

Botting, Fred, *Gothic* (London: Routledge, 1996)

Brice, Ben, *Coleridge and Scepticism* (Oxford: Oxford University Press, 2007)

Brisman, Leslie, *Romantic Origins* (Ithaca: Cornell University Press, 1978)

—— 'Coleridge and the Supernatural', *Studies in Romanticism* 21 (1982): 123–59

Brooks, Linda Marie, 'Sublimity and Theatricality: Romantic "Pre-Postmodernism" in Schiller and Coleridge', *MLN* 105 (1990): 939–64

—— *The Menace of the Sublime to the Individual Self: Kant, Schiller, Coleridge and the Disintegration of Romantic Identity* (Lewiston: Edwin Mellon Press, 1995)

Brown, Dennis, 'Coleridge's "Romanticism" and Psychotherapy: Primal Scene, Crime and Reparation', *English* 52 (2003): 203–19

Brown, Lee Rust, 'Coleridge and the Prospect of the Whole', *Studies in Romanticism* 30 (1991): 235–53

Brown, Robert F., 'The Transcendental Fall in Kant and Schelling', *Idealistic Studies* 14 (1984): 49–66

Burley, Stephen, 'The Silenced Voice: Curses and Law in Coleridge's Poetry', *Coleridge Bulletin* 20 (2002): 54–62

Burwick, Frederick (ed.), *Coleridge's Biographia Literaria: Text and Meaning* (Columbus: Ohio State University Press, 1989)

Cadava Eduardo et al. (eds) *Who Comes After the Subject?* (London: Routledge, 1991)

Chandler, David, 'Southey's "German Sublimity" and Coleridge's "Dutch Attempt"', *Romanticism on the Net* 32–3 (2003–4) (http://www.erudit.org/revue/ron/2003/v/n32-33/009257ar.html) (accessed 17 October 2009)

Chase, Cynthia, *Decomposing Figures: Rhetorical Readings in the Romantic Tradition* (Baltimore: Johns Hopkins University Press, 1986)

Chrétien, Jean-Louis, 'The Wounded Word: The Phenomenology of Prayer', in Dominique Janicaud et al., *Phenomenology and the 'Theological Turn': The French Debate*, trans. Bernard G. Prusach (New York: Fordham University Press, 2000), 147–75

Christensen, Jerome C., 'Coleridge's Marginal Method in the *Biographia Literaria*', *PMLA* 92 (1977): 928–40

—— 'The Symbol's Errant Allegory: Coleridge and his Critics', *ELH* 45 (1978): 640–59

—— *Coleridge's Blessed Machine of Language* (Ithaca: Cornell University Press, 1981)

—— '"Like a Guilty Thing Surprised": Coleridge, Deconstruction, and the Apostasy of Criticism', in *Coleridge's Biographia Literaria: Text and Meaning*, ed. Frederick Burwick (Columbus: Ohio State University Press, 1989), 171–90

Clark, Timothy, *The Theory of Inspiration* (Manchester: Manchester University Press, 1997)

—— *The Poetics of Singularity: The Counter-Culturalist Turn in Heidegger, Derrida, Blanchot and the later Gadamer* (Edinburgh: Edinburgh University Press, 2005)

Clemens, Justin, *The Romanticism of Contemporary Theory: Institution, Aesthetics, Nihilism* (Aldershot: Ashgate, 2003)

Courtine, Jean-François et al., *Of the Sublime: Presence in Question*, trans. Jeffrey S. Librett (Albany: SUNY Press, 1993)

Critchley, Simon, *The Ethics of Deconstruction: Derrida and Levinas* (Oxford: Blackwell, 1992)

Critchley, Simon and Dews, Peter (eds), *Deconstructive Subjectivities* (Albany: SUNY Press, 1996)

Crowther, Paul, *The Kantian Sublime: From Morality to Art* (Oxford: Clarendon Press, 1989)

—— *Critical Aesthetics and Postmodernism* (Oxford: Clarendon Press, 1993)

Culler, Jonathan, 'The Hertzian Sublime', *MLN* 120 (2005): 969–85

Curran, Stuart, *Poetic Form and British Romanticism* (Oxford: Oxford University Press, 1986)

Cutsinger, James S., *The Form of Transformed Vision: Coleridge and the Knowledge of God* (Macon: Macon University Press, 1987)

Davidson, Graham, *Coleridge's Career* (Basingstoke: Macmillan, 1990)

De Bolla, Peter, *The Discourse of the Sublime: Readings in History, Aesthetics and the Subject* (Oxford: Blackwell, 1989)

De Luca, Vincent, *Words of Eternity: Blake and the Poetics of the Sublime* (Princeton: Princeton University Press, 1990)

De Man, Paul, *Allegories of Reading: Figural Language in Rousseau, Nietzsche, Rilke and Proust* (New Haven: Yale University Press, 1979)
—— *Blindness and Insight: Essays in the Rhetoric of Contemporary Criticism*, 2nd edition (London: Methuen, 1983)
—— *The Rhetoric of Romanticism* (New York: Columbia University Press, 1984)
—— 'Phenomenality and Materiality in Kant', in *The Textual Sublime: Deconstruction and its Differences*, ed. Hugh J. Silverman and Gary E. Aylesworth (Albany: SUNY Press: 1990), 87–108
—— *Aesthetic Ideology*, ed. Andrzej Warminski (Minneapolis: University of Minnesota Press, 1996)
De Paolo, Charles, *Coleridge's Philosophy of Social Reform* (New York: Peter Lang, 1987)
De Vries, Hent, *Philosophy and the Turn to Religion* (Baltimore: Johns Hopkins University Press, 1999)
Deguy, Michel, 'The Discourse of Exaltation: Contribution to a Rereading of Pseudo-Longinus', in *Of the Sublime: Presence in Question*, trans. Jeffrey S. Librett (Albany: SUNY Press, 1993), 5–24
Dekker, George, *Coleridge and the Literature of Sensibility* (London: Vision Press, 1978)
Derrida, Jacques, *The Truth in Painting*, trans. Geoffrey Bennington and Ian McLeod (Chicago: University of Chicago Press, 1987)
—— *Limited Inc*, ed. Gerald Graff (Evanston: Northwestern University Press, 1988)
—— 'How to Avoid Speaking: Denials', trans. Ken Frieden, in *Languages of the Unsayable: The Play of Negativity in Literature and Literary Theory*, ed. Sanford Budick and Wolfgang Iser (New York: Columbia University Press, 1989), 3–70
—— *The Monolingualism of the Other; or, The Prosthesis of Origin*, trans. Patrick Mensah (Stanford: Stanford University Press, 1998)
—— 'In Memoriam: Of the Soul', in *The Work of Mourning*, ed. Pascale-Anne Brault and Michael Naas (Chicago: University of Chicago Press, 2001)
—— *Writing and Difference*, trans. Alan Bass (London: Routledge, 2001)
Dickie, George, *The Century of Taste: The Philosophical Odyssey of Taste in the Eighteenth Century* (Oxford: Oxford University Press, 1996)
Dilworth, Thomas, 'Symbolic Spatial Form in *The Rime of the Ancient Mariner* and the Problem of God', *Review of English Studies* 58 (2007): 500–30
Duffy, Cian, 'Mont Blanc's Revolutionary "Voice": Shelley and the Discourse on the Sublime', in *Silence, Sublimity and Suppression in the Romantic Period*, ed. Fiona L. Price and Scott Masson (Lewiston: Edwin Mellon Press, 2002), 15–36
Economides, Louise, '"Mont Blanc" and the Sublimity of Materiality', *Cultural Critique* 61 (2005): 87–114
Eilenberg, Susan, *Strange Power of Speech: Wordsworth, Coleridge, and Literary Possession* (Oxford: Oxford University Press, 1992)
Ende, Stuart, *Keats and the Sublime* (New Haven: Yale University Press, 1976)
Engell, James, *The Creative Imagination: Enlightenment to Romanticism* (Cambridge, MA: Harvard University Press, 1981)
—— 'Coleridge (and His Mariner) on the Soul: "As an exile in a far distant land"', in *The Fountain Light: Studies in Romanticism and Religion*, ed. J. Robert Barth (New York: Fordham University Press, 2002), 128–51

Epp, Len, 'Coleridge and the Non-empirical Imagination', *Coleridge Bulletin* 16 (2000): 40–8

Esterhammer, Angela, *The Romantic Performative: Language and Action in British and German Romanticism* (Stanford: Stanford University Press, 2000)

Etlin, Richard A., 'Aesthetics and the Spatial Sense of Self', *JAAC* 56 (1998): 1–19

Everest, Kelvin, *Coleridge's Secret Ministry: The Context of the Conversation Poems* (Hassocks: Harvester Press, 1979)

Fackenheim, Emil L., 'Schelling's Philosophy of the Literary Arts', *Philosophical Quarterly* 4 (1954): 310–26

Fairer, David, 'Coleridge's Sonnets from Various Authors (1796): A Lost Conversation Poem?', *Studies in Romanticism* 41 (2002): 585–604

Feder, Helena, 'Ecocriticism, New Historicism, and Romantic Apostrophe', in *The Greening of Literary Scholarship: Literature, Theory, and the Environment*, ed. Steven Rosendale (Iowa City: University of Iowa Press, 2002), 42–58

Fenves, Peter, 'Taking Stock of the Kantian Sublime', *Eighteenth-Century Studies* 28 (1994): 65–82

Ferguson, Frances, 'A Commentary on Suzanne Guerlac's "Longinus and the Subject of the Sublime"', *NLH* 16 (1985): 291–97

—— *Solitude and the Sublime: Romanticism and the Aesthetics of Individuation* (New York: Routledge, 1992)

Ferris, David S., 'Coleridge's Ventriloquy: The Abduction from the *Biographia*', *Studies in Romanticism* 24 (1985): 41–84

—— *Silent Urns: Romanticism, Hellenism, Modernity* (Stanford: Stanford University Press, 2000)

Foakes, R. A., 'Coleridge, Violence and "The Rime of the Ancient Mariner"', *Romanticism* 7 (2001): 41–57

Ford, Jennifer, *Coleridge on Dreaming: Romanticism, Dreams and the Medical Imagination* (Cambridge: Cambridge University Press, 1998)

Freud, Sigmund, *On Metapsychology: The Theory of Psychoanalysis*, ed. Angela Richards, Penguin Freud Library 11 (London: Penguin, 1984)

Fry, Paul H., *The Poet's Calling in the English Ode* (New Haven: Yale University Press, 1980)

—— 'The Possession of the Sublime', *Studies in Romanticism* 26 (1987): 187–287

Fulford, Tim, *Coleridge's Figurative Language* (Basingstoke: Macmillan, 1991)

—— (ed.), *Romanticism and Millenarianism* (Basingstoke: Palgrave Macmillan, 2002)

Fulford, Tim and Paley, Morton D. (eds), *Coleridge's Visionary Languages* (Cambridge: Brewer, 1993)

Gallant, Christine (ed.), *Coleridge's Theory of Imagination Today* (New York: AMS Press, 1989)

Garrett, Clarke, 'Joseph Priestley, the Millennium, and the French Revolution', *Journal of the History of Ideas* 34 (1973): 51–66

Gasché, Rodolphe, 'On Mere Sight: A Response to Paul De Man', in *The Textual Sublime: Deconstruction and its Differences*, ed. Hugh J. Silverman and Gary E. Aylesworth (Albany: SUNY Press, 1990), 109–15

Gilbert-Rolfe, Jeremy, *Beauty and the Contemporary Sublime* (New York: Allworth, 1999)

Goodson, A. C., *Verbal Imagination: Coleridge and the Language of Modern Criticism* (Oxford: Oxford University Press, 1988)

Greene, Thomas M., 'Coleridge and the Energy of Asking', *ELH* 62 (1995): 907–31

Guerlac, Suzanne, 'Longinus and the Subject of the Sublime', *NLH* 16 (1985): 275–89

Guyer, Paul, *Kant and the Experience of Freedom: Essays on Aesthetics and Morality* (Cambridge: Cambridge University Press, 1996)

—— *Kant and the Claims of Taste*, 2nd edition (Cambridge: Cambridge University Press, 1997)

Halmi, Nicholas, 'When is a Symbol not a Symbol? Coleridge on the Eucharist', *Coleridge Bulletin* 20 (2002): 85–92

Hamilton, Paul, *Coleridge's Poetics* (Oxford: Blackwell, 1983)

—— *Metaromanticism: Aesthetics, Literature, Theory* (Chicago: University of Chicago Press, 2003)

—— *Coleridge and German Philosophy: The Poet in the Land of Logic* (London: Continuum, 2007)

Harding, Anthony John, *Coleridge and the Idea of Love: Aspects of Relationship in Coleridge's Thought and Writing* (Cambridge: Cambridge University Press, 1974)

—— *Coleridge and the Inspired Word* (Kingston: McGill-Queen's University Press, 1985)

Heidegger, Martin, *Being and Time*, trans. John Macquarrie and Edward Robinson (Oxford: Blackwell, 1962)

—— 'What is Metaphysics', in *Basic Writings*, ed. David Farrell Krell (San Francisco: HarperCollins, 1977), 93–110

Hertz, Neil, *The End of the Line: Essays on Psychoanalysis and the Sublime* (New York: Columbia University Press, 1985)

Hodgson, John A., 'Coleridge, Puns, and "Donne's First Poem": The Limbo of Rhetoric and the Conception of Wit', *John Donne Journal* 4 (1985): 181–200

Holmes, Richard, *Coleridge: Darker Reflections* (London: Harper Perennial, 2005)

—— *Coleridge: Early Visions* (London: Harper Perennial, 2005)

Hume, Robert D., 'Kant and Coleridge on Imagination', *JAAC* 28 (1970): 485–96

Hurtrez, Lionel, 'Nature and Subjectivity; Coleridge and Fichteanism', *The Coleridge Bulletin* 18 (2001): 1–15

Jackson, J. R. de J., *Method and Imagination in Coleridge's Criticism* (London: Routledge, 1969)

—— (ed.), *Coleridge: The Critical Heritage* (London: Routledge, 1970)

Jackson, Noel B., 'Critical Conditions: Coleridge, "Common Sense", and the Literature of Self Experiment', *ELH* 70 (2003): 117–49

Janicaud, Dominique et al., *Phenomenology and the 'Theological Turn': The French Debate*, trans. Bernard G. Prusach (New York: Fordham University Press, 2000)

Janowitz, Anne, 'Coleridge's 1816 Volume Fragment as Rubric', *Studies in Romanticism* 24 (1985): 21–39

Jarvis, Simon, *Wordsworth's Philosophical Song* (Cambridge: Cambridge University Press, 2006)

Jasper, David (ed.), *The Interpretation of Belief: Coleridge, Schleiermacher and Romanticism* (Basingstoke: Macmillan, 1986)

Jones, Mark, 'Alarmism, Public-Sphere Performatives and the Lyric Turn: Or, What is "Fears in Solitude" Afraid of?', *Boundary 2* 30 (2003): 67–105

Kantor, Alon, 'Levinas's Law', *American Imago* 56 (1999): 357–85

Kearney, Richard, 'Deconstruction and the Other: Dialogue with Derrida', in *Dialogue with Contemporary Continental Thinkers: The Phenomenological Heritage* (Manchester: Manchester University Press, 1984)

Kessler, Edward, *Coleridge's Metaphors of Being* (Princeton: Princeton University Press, 1979)

Kirwan, James, *The Aesthetic in Kant* (London: Continuum, 2004)

—— *Sublimity: The Non-Rational and the Irrational in the History of Aesthetics* (London: Routledge, 2005)

Kitson, Peter, 'Coleridge, the French Revolution, and "The Ancient Mariner": Collective Guilt and Individual Salvation', *Yearbook of English Studies* 19 (1989): 197–207

—— '"To Milton's Trump": Coleridge and the Unitarian Sublime', in *Romanticism and Millenarianism*, ed. Tim Fulford (Basingstoke: Palgrave Macmillan, 2001), 37–52

Klancher, Jon P., *The Making of English Reading Audiences* (Wisconsin: University of Wisconsin Press, 1987)

Knapp, Steven, *Personification and the Sublime* (Cambridge, MA: Harvard University Press, 1985)

Kneale, Douglas J., 'Romantic Aversions: Apostrophe Reconsidered', *ELH* 58 (Spring, 1991): 141–65

Knight, G. Wilson, *The Starlit Dome: Studies in the Poetry of Vision* (Oxford: Oxford University Press, 1941)

Kramer, Lawrence, 'That Other Will: The Daemonic in Coleridge and Wordsworth', *Philological Quarterly* 58 (1979): 298–320

Kristeva, Julia, *Powers of Horror: An Essay on Abjection*, trans. Leon S. Roudiez (New York: Columbia University Press, 1982)

Lacoue-Labarthe, Philippe and Nancy, Jean-Luc, *The Literary Absolute: The Theory of Literature in German Romanticism*, trans. Philip Barnard and Cheryl Lester (Albany: SUNY Press, 1988)

Lamb, Jonathan, 'Hartley and Wordsworth: Philosophical Language and Figures of the Sublime', *MLN* 97 (1982): 1064–85

Leask, Nigel, *The Politics of Imagination in Coleridge's Critical Thought* (Basingstoke: Macmillan, 1988)

Leighton, Angela, *Shelley and the Sublime: An Interpretation of the Major Poems* (Cambridge: Cambridge University Press, 1984)

Levinson, Marjorie, *The Romantic Fragment Poem: A Critique of a Form* (Chapel Hill: University of North Carolina Press, 1986)

Lipowitz, Ina, 'Inspiration and the Poetic Imagination: Samuel Taylor Coleridge', *Studies in Romanticism* 30 (1991): 605–31

Loesberg, Jonathan, 'Materialism and Aesthetics: Paul de Man's Aesthetic Ideology', *Diacritics* 27 (1997): 87–108

Lyotard, Jean-François, *The Inhuman: Reflections on Time*, trans. Geoffrey Bennington and Rachel Bowlby (Cambridge: Polity Press, 1991)

—— *Lessons on the Analytic of the Sublime*, trans. Elizabeth Rottenberg (Stanford: Stanford University Press, 1994)

Macovski, Michael, *Dialogue and Literature: Apostrophe, Auditors, and the Collapse of Romantic Discourse* (Oxford: Oxford University Press, 1994)

Magnuson, Paul, *Coleridge's Nightmare Poetry* (Charlottesville: University Press of Virginia, 1974)

—— *Coleridge and Wordsworth: A Lyrical Dialogue* (Princeton: Princeton University Press, 1988)

—— 'The Politics of "Frost at Midnight"', *Wordsworth Circle* 22 (1991): 3–11

Mahoney, John L., 'The Classical Tradition in Eighteenth Century English Rhetorical Education', *History of Education Journal* 9 (1958): 93–7

Marion, Jean-Luc, *God Without Being: Hors-Texte*, trans. Thomas A. Carlson (Chicago: University of Chicago Press, 1991)

—— *Being Given: Toward a Phenomenology of Givenness*, trans. Jeffrey L. Kosky (Stanford: Stanford University Press, 2002)

Marsh, Robert, 'The Second Part of Hartley's System', *Journal of the History of Ideas* 20 (1959): 264–73

Martin, Wayne M., *Idealism and Objectivity: Understanding Fichte's Jena Project* (Stanford: Stanford University Press, 1997)

Martis, John, *Philippe Lacoue-Labarthe: Representation and the Loss of the Subject* (New York: Fordham University Press, 2005)

Marx, Werner, *The Philosophy of F. W. J. Schelling: History, System, and Freedom*, trans. Thomas Nenon (Bloomington: Indiana University Press, 1984)

Matheson, Ann, 'The Influence of Cowper's *The Task* on Coleridge's Conversation Poems', in *New Approaches to Coleridge: Biographical and Critical Essays*, ed. Donald Sultana (London: Vision Press, 1981), 137–50

Mattick, Jr., Paul (ed.), *Eighteenth-Century Aesthetics and the Reconstruction of Art* (Cambridge: Cambridge University Press, 1993)

Maxwell, Catherine, *The Female Sublime from Milton to Swinburne: Bearing Blindness* (Manchester: Manchester University Press, 2001)

McFarland, Thomas, *Coleridge and the Pantheist Tradition* (Oxford: Clarendon Press, 1969)

McGann, Jerome, 'The Meaning of The Ancient Mariner', *Critical Inquiry* 8 (1981–2): 217–52

—— *The Romantic Ideology: A Critical Investigation* (Chicago: University of Chicago Press, 1983)

McKusick, James C., *Coleridge's Philosophy of Language* (New Haven: Yale University Press, 1986)

McLean, Karen, 'Plotinian Sources for Coleridge's Theories of Evil', *Coleridge Bulletin* 20 (2002): 93–104

McNiece, Gerald, *The Knowledge That Endures: Coleridge, German Philosophy and the Logic of Romantic Thought* (Basingstoke: Macmillan, 1992)

Mee, Jon, *Romanticism, Enthusiasm, and Regulation: Poetics and the Policing of Culture in the Romantic Period* (Oxford: Oxford University Press, 2003)

Mellor, Anne K., 'Coleridge's "This Lime-Tree Bower My Prison" and the Categories of English Landscape', *Studies in Romanticism* 18 (1979): 253–70

—— *English Romantic Irony* (Cambridge, MA: Harvard University Press, 1980)

Miall, David S., 'The Meaning of Dreams: Coleridge's Ambivalence', *Studies in Romanticism* 21 (1982): 57–71

—— 'Guilt and Death: The Predicament of The Ancient Mariner', *Studies in English Literature, 1500–1900* 24 (1984): 633–53

Miller, J. Hillis, *The Disappearance of God: Five Nineteenth-Century Writers* (Cambridge, MA: Harvard University Press, 1963)

Milnes, Tim, 'Eclipsing Art: Method and Metaphysics in Coleridge's *Biographia Literaria*', *Journal of the History of Ideas* 60 (1999): 125–47

Mishra, Vijay, *The Gothic Sublime* (Albany: SUNY Press, 1994)

Modiano, Raimonda, 'Words and "Languageless" Meanings: Limits of Expression in *The Rime of the Ancient Mariner*', *Modern Language Quarterly* 38 (1977): 40–61

—— 'Coleridge and the Sublime: A Response to Thomas Weiskel's *The Romantic Sublime*', *Wordsworth Circle* 9 (1978): 110–20

—— *Coleridge and the Concept of Nature* (Basingstoke: Macmillan, 1985)

—— 'Humanism and the Comic Sublime: From Kant to Friedrich Theodor Vischer', *Studies in Romanticism* 26 (1987): 231–44

Monk, Samuel H., *The Sublime: A Study of Critical Theories in XVIII-Century England* (Ann Arbor: University of Michigan Press, 1960)

Moore, A.W., *The Infinite*, 2nd edition (London: Routledge, 2001)

Morris, David B., *The Religious Sublime: Christian Poetry and Critical Tradition in 18th-Century England* (Lexington: University of Kentucky Press, 1972)

—— 'Gothic Sublimity', *NLH* 16 (1985): 299–319

Morrow, John, *Coleridge's Political Thought* (New York: St. Martin's Press, 1990)

Nancy, Jean-Luc, *The Inoperative Community*, ed. Peter Connor, trans. Peter Connor et al. (Minneapolis: University of Minnesota Press, 1991)

—— *The Experience of Freedom*, trans. Bridget McDonald (Stanford: Stanford University Press, 1993)

—— 'The Sublime Offering', in *A Finite Thinking*, ed. Simon Sparks (Stanford: Stanford University Press, 2003), 211–44

Orsini, G. N. G., *Coleridge and German Idealism* (Carbondale: Southern Illinois University Press, 1969)

Paley, Morton D., *Coleridge's Later Poetry* (Oxford: Clarendon Press, 1996)

—— *Apocalypse and Millennium in English Romantic Poetry* (Oxford: Clarendon Press, 1999)

Perry, Seamus, *Coleridge and the Uses of Division* (Oxford: Clarendon Press, 1999)

Pillow, Kirk, *Sublime Understanding: Aesthetic Reflection in Kant and Hegel* (Cambridge, MA: MIT Press, 2000)

Poetsch, Markus, *'Visionary Dreariness': Readings in Romanticism's Quotidian Sublime* (London: Routledge, 2006)

Powell, Grosvenor, 'Coleridge's "Imagination" and the Infinite Regress of Consciousness', *ELH* 39 (1972): 266–78

Prickett, Stephen, *Romanticism and Religion: The Tradition of Coleridge and Wordsworth in the Victorian Church* (Cambridge: Cambridge University Press, 1976)

Prins, Yopie, *Victorian Sappho* (Princeton: Princeton University Press, 1999)

Rajan, Tilottama, *Dark Interpreter: The Discourse of Romanticism* (Ithaca: Cornell University Press, 1980)

—— 'Displacing Post-Structuralism: Romantic Studies After Paul de Man', *Studies in Romanticism* 24 (1985): 451–74

—— *The Supplement of Reading: Figures of Understanding in Romantic Theory and Practice* (Ithaca: Cornell University Press, 1990)

Rajan, Tilottama and Wright, Julia M. (eds), *Romanticism, History, and the Possibilities of Genre* (Cambridge: Cambridge University Press, 1998)
Read, Herbert, *Coleridge as Critic* (London: Faber, 1949)
Readings, Bill, *Introducing Lyotard: Art and Politics* (London: Routledge, 1991)
Richards-Fisher, Leah, 'Where There's a Rime, Is There a Reason? Defining the Personae in Coleridge's *The Rime of the Ancient Mariner*', *Coleridge Bulletin* 20 (2002): 63–8
Robinson, Daniel, '"Work without hope": Anxiety and Embarrassment in Coleridge's Sonnets', *Studies in Romanticism* 39 (2000): 81–110
Roe, Nicholas, *Wordsworth and Coleridge: The Radical Years* (Oxford: Clarendon Press, 1988)
Rogozinski, Jacob, 'The Gift of the World', in *Of the Sublime: Presence in Question*, trans. Jeffrey S. Librett (Albany: SUNY Press, 1993), 133–56.
Royle, Nicholas, *Telepathy and Literature: Essays on the Reading Mind* (Oxford: Blackwell, 1991)
Rubasky, Elizabeth A., '"The Rime of the Ancient Mariner": Coleridge's Multiple Models of Interpretation', *Coleridge Bulletin* 24 (2002): 19–28
Sayre, Robert, 'The Young Coleridge: Romantic Utopianism and the French Revolution', *Studies in Romanticism* 28 (1989): 397–415
Scott, Matthew, 'The Circulation of Romantic Creativity: Coleridge, Drama, and the Question of Translation', *Romanticism on the Net*, 2 (1996) (http://www.erudit.org/revue/ron/1996/v/n2/005715ar.html) (accessed 17 October 2009)
Sedgwick, Sally (ed.), *The Reception of Kant's Critical Philosophy: Fichte, Schelling, and Hegel* (Cambridge: Cambridge University Press, 2000)
Seidel, George J., 'Creativity in the Aesthetics of Schelling', *Idealistic Studies* 4 (1974): 170–80
Shaffer, Elinor S., 'Coleridge's Revolution in the Standard of Taste', *JAAC* 28 (1969): 213–21
—— 'Coleridge's Theory of Aesthetic Interest', *JAAC* 27 (1969): 399–408
—— 'Metaphysics of Culture: Kant and Coleridge's *Aids to Reflection*', *Journal of the History of Ideas* 31 (1970): 199–218
—— *'Kubla Khan' and The Fall of Jerusalem: The Mythological School in Biblical Criticism and Secular Literature 1770–1880* (Cambridge: Cambridge University Press, 1980)
Shapiro, Gary, 'From the Sublime to the Political: Some Historical Notes', *NLH* 16 (1985): 213–35
Sheats, Paul D., 'Young Coleridge and the Idea of Lyric', *Coleridge Bulletin* 20 (2002): 14–31
Simpson, David, *Romanticism, Nationalism and the Revolt Against Theory* (Chicago: University of Chicago Press, 1993)
Simpson, Michael, 'The Morning (Post) After: Apocalypses and Bathos in Coleridge's "Fears in Solitude"', in *Romanticism and Millenarianism*, ed. Tim Fulford (Basingstoke: Palgrave Macmillan, 2002), 72–86
Sircello, Guy, 'How is a Theory of the Sublime Possible?', *JAAC* 51 (1993): 541–50
Siskin, Clifford, *The Historicity of Romantic Discourse* (Oxford: Oxford University Press, 1988)
Smith, Olivia, *The Politics of Language, 1791–1819* (Oxford: Oxford University Press, 1984)

Spivak, Gayatri Chakravorty, 'The Letter as Cutting Edge', *Yale French Studies* 55–6 (1977): 208–26

Stempel, Daniel, 'Revelation on Mount Snowdon: Wordsworth, Coleridge and the Fichtean Imagination', *JAAC* 29 (1971): 371–84

Sternbach, Robert, 'Coleridge, Joan of Arc, and the Idea of Progress', *ELH* 46 (1979): 248–61

Stokes, Christopher, 'Coleridge's Philosophy of Prayer: Responsibility, Parergon, Catachresis', *Journal of Religion* 89.4 (2009): 541–63

Sultana, Donald (ed.), *New Approaches to Coleridge: Biographical and Critical Essays* (London: Vision Press, 1981)

Sussman, Henry, *Psyche and Text: The Sublime and the Grandiose in Literature, Psychopathology and Culture* (Albany: SUNY Press, 1993)

Swiatecka, M. Jadwiga, *The Idea of Symbol: Some Nineteenth-Century Comparisons with Coleridge* (Cambridge: Cambridge University Press, 1980)

Terada, Rei, *Feeling in Theory: Emotion after the 'Death of the Subject'* (Cambridge, MA: Harvard University Press, 2001)

Thompson, G. R. (ed.), *The Gothic Imagination: Essays in Dark Romanticism* (Pullman: Washington State University Press, 1974)

Thompson, Judith, 'An Autumnal Blast, a Killing Frost: Coleridge's Poetic Conversation with John Thelwall', *Studies in Romanticism* 36 (1997): 427–56

Todorov, Tzvetan, *The Fantastic: A Structural Approach to a Literary Genre*, trans. Richard Howard (Cleveland: CWRU Press, 1973)

Trott, Nicola, 'The Coleridge Circle and the "Answer to Godwin"', *Review of English Studies* 41 (1990): 212–29

Twitchell, James B., *Romantic Horizons: Aspects of the Sublime in English Poetry and Painting, 1770–1850* (Columbia: University of Missouri Press, 1983)

Ulmer, William A., 'Necessary Evils: Unitarian Theodicy in The Rime of the Ancyent Marinere', *Studies in Romanticism* 43 (2004): 327–56

—— 'Virtue of Necessity: Coleridge's Unitarian Moral Theory', *Modern Philology* 10 (2005): 372–404

—— 'The Alienation of the Elect in Coleridge's Unitarian Prophecies', *Review of English Studies* 57 (2006): 526–44

Vallins, David, *Coleridge and the Psychology of Romanticism: Feeling and Thought* (Basingstoke: Macmillan, 2000)

Van den Abbeele, Georges, 'Lost Horizons and Uncommon Grounds: For a Poetics of Finitude in the Work of Jean-Luc Nancy', in *On Jean-Luc Nancy: The Sense of Philosophy*, ed. Darren Shepherd, Simon Sparks and Colin Thomas (London: Routledge, 1997), 12–18

Van Haute, Philippe, 'Law, Guilt and Subjectivity: Reflections on Freud, Nancy, and Derrida', in *Deconstructive Subjectivities*, ed. Simon Critchley and Peter Dews (Albany: SUNY Press, 1996), 185–200

Vanwinkle, Matthew, 'Fluttering on the Grate: Revision in "Frost at Midnight"', *Studies in Romanticism* 43 (2004): 583–98

Vickers, Brian, *Classical Rhetoric in English Poetry* (London: Macmillan, 1970)

Voller, Jack G., *The Supernatural Sublime: The Metaphysics of Terror in Anglo-American Romanticism* (DeKalb: Northern Illinois University Press, 1994)

Wallace, Catherine Miles, *The Design of* Biographia Literaria (London: Allen & Unwin, 1983)

Wang, Orrin N. C., 'Kant's Strange Light: Romanticism, Periodicity, and the Catachresis of Genius', *Diacritics* 30 (2000): 15–37

Warminski, Andrzej, '"As the Poets Do It": On the Material Sublime', in *Material Events: Paul de Man and the Afterlife of Theory*, ed. Tom Cohen et al. (Minneapolis: University of Minnesota Press, 2001), 3–31

—— 'Returns of the Sublime: Positing and Performative in Kant, Fichte, and Schiller', *MLN* 116 (2001): 964–78

Warren, Robert Penn, 'A Poem of Pure Imagination: An Experiment in Reading', in *Selected Essays* (London: Eyre and Spottiswoode, 1964), 198–305

Weiskel, Thomas, *The Romantic Sublime: Studies in the Structure and Psychology of Transcendence* (Baltimore: Johns Hopkins University Press, 1976)

Wheeler, Kathleen, *Sources, Processes and Methods in Coleridge's* Biographia Literaria (Cambridge: Cambridge University Press, 1980)

—— *The Creative Mind in Coleridge's Poetry* (Cambridge, MA: Harvard University Press: 1981)

Williams, Anne, 'An I for an Eye: "Spectral Persecution" in *The Rime of the Ancient Mariner*', *PMLA* 108 (1993): 1114–27

—— *Art of Darkness: A Poetics of Gothic* (Chicago: University of Chicago Press, 1995)

Wilson, Eric G., *Coleridge's Melancholia: An Anatomy of Limbo* (Gainesville: University Press of Florida, 2004)

Wlecke, Albert O., *Wordsworth and the Sublime* (Berkeley: University of California Press, 1973)

Wolfson, Susan J., '"Comparing Power": Coleridge and Simile', in *Coleridge's Theory of Imagination Today*, ed. Christine Gallant (New York: AMS Press, 1989), 167–95

Wood, Theodore, *The Word 'Sublime' and Its Context 1650–1760* (The Hague: Mouton, 1972)

Wyland, Russel M., 'An Archival Study of Rhetoric Texts and Teaching at the University of Oxford, 1785–1820', *Rhetorica* 21 (2003): 175–95

Youngquist, Paul, 'Rehabilitating Coleridge: Poetry, Philosophy, Excess', *ELH* 66 (1999): 885–909

Zöller, Günter, 'From Critique to Metacritique: Fichte's Transformation of Kant's Transcendental Idealism', in *The Reception of Kant's Critical Philosophy: Fichte, Schelling, and Hegel*, ed. Sally Sedgwick (Cambridge: Cambridge University Press, 2000), 129–46

Index